JOB

Norman Whybray

Sheffield Academic Press

To David Clines
whose commentary on the book of Job
prompted this more modest one

Copyright © 1998 Sheffield Academic Press

Published by Sheffield Academic Press Ltd
Mansion House
19 Kingfield Road
Sheffield S11 9AS
England

Typeset by Sheffield Academic Press
and
Printed on acid-free paper in Great Britain
by Bookcraft Ltd
Midsomer Norton, Bath

British Library Cataloguing in Publication Data

A catalogue record for this book is available
from the British Library

ISBN 1-85075-839-5
ISBN 1-85075-840-9 pbk

Readings: A New Biblical Commentary

General Editor
John Jarick

J O B

Contents

6   **Contents**

Preface

In accordance with the general character of the *Readings* series this commentary records my personal perception of the book of Job. There are no notes: the views of other scholars where I differ from them are occasionally referred to in the text, but not there named. Detailed accounts of the innumerable variety of interpretations that have been proposed would have increased the length of this commentary out of all proportion and would have tended to confuse the reader while making clarity of exposition difficult to achieve. Needless to say I have made constant use of what have seemed to me to be the most important commentaries and special studies on the book of Job; the details of these will be found in the bibliography.

The Hebrew in which the poetry of Job is composed is very strange and unlike that of any other Old Testament book. This is particularly true of the vocabulary, which includes a large proportion of words that occur only in this book and whose meaning is consequently debatable. This circumstance is one of the causes of the above-mentioned diversity of interpretations. The series does not require a new translation, and I have taken the New Revised Standard Version as the basic text while indicating my disagreement when this has seemed desirable.

The division of some parts of the Old Testament books into chapters and verses in modern versions is not always identical with that of the standard Hebrew text. In the book of Job there is only one passage where the two differ: 41.1-34 in NRSV and other modern versions correspond to 40.25–41.26 in the Hebrew. In this commentary I have followed the English rather than the Hebrew numeration both with regard to this passage and also in references to other Old Testament passages; readers of the Hebrew will be able to make the necessary adjustments for themselves.

Introduction

Job as Narrative

It is important to realize that the Book of Job is a *narrative*. That is, it is
arranged as a chronological account of a series of events. Formally it is a
mixture of prose and poetry, as is the Pentateuch. But unlike the Pentateuch it is an entirely fictional story. It tells of the experiences of an exceptionally blameless and pious individual who was also a very wealthy
and prosperous one, and how he was struck down as the result of an
argument in heaven between God and a subordinate heavenly being, the
Satan, losing his wealth, his family, his health and his self-respect and
social status. At first he humbly accepts these afflictions on the grounds
that God, who both gives and takes back human life, is entitled to do
whatever seems good to him and still deserves to be praised and worshipped. After a period of reflection, however, and after three friends
have come to visit and to comfort him, he begins to complain bitterly
about his misfortunes, cursing the day when he was born. The three
friends then in turn make their comments on his situation in a series of
speeches in which there is more of accusation than of sympathy, and
Job replies to each of their speeches in turn, defending his innocence of
any sin that would deserve such divine punishment and accusing God of
injustice and hostility towards him.

Another person, Elihu, then appears and makes his contribution to the
discussion. He is angry with Job for his assumption of innocence, but
also with the friends for accusing Job without being able to produce any
evidence against him. He speaks mainly in defence of God.

The story then takes a new turn. God manifests himself to Job and
addresses him directly—a confrontation for which Job had constantly
appealed, demanding that God should explain his conduct towards him
and recognize his innocence. But in fact when he speaks, God makes no
allusion whatever to Job's predicament, and indeed makes very little
reference to human beings and their fate. Rather, he speaks of his own
power as creator and maintainer of the world, and in particular of his
care for the wild animals that live entirely outside the human sphere. All
this discourse is apparently quite irrelevant to everything that has gone
before. Job, however, is deeply impressed by God's appearance and by
his words, and submits himself to him. Finally God does take notice of
what has been happening: he rebukes the friends for not speaking
rightly of him (that is, of God), and praises Job for doing so. He then
restores Job's wealth, giving him twice as much as he had had before,
and gives him a new family, a long life and many descendants.

This, then, is a complete narrative with a beginning, a complication and a conclusion that recalls the beginning, leaving Job a happy and prosperous man as he had been before.

The story is ostensibly a simple one: Job, an exemplary man, passed a test imposed by God to discover whether his piety was genuine. He was made to suffer and protested against God's treatment of him, but was eventually restored to his former state of prosperity and wellbeing. Many modern critics, however, have found the book as it now stands to be profoundly unsatisfactory, full of incongruities and inconsistencies, and have questioned its literary integrity. These questions will be examined in the following pages.

It is clear that this story was not told simply to provide entertainment. It was intended to provoke thought. It has often been supposed that its main concern is with the so-called 'problem of suffering'. But this is plainly an inadequate explanation. The experiences of Job have manifestly been used as a peg on which the author has hung a series of discussions on theological themes of the most profound and wide-ranging kind concerning the nature of God, the nature of man and the relationship between God and man. The dialogues, which occupy the major part of the book, are not, however, purely academic exercises: they are highly polemical, and deal with matters of crucial importance for human existence. Job and his friends are made to represent respectively two very different understandings of God's treatment of his human creatures, and also of the human capacity to comprehend the divine nature. It is evident that behind these dialogues lies a real controversy to which the author of the book has made a decisive contribution. The central character, Job, is not precisely his mouthpiece; he is nevertheless made to challenge a fundamental belief about God that had been taken for granted in Israel: that, as the supreme arbiter of human destiny, God deals with his human creatures precisely as they deserve. This belief is already questioned in the Prologue at the beginning of the book. But the dialogue that follows provides no definitive answer to the question, and, in the speeches that the author puts into the mouth of God at the conclusion of the dialogue, he sets the matter in an entirely different light: he argues, by implication, that human concerns are absurdly petty when set against God's universal sovereignty over the universe. Finally in the Epilogue he reinforces this lesson: he returns to Job, who has now learned his lesson (42.1-6), and the book ends with a further demonstration of God's freedom to behave precisely as he chooses towards his human creatures.

These questions, then, are discussed in every part of the book: it manifests a unity of theme as well as a single 'story line'. But does it also express a single point of view? Or is it a collection of disparate pieces by different writers, who may or may not have been contemporaries, that have been attached to the legendary figure of Job in order to put forward their own quite different theological views? In other words, are there no grounds for attributing the book to a single author? In order to determine this question it is necessary to assess each part of the book and to examine the relationship of each part to the others in the context of the structure of the book as a whole.

The Prologue (1.1-2.13)

The fact that the book begins in prose but continues in poetical form should occasion no question as regards unity of authorship. Prose is the most appropriate form for narrative: nothing in the Old Testament suggests that ancient Israel knew a tradition of epic poetry. It is equally appropriate that the remainder of the book, apart from the continuation and conclusion of the narrative in the Epilogue, should be in poetical form, for poetry is more suitable than prose for the expression of complex emotional scenes. This arrangement—the encapsulation of an extended poem within a prose narrative—is by no means a unique phenomenon in ancient Near Eastern literature.

The Prologue, an example of impeccable classical Hebrew prose style, has the character of a folk-tale. It has only three principal characters, and in each scene only two of these are involved: Yahweh and the Satan (1.6-12; 2.1-8), the messenger and Job (1.13-19), Job and his wife (2.9-10). Some scenes (the conversations between Yahweh and the Satan) are repeated with appropriate variations, and there is also much repetition of phraseology and description (1.6-8 and 2.1-3; the four disasters of 1.13-19). Certain numbers are repeated (seven, 1.2, 3; 2.13; three, 1.2, 4, 17; 2.11). The story is one in which people are depicted in absolute terms: Job is faultless; his wife's brief intervention is dismissed as stupid; the Satan is a schemer and a tempter. Only God's character is ambiguous. The plot, too, is conceived in absolute terms: the sudden and improbable reversal of Job's fortunes from unheard of wealth and prosperity to utter poverty and misery, and, in the Epilogue, back again to even greater wealth and prosperity.

But the folk-tale genre is not to be taken as indicating that the Prologue is the product of an earlier, simpler age than is the rest of the book. There are indications that it is a pastiche: a relatively late composition incorporating features that merely purport to come from an earlier period. The most obvious of these features is the portrayal of Job's 'patriarchal' way of life (1.1-3). The statement in 1.3 that Job's great wealth consisted of vast flocks and herds bears a remarkable resemblance to what is said in Genesis of Abraham, Isaac and Jacob (e.g. Gen. 12.16; 13.2; 14.14; 24.35; 26.12-13; 36.7). This suggests that these verses of Job have been deliberately modelled on the Genesis stories; the way of life of Job described in Job 29 also has 'patriarchal' features.

It is clear that in its present form—if, indeed, there ever was an earlier form, a matter that is open to doubt—the Prologue is closely related to the poetical dialogue that follows it. Without it the dialogue would be incomprehensible. The Prologue sets the scene for the dialogue, introducing the central character, Job, describes his situation and tells of the arrival of Job's three friends whose dialogue with Job is to form the substance of the following chapters. The Prologue is thus an essential part of the book: it provides the readers with the information they need. Whether the author of the dialogue composed the Prologue on the basis of an already existing story or used the name of the legendary Job (cf. Ezek. 14.14) to attach to it an entirely original piece of fiction is immaterial for the understanding of the book.

That Prologue and Epilogue—the two parts of the book composed in narrative prose—are closely related, and that the latter is in some sense the completion of the former may be accepted in general terms. However, their relationship is not entirely straightforward. This is not simply the case of a single narrative split into two to accommodate a substantial interpolation: the two parts cannot be joined together to form a complete story. Nor could this supposed story have ever been independent of the rest of the book. Its plot is incomplete. The Prologue ends (2.13) with the three friends sitting silently on the ground; no word has yet been spoken, either by them to Job or by Job to them. Nor has God spoken to Job. But the Epilogue begins (42.7-9) with a reference to words spoken by God to Job and also to words spoken *about* God, both by Job and the friends. The Epilogue thus presupposes either chs. 3–41 as they stand now or some other account of words spoken by God, Job and the friends that has been omitted at some stage from the book. Of these two possibilities the former is the more plausible. Just as the Prologue and Epilogue together presuppose the dialogue and the speeches by Yahweh, so the Epilogue presupposes the Prologue. It is not possible to envisage the one part of the book without the other.

Yahweh and the Satan
It has frequently been alleged that the two scenes in which the Satan figures (1.6-12; 2.1-8) have been interpolated into an original version of the Prologue that lacked them. But the omission of these two episodes would leave simply a story (Prologue plus Epilogue) about a wealthy and pious man who was afflicted by terrible misfortunes that destroyed his family, his wealth and his health, but on whom God later took pity, restoring to him everything that he had lost and more. This would be a pointless story devoid of dramatic interest. The episodes with the Satan provide all that the story has to offer of narrative interest. The fascinating glimpses into events in the heavenly sphere and of decisions made there, alternating with corresponding events on earth, could hardly fail to arouse the interest of the readers. Above all, it is only in the episodes

with the Satan that the question is raised that gives point not only to the prose story but also to the whole book: 'Does Job fear God for nothing?'

Another feature of these episodes that affects the interpretation of the whole book is their dramatic irony: the fact that Job is unaware of what the reader knows, that is, the reason for his suffering. This not only stimulates the interest of the reader but also heightens the pathos of Job's struggle for an explanation of his predicament in the dialogue chapters.

The chief reason put forward for the view that these Satan episodes are interpolated is not stylistic: the same classical prose style prevails throughout the Prologue. It is rather that the Satan never appears again, either in the Epilogue or elsewhere in the book. His only part in the events is to initiate and set them in motion. This fading of the Satan from the scene after ch. 2, it is alleged, is difficult to account for in terms of the unitary authorship of the book as a whole. However, it is difficult to envisage what would have been the shape of the book if the Satan had continued to be a character in it. It would certainly have been very different, probably involving some kind of dualism, with the crucial question about the nature of God marginalized. In fact, the other references to the Satan in the Old Testament are so few and so brief that such a role can hardly be meaningfully discussed. It would seem probable that the introduction of the Satan into the Prologue was made simply to account (for the benefit of the readers) for God's action in permitting Job's misfortunes. That role performed, there was no reason why he should be mentioned further.

It has also been argued that the very introduction of the figure of the Satan is proof that these episodes are a late interpolation into the Prologue. This argument is hardly a convincing one in view of the fact that there is no scholarly agreement about the earliest appearance of this figure in the Israelite religious tradition. In fact, it would be equally possible to argue for an *early* date for these episodes: the concept of a heavenly court where subordinate heavenly beings, sometimes called 'sons of God' as here, participate in the making or implementation of divine decisions about events on earth could be taken to be an indication of an early rather than a late date. This concept is at home in the religious world of the ancient Near East and is found in a number of Old Testament passages that are probably to be dated relatively early. These contrary indications suggest that it would be unwise to take either of these two features—the Satan and the heavenly court—as a true reflection of the author's own religious beliefs and so as evidence for the date of the passages in question. A late writer wishing to pose as an ancient one could well have deliberately introduced the anachronism of a heavenly court into his narrative while also making use for the sake of his plot of the somewhat different figure of the Satan. The fact that the Satan plays no further part in the book may suggest that he is simply a literary device (a kind of *Satanas ex machina*?) to set the story in motion.

A further point in favour of the originality of the scenes in which the Satan appears is that apart from them there would be no account in the book of Job's second affliction, the loathsome disease. It is specifically stated in 2.7 that this was the work of the Satan. Yet that Job did suffer from such a disease is presupposed in the dialogue (e.g. 7.5; 30.17). Job's despair and longing for death are also easier to account for if he was suffering from such a disease.

The Prologue as a Whole
As has been indicated above, the Prologue is no simple folk-tale. It raises important theological questions that will be discussed in the dialogue between Job and the friends that follows. These mainly concern the nature of God and his relationship to his human creatures, but also the imperfect nature of man. The question of the universality of God's rule is raised in the Prologue, though only obliquely, by the fact that Job is evidently not an Israelite. Although he seems to possess all the virtues and so could stand as a model of an ideal Israelite, he is a resident of the land of Uz. This statement in 1.1 is more significant than might be supposed. It is not merely incidental to the story, and would not have escaped the attention of the first, Israelite, readers.

It is made clear in 1.1 that the antecedents of Job are obscure. The complete absence of any indication of his tribe, or even the name of his father, is an almost unique feature in Hebrew narrative: we may compare, for example, 1 Sam. 1.1, where a somewhat similar story in the manner of a folk-tale begins with a most elaborate notice of the provenance and family descent of the protagonist Elkanah. The location of the land of Uz was probably as obscure to the original readers of the book of Job as it is to modern readers: it will have suggested to them a remote, mysterious region, if indeed it existed at all, and would have indicated that what followed would be a tale of the imagination despite its matter-of-fact beginning. Wherever Uz was located it was not in Israel. The fact that nothing is said that could suggest any particular historical circumstances also added to the impression that Job was not an Israelite, and the clearly non-Israelite provenance of the three friends (2.11) further supports this impression. It is therefore clear that, whether or not he is called by his name Yahweh (as he is in the Prologue and Epilogue and the speeches by Yahweh but not elsewhere in the book) God is presented as the sole deity, who is yet also concerned with all his human creatures. The characteristic particularism of the main Old Testament tradition is, as it is also in the wisdom books Proverbs and Ecclesiastes, entirely lacking.

The Prologue: Themes

It was not, however, the primary intention of the author of the Prologue or of the rest of the book to teach the universal nature of God. This was evidently taken for granted. The Prologue introduces the reader to other issues.

The first scene with the Satan introduces a crucial issue that will continue to be debated throughout the book: that of theodicy. Yahweh is here depicted as a God who—whether by personal observation or through his agents—keeps watch over the behaviour of human beings: a watch so meticulous that he is able to inform the Satan that Job's perfect qualities are unparalleled (1.8). But the Satan raises the question of a connection between Job's wealth and his piety. Is one of these the cause of the other? The Satan suggests that Job's piety is not genuine but conditional on Yahweh's continuing to confer worldly goods on him. So Yahweh allows himself to be tempted by the Satan to permit him to make a test. But in fact it is obvious to the reader that this is as much a test of Yahweh as of Job. If even the ostensibly perfect Job fails the test, this means that no true, disinterested fear of God exists in the world; and if this is so, Yahweh's entire plan for humanity falls to the ground and is revealed as worthless.

In the event Job passes not only the first test but also a second, more demanding one. His piety is thus shown to be genuine: it has nothing to do with his wealth, but is based on a simple faith in God as the one who in his sovereign freedom can—and is justified in doing so—take away from human beings those gifts that he has previously given them just as he pleases, even without a sufficient reason (1.21; 2.10).

Job's acceptance of this would appear to exonerate God. Can this kind of theology be reconciled with the rest of the book? Of course in the dialogue (chs. 3-31) Job adopts a radically different attitude and accuses God of injustice; but it is not in the dialogue that the author's theology is to be found. Rather, the author's own position is expounded in the words that he gives Yahweh to speak when he brings him on to the scene (chs. 38-41). This is very much in line with the theology implied in the Prologue, where Job asserts that it is not for human beings to question God's actions. And when in 42.2-6 Job, after listening to Yahweh's exposition of his sublime and mysterious activities, makes his submission to him, he has returned to his original position; his recognition of God's right to treat human beings as he pleases has actually been strengthened by what he has discovered about him and about his own ignorance.

The Dialogue

The dialogue between Job and his friends is often described as comprising three rounds of speeches in which Job replies to each speech of each of the friends in turn. This description, however, does not adequately represent the actual sequence of the speeches, nor does it set the dialogue in its proper setting. In fact the dialogue is set in motion not by one of the friends but by Job himself (ch. 3). Thus the first speech by Eliphaz is a reply to Job's soliloquy. Eliphaz's opening words are addressed not to the patient Job but to a 'new' impatient and desperate Job who has cursed the day of his birth and who wishes that he had never been born (4.5).

The series thus inaugurated continues with a succession of speeches, first by Job to Eliphaz (chs. 6–7) and then alternatively between each friend and Job until from ch. 25 it peters out with a third very short speech by Bildad (25.1-6) and no third speech by Zophar at all. A further speech by Job follows in ch. 26, clearly addressed to Bildad alone (note the second person singular address in 26.2-4); but then Job continues to speak in a separate speech in ch. 27 in which he addresses the three friends as a group (plural verbs in 27.5, 11, 12). But this is not the end of the speeches: Job still continues to speak uninterruptedly, presumably still addressing the friends, until the end of ch. 31, at which point (31.40) it is stated that his words have come to an end. This uninterrupted speech must be taken to include ch. 28, which is often considered to be a later addition to the book (see below), since there is nothing in the text to indicate a change of speaker. Similarly chs. 29–31, in which Job speaks of his past and present situations and then makes a detailed declaration of his innocence, are clearly intended to be taken as addressed to the friends.

The main topic of discussion in the debate (chs. 3–31) is whether God rewards human beings exactly according to their deserts. The author's own position on this point is made clear by the prominence that he gives to the speeches of Job. These taken together amount to 20 whole chapters (513 verses), while Eliphaz's speeches account only for four chapters (113 verses), Bildad's three (49 verses) and Zophar's two (also 49 verses).

If Job's speeches express the author's own point of view, we must ask what is the function of the speeches of the friends. Must we conclude that their arguments are to be regarded from the author's point of view as simply erroneous and futile? Are the friends, in other words, no more than dummies set up only to be knocked down? This can hardly be the case. They are obviously essential to the literary form that the author has chosen for his book: the dialogue form. No doubt the author might have chosen a different way of expressing his views. An example of such an alternative method is to be found in the Old Testament in the book of Ecclesiastes (Qoheleth). There the author speaks directly to the reader in his own person, setting forth his arguments in a single uninterrupted discourse. The questions with which he deals are to a large extent the same as those raised in the book of Job, and his views about them are sufficiently similar to distinguish these two books as unique in the Old Testament. Like the author of Job, Qoheleth frequently alludes, though in an indirect manner, to other views prevailing in his time that it is his purpose to refute. But he expresses his opinions coldly and dispassionately in the manner of a schoolmaster or lecturer. The author of Job, on the contrary, is all passion. In their speeches his characters, in expounding their respective views, give vent to a whole range of passionate feelings against one another: resentment, anger, hostility, irony, contempt. In this way their various viewpoints come vividly to life. These are no opponents in a purely academic debate. It is easy to imagine—though we have no proof of this—that live debates of this kind may actually have taken place in the time of the author of the book. At any rate, the debate or dialogue form that is the central feature of the book was effective as a way of arousing a lively interest in the issues concerned.

But the principal function of the friends' speeches is to restate a traditional understanding of the nature of God, and one that would have been held by many, if not most, of the first readers of the book, and taken for granted as a fundamental principle on which their lives had always been based and on which they had thought that they could rely: that God is a just God, who is concerned with the lives of ordinary individual human beings and who always rewards the righteous and punishes the wicked. The readers would recognize in the speeches of the friends the expression of this familiar, fundamental doctrine. These speeches, then, were intended to be taken seriously by the readers as statements of what they had always believed. This belief had, however, already been called into question by the scenes in heaven, which depicted God as inflicting misery and suffering on a paragon of righteousness in the person of Job. Now, in the dialogue, this questioning is carried further. Here the readers encounter this same innocent but wretched person no longer quietly accepting his fate but inveighing bitterly against his treatment. Seen in this context the friends' speeches in God's defence, spoken in ignorance of the events described in the Prologue, appear overwhelmed by the testimony of the speeches of Job, who appeals, apparently in vain, against his treatment. At this stage in the book God is apparently inaccessible and not to be moved by Job's desperate appeal.

Chapter 3, with which the dialogue begins, was clearly designed to excite the compassion of the reader. It begins with a curse; but it is not God whom Job curses, as had been predicted by the Satan (1.11; 2.5) and urged by Job's wife (2.9). Although in his speeches Job attacks God and regards him as his enemy, he never commits the terrible sin of cursing him. Rather, he expresses his utter despair by cursing the fact that he was born. He desires death rather than the continuation of his wretched life. Such a desire for death is extremely rare in the Old Testament. That Job has been driven to this extreme is an indication of the hopelessness into which God has driven him.

The surprising transformation of the silent, resigned and wholly acquiescent Job of the Prologue, who simply recognized God's right to take away all that had made his life worthwhile and continued to offer praise to him, into the outspoken Job of the dialogue who defiantly proclaims his innocence and rails against God as the author of his misery can, in terms of the narrative sequence, be accounted for by the considerable but unspecified interval between the infliction of his disease and his words beginning with ch. 3. There was evidently time for the friends to hear of his affliction and to arrive from their distant homes (2.11), and then a further period of seven days and nights during which they all sat together in silence (2.13). It was 'after this' (3.1) that Job began to speak. A psychological explanation of Job's transformation is therefore possible: the author may have intended this interval of time to be seen as having given Job the opportunity to reflect on his situation. The immediate shock caused by the successive blows that he had received had prompted an 'automatic' response: Job's initial reactions were those that came naturally to him as a sincere believer who trusted God in all things; but when he came to consider the matter more deeply he realized that the suddenness and intensity of the calamities that had fallen on him made this automatic response inadequate. He began to think that God must have singled him out with malicious intent, behaving in a way that was completely at variance with the traditional belief in his justice.

The author, however, does not even hint at Job's thoughts during that interval. The change in Job's attitude towards God comes with as devastating suddenness as had the calamities themselves. It undoubtedly came as a shock to the readers.

Chapter 28

This chapter is regarded by many modern scholars as an interpolation. In order to consider that view it is first necessary to pay regard to its position in its present context. The dialogue with the friends ends, properly speaking, with ch. 26, in which Job replies to the final speech spoken by a friend (Bildad) in ch. 25. But there is no textual indication that the dialogue has come to an end, except that in ch. 27 Job addresses all the friends together, and that ch. 27 is prefaced by a new heading: 'And Job again took up his discourse ($m^e\check{s}\bar{a}l\hat{o}$) and said...' This heading is exactly repeated at the beginning of ch. 29. It should also be noted that only in these two verses in the book are Job's words described as a $m\bar{a}\check{s}\bar{a}l$. Since neither ch. 28 nor ch. 30 (or ch. 31) is provided with a separate heading, it appears that the author intended chs. 27-28 and 29-31 respectively to be understood as constituting two distinct speeches.

Chapter 28, then, is presented in the text as the continuation of ch. 27, and thus as addressed, like ch. 27, to all the friends, although the friends are not specifically named in it. The view that ch. 28 is a quite distinct entity that was subsequently incorporated into the original book is based not on the sequence of the speeches presented in the text but on other grounds: that its contents bear no relation to what precedes or to the content of the book as a whole. On the other hand, ch. 27, to which it is clearly intended to be linked, presents problems of its own. (At least 27.13-23 unaccountably express views that are virtually identical with those of the friends, but contrary to those of Job; and it has been widely supposed that this chapter, or a large part of it, is in fact the 'lost' third speech of Zophar, which has been misplaced.) These problems, however, do not directly affect the assessment of ch. 28. The argument against its originality is principally that it cannot be the original continuation of ch. 27 because of its theme. It is a quiet, reasoned and impersonal academic discussion of wisdom and its inaccessibility to human beings; wisdom is depicted as an 'object' whose 'location' is known only to God. This, it is alleged, is a theme that has no relevance to the dispute between Job and his friends. It is urged that the chapter is a well-structured and self-contained literary unity, a literary 'set piece' that would be more at home with the discourses about a personified Wisdom in Proverbs 1–9 than in its present position in the book of Job. (An alternative theory is that it has somehow been misplaced and would be more appropriately situated after the speeches by Yahweh.)

The claim that ch. 28 as a treatise on the nature of wisdom is irrelevant to the preceding debate betrays a misunderstanding of the nature of that debate. The fact that the root *ḥkm* occurs some 24 times in the book apart from ch. 28 is itself sufficient to suggest that there *is* a connection between that chapter and the rest of the book; and this is confirmed by an analysis of the contexts in which wisdom is mentioned in the dialogue. Indeed, it may be claimed that in a real sense the question of wisdom is the main issue of the dialogue. The dialogue is a dispute about who is in the right—that is, about who among the disputants possesses wisdom. All the disputants claim either specifically or by implication to possess superior knowledge; Job in particular specifically disputes the wisdom of the friends and mocks their pretensions to possess it (12.12; 13.5; 17.10; 26.3). There is also a dispute about the claim that the aged have a monopoly of wisdom; this is asserted by Eliphaz (15.10) but denied by Job (12.12) and by Elihu, who maintains that, on the contrary, the young are wiser than the old and that that gives him, as a young man, the right to speak (32.6-11, 16-18). Eliphaz makes an opposite claim: he maintains that the truly authoritative wisdom is that of the wise men of old, and claims that his own opinions are based on that traditional wisdom.

Beyond these disputes as to who among the disputants possesses wisdom there is a more fundamental discussion in the dialogue about the source and the nature of wisdom. Despite their personal claims to it, all agree that in some more fundamental sense only God possesses wisdom: so Job (9.4; 12.13), while Eliphaz asserts (4.21) that mortal men all die without attaining it, and taunts Job by enquiring ironically whether he has been uniquely privileged to hear what is spoken in God's council (*sôd*), so becoming the only person to share in God's wisdom. This question, whether wisdom is ever attainable by human beings, is precisely the theme of ch. 28, which asserts that wisdom is in fact the sole prerogative of God.

The theme of wisdom also provides a link between ch. 28 and the speeches of Elihu (chs. 32–37), who has much to say on the subject. Elihu claims to possess superior wisdom (ch. 32) and maintains that God himself teaches it to human beings (35.11). (37.24 is a disputed verse; it may mean that God will not recognize the wisdom of those who claim to possess it.)

There is also a thematic link between ch. 28 and the speeches of Yahweh (chs. 38–41). In his speeches God's rehearsal of his acts of creation, which are incomprehensible to his human creatures and cannot be matched by them, constitutes an assertion that he alone possesses wisdom, even though the word *ḥokmâ* itself occurs only once in these chapters, when he ironically demands who in his wisdom can count the clouds (38.37). Yahweh's speeches are thus an illustration of the fact, adumbrated in the dialogue but fully expressed in ch. 28, that wisdom is God's sole prerogative. It is then, clear that the question of wisdom and the possession of wisdom is a major topic linking dialogue, ch. 28 and the Yahweh speeches.

A further argument that has been employed against the authorial authenticity of ch. 28 is that it interrupts the flow of discourse between the dialogue and Job's final speech in chs. 29–31 while contributing nothing to the argument. With regard to the immediate context—specifically the relationship of ch. 28 with ch. 27—there is some reason to suppose that at least one common topic links them together. Reference is made in 27.16-17 to the accumulation of wealth by the wicked: they 'heap up silver like dust', but their wealth will be taken from them and given to the innocent. It may be significant that ch. 28 begins with a reference to the acquisition—though in a different sense—of silver (and other precious objects). In 28.1-11 the mining of these precious objects is described. The same word 'dust' (*'āpār*) employed in 27.16 occurs again here twice, in vv. 2 and 6. Since it is the purpose of 28.1-11 to emphasize the ingenuity of human technology and the lengths to which men will go to acquire these sources of wealth, only to point out in vv. 14-19 that the most precious treasure of all, namely wisdom, is the one thing that they cannot obtain, this may be seen as a comment on the futility of those who, like the wicked of ch. 27, value material wealth above all else.

There are also further points of contact between ch. 28 and the Yahweh speeches and between that chapter and the speeches of Elihu. In 28.24-27 there is a list of certain creative acts of God: the weighing of the wind, the apportioning of the waters and the creation of the rain and the thunder. Such passages about God's creation of and control over the natural phenomena are in fact scattered throughout the book. They appear in the dialogue (9.8-9; 12.15, 22; 26.7-13) and also in the Elihu speeches (36.27-33; 37.2-24). They are a principal theme of the Yahweh speeches, where there are references to God's measuring of the earth (38.5), his setting of a limit to the sea (38.10), his creation of the rain and the thunder (38.25, 35). All these passages belong to a specific wisdom genre of which the wisdom poem of Prov. 8.22-31 is an outstanding example. In Job the creation passage in ch. 28 stands especially close to ch. 38. In one sense all of these earlier passages, including ch. 28, can be seen as anticipations of the great Yahweh speeches of chs. 38–41.

Beyond such affinities, some of which could admittedly be explained as due to the deliberate adaptation of the style and themes of the work of one writer by another, it is possible to make out a good case for a positive function of ch. 28 in the context of the book as a whole. Whatever may have been the original function of ch. 27, ch. 28 can be seen as Job's final comment on the problem of the possession or lack of wisdom that had caused so much acrimony in the dialogue. Taking up earlier hints in those chapters that true wisdom resides in God alone, Job now assesses the matter calmly, dispassionately and at an elevated theological level. He shows himself to be already on the way towards the self-assessment that he will make in ch. 42, when he will at last have encountered God and listened to God's account of himself. He now declares his conclusion, that neither he nor the friends nor any human being possesses wisdom at all. Wisdom is the possession of God alone, and human beings, however hard they try and whatever ingenuity they may display, can never attain to it. The concluding verse of the chapter (v. 28) has often been regarded as an interpolation which contradicts all that the rest of the chapter is concerned to affirm; however, it may be argued that, far from contradicting it, v. 28 confirms it. This verse indicates that much of the previous discussion has been misguided because it has not distinguished between human and divine wisdom. It implies that although God, who created the world by his power and who 'sees everything under the heavens' (v. 24), is incomprehensible to human beings and is the only one to possess the secret of the universe, he has given mankind another kind of wisdom that is sufficient for them: this consists of the fear of Yahweh and the rejection of evil.

With this verse we revert to the Job of the Prologue, who, as is
specifically stated in 1.1, possessed this latter kind of wisdom that has
now been defined in 28.28 in that he *did* fear Yahweh and turn from
evil. Chapter 28, then, it seems, might have been the original conclusion
of the book, since its final verse forms an inclusio with the first sentence
in the book; this is what gives the view of those who suppose the chapter to have been misplaced from after the Yahweh speeches some plausibility. But in fact the story of Job has one more twist: until he has 'seen
God' and listened to God's own words, Job's 'conversion' from what he
had said in the dialogues is still not quite complete. He remains convinced of his innocence and of the injustice of his treatment by God,
and is still determined to maintain his case. Chapters 29–31 are the
expression of this determination.

The Speeches of Elihu (32-37)
Elihu's speeches present a greater challenge to the theory of single authorship of the book than does ch. 28. The arguments that they are an
interpolation are formidable. Elihu is never mentioned elsewhere in the
book, not even in the Epilogue, where Yahweh speaks of the *three*
friends and ignores his existence (42.7). Further, it has been argued that
Elihu's arguments add nothing to those presented in the dialogue. Equally important is the argument that his speeches disrupt the sequence of
events. They occur at the moment when Job has thrown down his final
challenge to God, swearing with an oath that he is innocent of every sin
of which he could be accused (ch. 31). At this point the reader, now
anxious for a conclusion to the whole affair and avid to know its outcome, would naturally suppose that if ever God was going to appear on
the scene and bring about the denouement of the plot, this was the
obvious moment for that to occur. But the reader would be disappointed. Instead of a solution he is confronted by yet another lengthy
discourse, spoken by an interloper whose very existence he had never
suspected, who seems simply to repeat the preceding arguments for and
against Job. This interruption, which thus delays the denouement, it is
argued, is not only unexpected but intolerably disrupts the flow of
events. These arguments have appeared to many scholars to constitute
overwhelming proof that the Elihu chapters did not belong to the book
in its original form.

One matter on which there is general agreement among the critics is
that the Elihu speeches are not an independent composition unrelated
to the theme of the book. Their author shows himself to be fully aware
of Job's situation, and is especially familiar with the dialogue section of
the book. He refers in some detail to Job's previous speeches, especially
to his claim to be guiltless and to his complaint of God's treatment of
him, often citing his actual words (e.g. 33.9-11; 34.5-6; 35.2-3); and he
also alludes to the speeches of the friends. His own arguments are often

similar to those already put forward by them. His main substantially new contribution—though in fact this has already been briefly mentioned by Eliphaz in 5.17—is his attempt to defend God by interpreting his punitive actions as educative: as warnings intended to frighten human beings into righteous behaviour.

In fact it can be argued that Elihu's theology is more distinctive than it at first appears to be. It can also be argued that his intervention does *not* weaken the dramatic sequence by interrupting it: that the author has deliberately retarded the denouement in order to leave the reader in suspense—a device familiar to readers of fiction. It can even be maintained that his words mark an essential stage in the drama: that Elihu, whose name—'My God is He'—is, as it were, a forerunner of the God who reveals his true nature in chs. 38-41, as well as supplying a corrective to the academic arguments of the friends. Elihu claims that his own wisdom is derived directly from God himself (32.8) rather than from the conventional theology of the friends.

As has long been observed, as Elihu's speeches proceed the accent is laid less and less on Job's sufferings and more and more on the majesty of God, so that by ch. 37 he is already speaking in language that is almost identical with the words spoken by God himself in chs. 38-41. The fact, too, that he is the only human speaker who is permitted to speak at great length with no interruptions either from Job or the friends suggests that he was regarded as making a substantial contribution to the debate.

Elihu is perhaps best seen as a transitional figure who quite properly disappears once his role has been played out—a counterpart to that other figure, the Satan, for whom also there was no further role in the author's scheme. The lack of reference to Elihu in the Epilogue, when the friends reappear to be castigated by Yahweh, may be thought strange; but the final chapter ought not to be thought of as a complete round up of the 'cast' as at the end of a theatrical performance: it has the limited function of concluding the story of Job with an account of his rehabilitation, together with an act of divine mercy towards those who have erred by refusing to believe in Job's innocence and so speaking wrongly about God; and in that design Elihu, the spokesman for God, had no role to play.

The arguments for and against the Elihu speeches as an integral part of the book have each their own plausibility; but inasmuch as the onus of proof lies upon the proponents of a negative judgment, it may be concluded that their case is not proven.

Yahweh's speeches (38.1-39.30; 40.6-41.34)

These two speeches comprise Yahweh's answer to Job, who had made his final appeal to him in ch. 31. On reading 38.1, 'Then Yahweh answered Job from the whirlwind', the reader would no doubt suppose that Yahweh had come down to earth from his heavenly dwelling in order to accept Job's plea of innocence and to account for his own treatment of him. But on reading further he would receive a shock, for in his very first words Yahweh accuses Job of speaking without knowledge and so of obscuring his 'design' ('ēṣâ), probably meaning his way of operating in the universe.

Throughout these two speeches Yahweh never alludes to Job's situation or to his claim to be guiltless. Instead, he demands that Job should answer a series of questions. The questions that he asks appear to have nothing whatever to do with the concerns that have been central to the book up to this point. Even more astonishing is the fact that he does not speak about human beings and their concerns at all. Rather, his questions are about the 'design' or 'plan' to which he has referred in v. 2—his governance of the world. Their relevance to human concerns can only be surmised; Elihu already gave a hint of this when he drew Job's attention away from the problem of Job's troubles towards a contemplation of God's majesty and incomprehensibility to mankind, urging him to 'stop' (ʿᵃmōd), listen and 'consider the wondrous works of God' (37.14).

Yahweh's speeches are an example of irony on a large scale. The intention of the author here was clearly to demonstrate the utter insignificance of human beings in God's sight. It seems that the human concern for divine justice is after all of no importance to God, as if it is not worthy of his attention. There could hardly be a greater reversal in literature of the reader's expectations; but the theological significance of what Yahweh has to say can scarcely be missed. Significantly, these speeches of Yahweh express a theology that comes close to the teaching of Ecclesiastes.

The fact that Yahweh's reply to Job is delivered not in a single speech but in two has led some interpreters to suppose that one of them is not part of the original version of the book. In fact they complement one another. Although each is prefaced with an identical statement (38.1; 40.6), the second speech, which consists mainly of descriptions of the two monstrous creatures, Behemoth and Leviathan—whether these are to be seen as real creatures or in mythological terms is not relevant in this connection—constitutes the continuation and climax of the catalogue of created creatures (the wild ass, the ostrich, the horse and the hawk and so on) with which the first speech concludes (39.5-30). Between these two parts of the catalogue there is an interlude (40.1-14) consisting of an address to Job and a reply by Job, before Yahweh resumes his interrogation. If these chapters do contain an interpolation it is more likely to be 40.1-14, in which Yahweh ironically invites Job to assume his own powers and punish the wicked, though the authenticity of that passage also can be defended.

Job's Replies to Yahweh (40.4-5; 42.2-6)

Job's reaction to Yahweh's words evolves gradually in two stages. In 40.4-5, in answer to the great series of rhetorical questions that Yahweh has posed in order to demonstrate that as a mere human being Job is powerless and insignificant, Job admits that this is so: 'I am of no importance' (qallōtî). He has in the past tried to dispute with God (he has been, in God's words, a rōb 'im-šadday), but he now finds that he is unable to do so: there is no reply that he can make. God has overwhelmed him; yet at this stage it is not stated that he has abandoned his demand for vindication: he merely says that he will now make no further attempt to argue with this God of infinite power. Yahweh, however, is clearly not satisfied with this reply. In 40.7-8 he reverses the tables and makes his own one and only complaint against Job: he accuses him of denying his (God's) justice (tāpēr mišpāṭî) and of putting him in the wrong in order to maintain his own righteousness (taršî'ēnî l^ema'an tiṣdāq).

In 40.9, therefore, Yahweh resumes his ironical interrogation, once again challenging Job to perform actions that only he can perform and promising that if Job can do so he will acknowledge his superiority (vv. 9-14). He faces him with the most awe-inspiring monsters that he has created (40.15–41.34). When Job speaks again (42.2-6) he has quite changed his demeanour, although God has not used any substantially new arguments to persuade him to do so. This change in Job, however, should not take the reader entirely by surprise: it attests the author's psychological subtlety. Just as at the beginning of the book the patient Job of the Prologue had changed after an interval of reflection to the impatient and quarrelsome Job of the dialogue, so at the end, again after an opportunity for reflection, the browbeaten but unrepentant Job of the first reply to God becomes the repentant Job of the second.

The reason for Job's changed attitude in his second reply is made clear in 42.5, where he speaks of the contrast between hearing and seeing. By 'hearing' he means the traditional teaching of the sages (deployed by the friends in their speeches), which he has come to reject as contrary to his own experience. But he now claims to *see* Yahweh, and confesses that this 'sight' of him has entirely changed his attitude. (We should probably take the phrase 'but now my eye sees you' in the extended sense of 'seeing', that is, seeing with the inward eye, since it is not stated in the text [38.1] that God made himself literally visible to Job when he spoke to him from the whirlwind. Nevertheless this was a genuine encounter.) Job has now obtained what he had previously longed for (cf. 19.26). But this 'vision' proved to be quite different from what he had expected: and it is precisely because of this ('al-kēn) that Job, now completely overwhelmed, declares that he rejects or revokes ('em'as, niḥamtî) all that he had previously spoken.

The Epilogue (42.7-17)
In the Epilogue the prose folk-tale style of the Prologue is resumed. In a sense, as has been pointed out above, it is to be seen as the conclusion of the story begun in the Prologue: but it is more than that: it shows knowledge of the dialogue, if not also of Elihu's speeches and the speeches by Job made subsequent to the conclusion of the dialogue proper. The unexpected restoration of Job's fortunes (vv. 10-17) probably also presupposes a knowledge of the test of the genuineness of Job's righteousness that is described in the Satan episodes of 1.6-12 and 2.1-7, though the Satan does not himself reappear. (It is important to observe that the Epilogue brings no solution to the universal problem of human suffering, since God's treatment of Job in these verses is evidently entirely exceptional, and it is unreasonable to suppose that the readers would have thought it possible to draw from the restoration of Job's fortunes any parallel with their own expectations from life. Indeed, the book as a whole offers no solution to this problem.)

Is the Epilogue, then, intended to be no more than a 'happy ending', bringing the story to a close with the appearance of a *deus ex machina*—a device in the folk-tale style to relieve the anxiety of the readers whose sympathies were with Job, and to reassure them that in the end God proves after all to be just and that he never intended Job to suffer indefinitely? This can hardly be the case. The Epilogue, like so much else in the book, has ironical features that suggest that it is not a simple, straightforward story. A mere 'happy ending' would solve no problems and would be a very trivial conclusion to a book of such high dramatic and philosophical character. Readers who were able to appreciate the subtleties of the dialogue and other speeches in the book would not have been lacking in the ability to discern deeper meanings lying behind the apparently simple narrative.

There is certainly irony in Yahweh's treatment of both the friends and Job in 42.7-8. Their relative situations have been completely reversed. The friends have treated Job as a sinner who deserved his punishment, but are now arraigned before God as being themselves the ones who have sinned, and who need the intercession of Job, whom God, using again the title that he had conferred on him in 1.8 and 2.3, designates 'my servant'—a title that he had given him because he was 'blameless and upright, fearing God and turning away from evil'.

It is by their *speech* that Yahweh judges both Job and the friends here: on whether they have spoken about God what was correct (*nᵉkônâ*). This shows that the main issue in the book is of *different concepts of God*; and this is clearly not simply a theological question to be discussed dispassionately in an academic manner. To speak wrongly about God is blasphemy, deserving public humiliation (*nᵉbālâ*, v. 8) that can only be averted by the prayers of a righteous man and by the offering of propitiatory sacrifices. This, then, is the crucial issue of the whole book, now brought to a head: the nature of God and the right way to think about him. It is not denied here that God has brought suffering (*rā'â*, 'evil') on an innocent person: this is openly admitted here by the narrator (v. 11). The point is that his sovereign will is not to be questioned.

The text of 42.7, 8 offers no clue to the nature of the friends' failure to speak rightly about God or of Job's doing so. But it is clear that the fault of the friends lay in a false concept of God. In the dialogue they had frequently attempted to *defend* God against the accusations made against him by Job, but they get no credit for this: they are condemned because they have made the assumption that God will always punish the wicked and reward the righteous because he is bound by his very nature to do so, though he is also bound to heal them if they repent. This is to deny God's freedom. That he is not to be thought of as having justice toward human individuals as his primary concern has been stated by implication in his own speeches in chs. 38–41, where human beings and their problems are not even mentioned as part of his activities. He is not to be confined by *a priori* concepts of how he *must* behave.

Job, on the other hand, although he has railed against God and claimed that he was treated by God as an enemy, has never doubted God's freedom. He has not allowed his sense of injustice to shake his trust in God; he has frequently affirmed his confidence that if only he could meet him face to face he could justify himself. It is for this reason that Yahweh commends him. The author, then, tacitly represents Yahweh as approving Job's outspokenness; it is not the acquiescent Job of the Prologue who wins his approval but the Job who had dared to argue against him.

It is noteworthy that already in 13.7-11 Job had accused the friends of speaking falsely about God. In his two final replies to Yahweh he indicates that it is not for mortal beings to make confident pronouncements about him. This realization, that God's mysterious ways are not available for human scrutiny, is the real lesson of the book. This is a belief very close to that of the thought of Qoheleth.

These questions about the authorship of the book will not be further discussed in the body of this commentary. Whether or not its various parts were the work of different writers, its composition cannot have been the result of chance. Those who gave it its final form knew what they were doing; they perceived it as having a single theme, though one with many facets—the nature of God and his relationship to his human creatures.

Job 1

An obvious purpose of the Prologue (chs. 1 and 2) is to introduce the principal characters and to set the scene for the dialogue that follows. But it would be a mistake to read these chapters as if they were just a simple, naive tale. They already raise, and in acute form, two important theological and ethical questions with which the whole book will be concerned: whether human concepts of justice are the same as God's, and how men and women ought to react to unexplained misfortunes.

Chapter 1 is heavily ironical. This is especially true of the scene in heaven (vv. 6-12), which describes an imaginary dialogue between God (here identified as Yahweh) and a figure called 'the Satan' concerning the genuineness of Job's religious faith. Part of the irony consists of the way in which, although Yahweh's absolute power over the world and over his human creatures is never in question, the two participants are made to converse almost as equals. The Satan addresses God without the usual deferential formalities, questions his judgment and persuades him, apparently against his will, to submit Job to a severe test.

It cannot be said that Yahweh comes well out of the encounter. His apparently ignorant enquiry about the Satan's previous whereabouts (v. 7) may be no more than a way of opening the conversation; but after an initial strong assertion of Job's outstanding virtues he exhibits weakness in allowing himself to be seduced by the Satan's cynicism, and subjecting Job to a humiliating and painful test. This caricature, which is reminiscent of the informal and sometimes comic scenes in polytheistic myths, can hardly be a true representation of the author's own concept of God. One of the purposes of the scene was to create a dramatic irony that would persist throughout the book—that the reader knows what Job does not: that his misfortunes are due to a decision made in heaven to test him. But the introduction of the Satan may have been intended to draw attention to the theological problem of the risk taken by God when he created mankind. The Satan himself is not a substantial figure—merely a fiction serving a limited purpose. He disappears after ch. 2, never to reappear. But these scenes with their pretended claim to provide a glimpse into God's mind are probably not intended to be taken seriously, though they add spice to the reader's enjoyment.

Verses 1-3 introduce the man Job as a person of princely wealth who was also a model of goodness and piety. 'The sons of the east' is a rather vague term designating the inhabitants of regions bordering on the eastern desert. But despite his possession of herds and flocks, Job did not live a nomadic life. Even his sons, as befitted their princely status,

had their own houses and establishments. The description of the frequent parties or banquets organized by Job's sons for themselves and their sisters and of Job's protective actions on their behalf each morning following one of these parties (vv. 4-5) reflects the harmonious relationships of a patriarchal family, but it also suggests that the sons were irresponsible; nothing is said about their participation with their father in the management of his vast enterprises.

The use of the word *mište* for the brothers' banquets shows that these were not religious feasts but simply examples of the self-indulgence of the really rich. But the brothers are only of peripheral importance in the story, and no other reference is made to them apart from the notice of their deaths, which occurred when they were, typically, eating and drinking (vv. 18-19). The real purpose of vv. 4-5 was to illustrate with a concrete example the initial statement about Job's piety. He acts with great scrupulousness, offering sacrifices on behalf of his sons not for sins that he knows them to have committed but for sins that they *might* have committed in the course of their feasting: blasphemy, described as 'cursing God in their hearts' (this verb has the literal meaning of 'bless': but here, as also in v. 11 and 2.5, it is a euphemism, having this opposite meaning). Job is seen here in his patriarchal role, assuming responsibility for his whole family.

The scene now shifts abruptly to heaven, where Yahweh, as supreme king, holds court (vv. 6-12). This scene, of which there is no further hint beyond ch. 2, draws on the notion of a heavenly court that is ultimately traceable to the polytheistic belief in an assembly of the gods under the presidency of a king of the gods. In the Old Testament this concept is found in an attenuated form (e.g. in 1 Kgs 22.19-23; Isa. 6) in which the members of the court are no longer to be thought of as gods but are subordinate heavenly (or 'angelic') beings. In some passages, as here, they have retained the old title 'sons of God', but their activities are completely subject to Yahweh's orders.

Verse 6 relates that these heavenly beings came on a certain day to 'present themselves' before Yahweh. It is not stated what were the nature and purpose of this assembly; but it may be presumed from the ensuing dialogue that they came to take their orders or to report on the various missions that they had undertaken. About them as a body no more is said beyond ch. 2: they are introduced here simply to provide the setting for a dialogue in which only one of them, the Satan, is singled out for detailed attention. (Though this is not specifically stated in the text, it may be presumed that the Satan is one of these 'sons of God', one who had been given the specialized function of visiting the earth and investigating and reporting on the characters and deeds of human beings. Compare Zech. 3.1-2 and 1 Chron. 21.1, the only other Old Testament passages in which the Satan appears.) Although he is evidently permitted to speak his mind, the Satan cannot act without Yahweh's permission; but he makes use of his privilege of speech to persuade Yahweh to change his mind.

After a probably otiose enquiry about the Satan's recent activities, Yahweh begins the discussion by referring to the case of Job. Using the same phraseology as that of the narrator in v. 1, he asserts that Job is without equal among human beings for piety and way of life, and enquires whether the Satan has paid special attention to him. The Satan disagrees with God's estimate, and poses the crucial question that re-echoes through the book: 'Does Job fear God for nothing (ḥinnām)?' He suggests that Job's piety is spurious; that Job only appears to be religious so that God may continue to confer prosperity on him. The Satan further accuses God of fostering this attitude of Job's by giving him special protection (v. 10), and claims that if Job's wealth were to be stripped from him God would discover the fraud: Job would then cease to serve God and would curse him instead. Yahweh, easily persuaded, gives the Satan as his agent full power to make the experiment. The only proviso is that there is to be no attack on Job's person, only on his wealth.

After the Satan left Yahweh's presence and returned to the earth, Job suffered a series of simultaneous blows to his happiness. They fell precisely at the time when Job's sons were eating and drinking at one of their banquets. They are stated, in true folk-tale style, to have followed immediately one after the other. The test of Job proposed by the Satan—'Stretch out your hand and strike everything that he possesses'—had been put into operation with a vengeance: Job's entire establishment—herds, servants, children—was wiped out. Two of the blows were inflicted by human agency in the form of attacks by tribes from the desert, here somewhat vaguely referred to as Sabeans and Chaldeans; two were natural disasters, the 'fire of God' (presumably a conflagration caused by lightning) and a 'great wind'. The author's attention is concentrated not on the loss of human life involved but on the effect of the disasters on the central figure, Job. That is what the readers had been anxiously waiting to discover: whether Satan's claim, that Job would react by cursing God, had been fulfilled; in other words, whether his piety would survive his material ruin.

With vv. 20-22 the denouement of the story seems to have been reached. Job's immediate reaction to his loss (tearing his clothes, shaving his head) was what was to be expected of a man suffering extreme grief. But then we are told that he prostrated himself and worshipped (the verb is hištaḥªwâ, literally, 'to bow down'). He then began to speak, first citing the general belief that human beings must eventually be deprived of their possessions and return to their prenatal state (cf., e.g., Gen. 3.19; Eccl. 12.7), and then applying this principle to his own more limited situation: even though he remained alive, God had already taken away from him everything that he had previously given. But he ended on a positive note: grateful for what God had given him in the past and not reproaching him for having taken it away again, he blessed the name of Yahweh. His faith was thus completely vindicated, the Satan proved wrong and the reader satisfied.

Verse 22, which sums up Job's reaction to his losses, appears to mark the conclusion of the story (note the first words, 'In all this'). But in remarking that Job did not attribute blame to God (or perhaps impropriety—the precise meaning of *tiplâ* is not certain, but it occurs again in 24.12 and certainly denotes some kind of disapprobation—the author is perhaps suggesting that he would have been justified in doing so. At least, the use of the word here may be a hint to the reader that there was something about God's conduct in the story that needed explanation. Although in terms of narrative intention the author no doubt expected the reader to assume that this was the end of the story, since the question of the genuineness of Job's piety was satisfactorily solved, this was in fact a false ending. The discovery that Job's persecution by God was not in fact over but was further intensified would surprise the reader and spur him to deeper reflection.

Job 2

The second scene in which Satan appears (vv. 1-7) is to a large extent a verbal repetition of the first. These verses are thus an example of the literary device known as repetition with variations which is a regular feature of folktales and fairy stories, but which came also to be characteristic of much more sophisticated narrative literature in the ancient Near East (we may compare the Ugaritic legends and, in the Old Testament, 2 Kings 1 and the account of the Plagues in Exod. 7-12). As a narrative device its purpose is to maintain the level of the reader's interest. In this case it may be said to be intended to revive that interest, since ch. 1 has given the impression of being a complete story beyond which there is nothing to be added. However, when he or she reads the first verses of ch. 2 the reader will have to revise this conclusion, and will now expect a further development. He or she may well wonder whether the new instalment will speak of a change of Yahweh's mind, leading to the restoration of Job's fortunes—in fact, anticipating the final chapter of the book. In any case, the interest in the sequel will now be intense.

The variations in these verses are, of course, the significant features. In v. 3 Yahweh repeats the question that he had asked in 1.8, reasserting his confidence in Job's integrity and still referring to him by the rare designation 'my servant'. He first appears to withdraw his approval of the Satan's test, since the latter's prediction that Job would react to the test by turning against God had proved to be groundless. By using again the word *ḥinnām*, here in the sense of 'for no reason' as in 1.9, where it means 'for nothing', the author stresses the contrast between Job's real character and the Satan's estimate of it. The Satan, however, is not only unrepentant, but even proceeds to argue that the earlier test had not been sufficiently searching. He now proposes that if an attack were made on Job's physical health ('strike his bone and his flesh') sufficiently crippling to put him in fear of death, his reaction would be different. The meaning of the phrase 'skin for skin', possibly a current idiom, is uncertain; but the meaning of the remainder of v. 4 and of v. 5 is clear. The Satan expresses the belief that even a pious person whose faith is not shaken by a sudden reversal of material fortune will nevertheless turn against God if threatened with death, since to die is to lose everything that makes life worth living. In making this assertion the Satan expresses a total cynicism about human nature: he implies that true piety among human beings does not exist. This is, in effect, a challenge to the whole enterprise of God's creation of mankind.

If the readers of the first part of the Prologue had expected that Yahweh would reverse the earlier damage that he had allowed to be inflicted on Job, they would be disappointed. Once again Yahweh deferred without argument to the Satan's new proposal, even though it would inflict much greater suffering on Job. Again, he made only one stipulation: this time it was that Job's life should be preserved. But it is reasonable to argue that this stipulation was not made out of kindness; rather, it was essential to the whole enterprise, since if Job were dead he could neither praise nor curse God. This time it is specifically stated that the Satan himself, on leaving Yahweh's presence, inflicted the agreed disease on Job, which took the form of an unspecified but particularly virulent skin disease in which the skin broke out in sores (v. 7). Job's reaction to this new affliction in sitting among the ashes is not unexpected: this was a customary sign of grief (compare Isa. 58.5; Jon. 3.6). Ashes, together with dust, also signified a recognition of personal unworthiness (42.6). In Job's case the ashes were presumably to be found in the vicinity of the rubbish dump of the village or city.

This time Job's verbal reaction occurred as a reply to his wife's advice (vv. 9-10). Otherwise he kept silent. This incident is tantalizingly brief. But Job's wife, who is mentioned only here, must have been directly and drastically affected by what had happened to him, though she had not herself suffered the fate of her family. With him she had borne the loss of their children and of all their wealth and possessions; but it was only when he was smitten by a terrible disease and suffered the additional loss of social status that she was impelled to speak. Her advice, 'Curse God, and die', is a deliberate echo of the Satan's predictions in 1.11 and 2.5; and, though its intention was probably to bring an end to her husband's suffering, it was a temptation to him to sin. She recognized his integrity, but called on him to abandon it. Nor surprisingly, she has been called 'the mouthpiece of Satan'. Like the Satan, she did not believe in piety for its own sake. Her advice was, in fact, an invitation to self-destruction, since to curse God would be considered as inviting retaliation by God, which in the circumstances could only take the form of death, since Job now had literally nothing to lose except his life.

What was the purpose of the insertion of this incident into the story? It could be considered simply as a pretext for the inclusion of a verbal reaction from Job; yet no such pretext was thought necessary after the first incident (1.21). Another way of looking at it might be in literary terms: Job's initial silence (v. 8) might be thought to create a tension that required a resolution before the narrative passed on to the visit of the friends which leads directly into the dialogue. In fact this incident also anticipates the ensuing dialogue, in that it constitutes the first negative reaction to Job's treatment by God—it is a foretaste of the plethora of human reactions that follows. It is also, more distantly, an anticipation of the final scene in the Epilogue, where Job's married state was obviously a precondition (though his wife is not, curiously, mentioned there) of the 'happy ending' in which he was blessed with a new family and ultimately with further descendants, so reaffirming his initial status as patriarch (42.13-16).

Job's reply (v. 10) to this new blow closely resembles his earlier reply in 1.21. In both verses the question concerns what one receives from God and how one should receive it: God gives, but also takes away (1.21); we receive both good and bad things from him (2.10), and we ought to respond without recrimination to what he gives (it is perhaps worth noting, however, that Job does not here repeat his words of blessing to God, and that no reference is made this time to an act of worship). Job rebuked his wife for giving him wicked advice, but gently: he did not accuse her directly of being an impious fool (of $n^e b \bar{a} l \hat{a}$), but only of speaking like one in her agony of mind. The verse ends, again, with what seems like a concluding summary ('In all this...'): Job committed no sin in his reaction to the second terrible blow. Whether the final 'with his lips' has a special significance is a moot point. On one level the phrase is obviously intended to distinguish between spoken sins (specifically curses) and sinful actions; but there has been no question in this scene of sinful actions, so the phrase seems redundant unless, as has been suggested, the distinction intended is between Job's pious words at this point and his subsequent raging against God in the dialogue; however, in fact, he never cursed God in the dialogue or elsewhere, and in 42.7 he was praised by God for speaking 'rightly' about him.

In fact, v. 10 is no more a conclusion to the story than 1.22. Verses 11-13 introduce the last essential element: the arrival of the three friends of Job who will be his partners in the dialogue that is to occupy the greater part of the book and who will reappear at the end (42.7-9). Verse 10 presupposes a considerable but indefinable period of time between the occurrence of Job's misfortunes and the arrival of the friends: the time to receive the news in their distant homes and to travel to Uz. When they arrived Job would have been sitting among the ashes, presumably in silence, ministered to by his wife, for weeks or even months. All this may be surmised, although the author, true to his chosen folk-tale style, leaves the details vague, not deeming it necessary or appropriate to supply them. He gives the friends somewhat outlandish names and places of origin: only Eliphaz the Temanite can certainly be placed, another Eliphaz having been one of the sons of Esau, the ancestor of the Edomites (Gen. 36.4), and Teman being a district of Edom. To the original readers of the book all these places were no doubt as remote and mysterious as was Job's own home in the land of Uz.

The word 'friend' does not entirely convey the fullness of meaning of the Hebrew word *rēa'*. This is a word that occurs many times in the book of Proverbs, which speaks of love and loyalty between friends (Prov. 17.17), of the relation between friends being closer even than that between members of the same family (Prov. 18.24) and of the good advice that one may expect to receive from a true friend (Prov. 12.26). Although we are not told by what means Job's friends had been able to form and maintain friendship with Job and with one another, we are left in no doubt that Eliphaz, Bildad and Zophar, who had left their own affairs and undertaken considerable journeys in order to do what they could for Job, are represented as possessing these qualities. We are told, again with no explanatory details, that before they arrived at his home they met together, perhaps to decide how best to comport themselves with him.

The friends came to do two things: to grieve with Job and to comfort him. The first of these (*nûd*) was expressed by external manifestations of grief similar to those of Job himself (1.20). These were normally performed over the dead (e.g. Jer. 22.10); and there may be a suggestion here that the friends thought of Job as very near death. But they also came to 'comfort' him. This word (*nḥm*) also has a more positive sense than its English counterpart: it can mean (and this is its probable meaning here) to encourage, that is, to persuade a despondent person that his trials are over and that there is hope for better things in the future (so, e.g., Isa. 40.1-2). In the dialogue the friends will, in fact, adopt this tone: they will assure Job that if he will confess that he is sinful and promise amendment God will restore and heal him (e.g. Eliphaz in 5.17-27).

The scene in vv. 12-13 is depicted with great poignancy. As they approached from a distance the friends looked for Job, but he was so changed in appearance that they did not at first recognize him. When they did, they mourned for him as for one dead. To sit on the bare ground was a symbol of grief or despair, an expression of humiliation (cf. Lam. 2.10; Isa. 3.26; 47.1); the friends' doing so (v. 13) was a gesture indicating that they fully participated in Job's grief. They were so overwhelmed by the sight of Job's suffering that for a whole week they were unable to carry out their second purpose of 'comforting' him. They could not even perform the customary greetings. But apart from its poignancy the unprecedented length of this period of total silence (which Job may already have been observing for much longer) serves an important rhetorical purpose. The profound quiet that prevails at the end of this scene can almost be felt. Then in 3.1 Job suddenly and dramatically shatters the silence, breaking into it with an utterly unexpected and bitter curse. At last, the reader may feel, we have encountered the 'real' Job.

Job 3

Verses 1 and 2 continue the prose narrative begun in the Prologue. Job's curse on the day of his birth, though in poetical form, is thus presented as an essential part of the story, carrying the plot further. It was this curse that provoked the hitherto silent friends to indignation and to speech; their words are thus to be seen as responses to him rather than the other way round. The reason for their indignation was that throughout his moving account of his misery Job never once admitted that it was the result of his own sin. Although in this chapter he did not directly accuse God of injustice, he came close to doing so. He presented himself as an innocent sufferer and so as a living testimony to the falsity of the principle that both he and the friends had always taken for granted as a fundamental fact of life, namely that the innocent enjoy God's blessing and that only the wicked are punished. Thus the author is here already challenging the reader either to approve the submissive Job of 1.21 and 2.10, who passively acknowledged the right of God to behave as he chose, or to side with the new militant Job of this and the succeeding chapters.

With v. 3 begins what is often called 'the poem of Job'; it continues without a break until 42.6, after which the prose narrative is resumed. The poem presents not a few difficult linguistic problems, but its literary excellence has been universally recognized. Chapter 3 stands by itself as a literary masterpiece. It is described in v. 1 as a 'curse', though in content it is more like a lament. A curse was properly speaking a form of speech employed to achieve a specific, negative effect on a particular individual or human group. But no such persons are named here. The 'curse' is directed, rather, against the day of Job's birth and the night when he was conceived: Job expresses the wish that they should 'perish'. He refers to those past moments of time as though they were alive and even still in existence. This poetic conceit is elaborated in vv. 4-10. In realistic terms these verses simply express Job's futile wish that he had never been born.

The lament is reminiscent of Jer. 20.14-18, where the prophet Jeremiah voices the same wish as Job. But despite some common imagery there is probably no direct connection between the two passages. Verses 3-10 play on the topics of day and night, light and darkness: Job wishes that the day of his birth would become dark, and the night when he was conceived be joyless, never seeing the dawn. Despite some of the language employed, there is no justification for interpreting these verses literally in the sense of a wish by Job that the process of creation as described especially in Genesis 1 should be reversed: Job's concern here is confined to his own personal situation. But there are mythical allusions of a literary kind, notably in v. 8, where 'curse the day' (*yôm*) ought perhaps to be emended to 'curse the sea' (*yām*), making a parallel with 'Leviathan' in the next line. This would seem to be an allusion to a Canaanite myth to which there are other allusions in the Old Testament (e.g. Ps. 74.14; Isa. 27.1), in which 'Sea' (Yam) and Leviathan (Lotan) are powerful allies. Job is represented as calling on powerful cosmic forces to assist him in implementing his 'curse'.

From v. 11 the curse gives way to pure lament, introduced by the characteristic 'Why?' (*lammâ*) as in many of the psalms of lamentation. Job wished that he had died soon after his birth (v. 11) or had been stillborn and so had never 'seen the light' even for an instant (v. 16), so escaping all suffering. In vv. 20-23 he speaks in more general terms of all those who have to endure intolerable suffering, asking why those who in their misery would rather die because they have 'lost their way' or been 'hedged in' by God are not allowed to do so. Finally in vv. 24-26 he reverts to his own situation.

Verses 13-19, which describe the state of the dead, are interrupted by v. 16, which may have been misplaced, probably from after v. 12. One indication of this is that the word 'There' (*šām*), which occurs repeatedly in vv. 17, 18 and 19, presumably referring to the place of the dead, has no antecedent unless v. 17 immediately follows v. 15. This positive picture of the place of the dead (often called 'Sheol' or 'the Pit' elsewhere in the Old Testament, but not named here) is virtually without parallel in the Old Testament: for Job at this moment it is a desirable place, a place of quiet and rest where all sleep together in peace. This depiction is totally contrary to the way in which it is conceived for example in Ps. 88.6-7 and Isa. 14.11, where it is terrifying, utterly repulsive and inhabited by worms and maggots. This negative view is shared by Job himself elsewhere in the book (10.18-22).

In presenting Job in two such different moods, the author shows his psychological subtlety. In 3.13-19, before the outbreak of the battle of words with his friends has begun, Job sees his case as hopeless, and feels the need above all for peace and rest, which death will bring him. This feeling has for the moment driven from his thoughts his normal repugnance towards death and its aftermath. But later, when he is in the thick of debate and no longer resigned to his fate but determined to fight his case against God's unjust treatment of him, and at least sometimes with a glimmer of hope for his vindication, he returns to that feeling of abhorrence.

Another surprising feature of vv. 13-19 is their enumeration of various types of person who together make up the number of the dead and share the same fate: kings and counsellors (v. 14), 'princes' (*šārîm*, v. 15), the wicked and the weary (v. 17), prisoners (v. 18), and finally the small, the great and the slaves (v. 19). These categories are not all of the same kind: they overlap to some extent, and they are clearly not intended to comprise all human types: there is, for example, no mention of the righteous to balance the wicked, nor of wise and foolish; nor is any differentiation made between those who die in peace and those who die by violence, a distinction that is considered to be particularly significant in other Old Testament texts. In fact the list serves a quite different purpose. The kings and their ministers (yō‘ṣîm, literally 'advisers'), who construct or restore great buildings, represent power; the 'princes' (śārîm, perhaps here 'merchant princes') with their gold and silver represent wealth. In reflecting that in death he would find himself in such company Job sought to find consolation in the fact that he would share a state common to all humanity, including even the wealthiest and most powerful.

But as in other Old Testament passages with a similar theme (Isa. 14.9-11; Ezek. 32.18-30) a note of social criticism can be detected here that is further pursued in the verses that follow. Although the text does not directly identify kings and millionaires with the wicked, such an identification may be implied in the reference to the wicked that immediately follows in v. 17. The second line of that verse, which sets the weary in parallel with the wicked, may also refer indirectly to the oppression of the weak. Verse 18 expresses a similar thought: death brings relief to those in prison, who no longer have to obey the commands of their taskmasters. Finally in v. 19 Job sums up all humanity in terms of three socio-economic classes: two kinds of free persons, small and great (that is, powerless and powerful) and the slaves. It is to the last of these that death comes as the greatest relief, as they are freed from the otherwise never-ending tyranny of their owners. In making these references to taskmasters and slave owners Job identifies himself with the most wretched of all human beings, for whom death would be preferable to life. This whole passage (vv. 18-23) is remarkable in that it gives indirect expression to the voice of the oppressed.

How do these verses fit into the general theological teaching of the book? What is the author's attitude towards the rich? Job himself, before the calamities that had fallen on him, had been, if not one of the 'kings of the earth', a very rich man, the owner of many slaves and one who had many 'small' people under his authority; he was, as the author points out in 1.3, one of the 'great' men. Now, reduced to the lowest state of degradation, destitute and suffering from a repulsive disease, he was experiencing a level of human existence that was new to him; even a slave might well have excited his envy. We are not told that this new experience led him to regret his past behaviour at the time of his affluence; on the contrary, he had a clear conscience about this, and towards the end of the book (ch. 31) he defended his record, claiming that he had behaved in an exemplary and generous manner towards his social inferiors (31.9-23).

It was not, then, a concern of the author to condemn the rich and powerful as such; yet, as we have seen, here in ch. 3 a note of disapproval towards them can be detected. How is this apparent discrepancy to be explained? That there is a certain ambiguity on this question in the book cannot be denied. But it can be explained by the fact that the author recognizes the existence of *two distinct kinds* of powerful and influential persons. On the one hand there are those who, like Job, lead exemplary lives, and on the other there are those who are identical with the 'wicked', who oppress and prey upon the weak and defenceless. Between the two types there appears to be no middle position. Such a polarization of the righteous and the wicked is not peculiar to the book of Job; it is especially characteristic of the book of Proverbs. There have been attempts by modern scholars to identify a particular social background to the book on the basis of this dichotomy; but no agreement has been reached about this. Such phenomena occur in almost every age; and if the presentation of them in this book has distinctive features, this is due to the literary character of the book rather than to an actual historical social phenomenon.

In the final verses of the chapter (vv. 24-26) Job identifies himself with those of whom he had spoken in vv. 20-23—those in misery and bitter in spirit (v. 20), longing for death (v. 21), who have 'lost their way' and are conscious of being 'hedged in' by God (v. 23). Sighing and groaning have become, as it were, his daily food (v. 24). The verbs in v. 25 are probably to be taken as past tenses: what he had most feared has now happened to him. It is not clear to what this fear refers; perhaps it reveals Job as a constitutional worrier, always afraid that some terrible calamity would ruin an apparently stable existence. There may be a hint of this in the account of his over-scrupulous, almost obsessional behaviour in 1.5. Or, the meaning may be that after the first series of blows Job had been fearful of a further disaster, which had now occurred when he was struck by disease. Verse 26 gives the reason for Job's longing for death: his world has been shattered. He has lost confidence in the meaning of life, and cannot find peace and rest but only ever-recurring turbulence or violence (*rōgez*, the word used of the activity of the wicked in v. 17). This word, significantly, is the final word of the chapter in Hebrew. This is a chapter that does not pose intellectual questions concerning such matters as the reason for human suffering or divine justice, but simply exposes the rawness of Job's feelings in a way that is very rare in the Old Testament.

Job 4

Eliphaz, who here begins his first reply to Job, is clearly intended to be seen as the leader of the friends and their chief speaker; his speeches are longer and more wide-ranging than those of the others. In v. 2 he makes it clear that while he has been provoked into speech by what he considers to be the unorthodox tenor of Job's lament ('Who can refrain from speaking?'), he is also aware that Job may not be willing to listen to what he has to say (it is not clear whether the first part of this verse is in question form or not; but it certainly expresses Eliphaz's unease). The tone of his speech is therefore, at least at the beginning, conciliatory and deferential, as befits the words of one friend to another. But the intention was to administer a gentle rebuke to Job in order to correct his mistaken attitude.

In vv. 3-6 Eliphaz acknowledges that Job has a deserved reputation as a wise man to whom people in distress would come for advice and from whom they would receive help: 'You have indeed instructed many [this verb is used in Prov. 19.18; 29.17 of the education of children] and have strengthened weak hands.' He has given support and encouragement to those who were uncertain and infirm of purpose. Precisely what were the personal problems facing these people is not stated, but some idea of these is conveyed in v. 5, when Eliphaz turns the tables on Job, who is now in the same state as his former clients but evidently unable to apply his own remedies to himself. 'It' (the word is undefined, but presumably denotes a predicament comparable with those with which he used to deal) has now happened to him; but, as he has clearly shown by his despairing lament, he is now finding that he does not have the resources to deal with an unbearable situation. In v. 6 Eliphaz, perhaps ironically, appeals to the very qualities for which Job is famous but in which he himself now appears to have no confidence: his piety (fear of God) and his integrity (*tōm*, cf. 1.1).

Eliphaz now produces what may be called a 'set piece' of wisdom teaching. He does not apply this directly to Job's case, and indeed does not mention him at all at this stage; but he evidently expects that Job will find encouragement in his words. Eliphaz speaks like a traditional wisdom teacher, or perhaps rather as one introducing an academic discussion. He begins (v. 7) with an appeal to universal experience couched in question form: he challenges Job to state whether he has known a case in which an innocent person suffered a premature death. The questions conceal what Eliphaz holds to be a self-evident truth: that such a thing has never happened. The modern reader may wonder whether

anyone can ever have really believed this; but there are other examples
of this doctrine, notably Ps. 37.25, where the psalmist goes even further
than Eliphaz, maintaining that in a long life he has never seen a case of a
righteous person in poverty. Eliphaz restricts himself to asserting that
the innocent will not die prematurely. His intention is to comfort Job by
assuring him that he will not die the death that is the lot of the wicked.
This assurance, however, is hardly calculated to meet Job's case, as Job
has said that he *wants* to die.

Verses 8–11 are a traditionally 'orthodox' statement about the truly
wicked, those who 'plow wickedness' and 'sow trouble'. Since it has
not been suggested that Job belongs to this category, they are completely irrelevant to his case. It is remarkable that of this whole section
(vv. 7-11) only one verse (7) is concerned with the innocent: the rest are
about the wicked and their fate. This lack of balance may be an instance
of an intention to caricature the tendency of traditional wisdom teachers
to adhere rigidly to their 'script', however irrelevant it might be to the
matter in hand. The assertion in v. 9 that the wicked will be blasted out
of existence is simply a more violent expression of what is frequently
stated in the book of Proverbs about their fate (e.g. Prov. 10.27; 12.7;
14.11; 21.12). The ravening lions of vv. 10-11 are evidently metaphorical, intended to symbolize these wicked persons.

In vv. 12-21 Eliphaz attempts to bolster his authority as a wisdom
teacher by claiming to be the recipient of a mysterious message from
the spiritual world. The circumstances of this visitation are built up in
considerable though somewhat obscure detail (vv. 12-16). The reader is
thereby led to expect some tremendous revelation; but when it comes it
consists only of a truism: that no human being is pure in God's sight
(v. 17). The following verses are merely an elaboration of this. Eliphaz
thus claims divine inspiration for his teaching. This is a most unusual
claim by a wisdom teacher, and the incident may be simply intended by
the author to be ironical.

The nature of this experience is far from clear. The message is described as a personal one for Eliphaz alone ('to me'), though he now
reveals it to Job. The coming to him of a 'word' (*dābār*) suggests an
oracle such as would have been revealed by God to a prophet. But the
unique use of the verb 'to steal' here (an idiom similar to the metaphorical use of the term in modern English) gives v. 12 a peculiarly
furtive character, particularly when associated with the word 'whisper'.
Verse 13 refers to the 'anxious thoughts' that occur in a 'night vision' (as
in 33.15, where Elihu refers to God's speaking to men in a dream or
vision, and also Dan. 2.19; 7.7, 13). In v. 14 Eliphaz speaks of the dread
that fell on him, a characteristic feeling of recipients of a divine visitation, and in v. 15 of a wind (*rûaḥ*) that passed before his face (we may
compare Ezekiel's stormy wind, Ezek. 1.4, and the wind from which
Yahweh appeared to Job in 38.1). In v. 16 Eliphaz stresses his inability

to discern the shape of what he saw; the silence followed by a voice speaking, however, is reminiscent of Elijah's experience when Yahweh appeared to him (1 Kgs 19.12). It is difficult to reconcile all these details, which seem to have been collected from a variety of sources; the author was probably not concerned to produce a coherent picture. Although these verses together suggest some kind of supernatural revelation, they reveal Eliphaz's inability to describe what he had seen, and add to the ironical effect of this incident.

There was nothing new about the contents of the supernatural message revealed to Eliphaz in v. 17, but it introduced a new factor into the discussion. It asserted the inadequacy of the simple division of humanity into two categories, that of the righteous or innocent and the wicked. Its implication was that since no human creature can be absolutely righteous or absolutely pure in God's sight, no person can entirely escape the consequences of the misdeeds that he must have committed. It might be true, as Eliphaz had implied in v. 7, that the innocent never perish; but this doctrine of *relative* guilt shared by all opened the way to a new perception of retributive justice. It was the lot of human beings to suffer misfortune; and so, by implication, Job was no exception. But once again Eliphaz completely failed to understand Job's situation. He meant to console Job, but only succeeded in trivializing his complaint and the disproportionate nature of what he had been made to endure.

Verses 18-21 are a series of comments on v. 17 made to reinforce its message. Whether these verses are a continuation of the message received by Eliphaz or belong to Eliphaz's own speech is not clear. Verse 18 takes the reader back to the concept of the heavenly court, though there is no further reference to the Satan. The members of the court are no longer called 'sons of God' but 'servants' and 'messengers' (that is, angels). The argument in this and the following verse is *a fortiori*: if even these subordinate heavenly beings, who are immortal, are capable of error and not entirely trustworthy, how much more must this be true of mere human mortals! The background to this statement about the angels is obscure. There is certainly no idea here of rebellious or 'fallen' angels as in some of the apocryphal literature and in later theology, though the myth of the 'sons of God' who intermarried with human women (Gen. 6.1-4) may belong to a similar tradition.

Verses 19-21 continue the argument, stressing the ephemeral nature of human beings in contrast with God and the angels. The 'houses of clay' (v. 19) are probably our physical bodies; the notion of human beings as consisting of clay and dust was a commonplace of ancient Near Eastern literature as well as of the Old Testament: see especially Gen. 2.7. These verses emphasize the fragility of human life, which can be extinguished in a moment never to be restored, 'without [anyone] paying attention'. This last phrase, which has no subject in the Hebrew, probably does not refer to God; rather, it means either that death may come without warning to its victims or that death is too commonplace to be especially remarked upon by others. The statement that 'they' die without wisdom in v. 21 is not an assertion that *all* human beings are foolish; it refers, rather, like the preceding statements, to what may happen to some. Eliphaz, if it is he and not his mysterious 'voice' speaking here, would certainly not regard himself as lacking wisdom. But in this verse, which is the first of many verses in the book that mention wisdom, the term probably does not signify more than the ability to manage one's life intelligently and successfully. Elsewhere in the book, as we shall see, it has other meanings.

Job 5

Eliphaz continues his speech and now again addresses Job directly. As in 4.2, 7 he begins by putting questions to him (v. 1). On the basis of Job's lament and curse pronounced on the day of his birth Eliphaz assumes that he will now appeal to heaven against his fate—presumably not against the death that he is threatened with, as death is what he longs for; but more probably in order to obtain some alleviation of his pain. But perhaps Eliphaz has once again simply failed to understand Job. At any rate, he implies that any such appeal would be futile: not one of the 'holy ones', that is, the angelic members of the heavenly court, will or can give him a satisfactory answer. Eliphaz's own advice to Job, expressed in v. 8, is that if Job has any chance at all of a favourable response he must appeal directly to God himself. Nevertheless in vv. 6 and 7 he warns him that misery (*'āmāl*) is endemic in human nature and cannot be avoided.

Verses 2-5 may strike the reader as totally irrelevant as they are concerned with the fool, who has up to this point never been mentioned, attesting the inevitability of his ruin. This apparent irrelevance is partly explained by the fact that in ancient wisdom thought there is often no clear distinction between fools and the wicked: the fool is not only self-destructive but also an enemy of society in that he disrupts the life of others just as does the evil person, and is duly punished. The word for fool here (*'ewîl*) frequently has such connotations (Prov. 10.10; 14.9; 20.3; Jer. 4.22; Ps. 107.17). Eliphaz, however, does not call Job a fool; in these verses he is only citing examples of the fact of *universal* human misery that is his main point (vv. 6-7). Resentment (*ka'aś*) and jealousy (*qin'â*, v. 2) are common human vices that can lead to disaster.

Verse 2 is a clear example of a proverb; v. 3 is an example of a particular kind of wisdom instruction in which an instructor teaches a moral lesson by describing a personal experience, real or fictitious ('I saw...', *rā'îtî*) and then the consequences of what he has seen (e.g. Ps. 37.25; Prov. 7.6-23; 24.30-34). But there is a textual problem in this verse: it is difficult to see why Eliphaz should have suddenly uttered a curse against the prosperity of the fools. It may be best to accept a slight emendation of v. 3 based on the LXX and read 'but suddenly their home became accursed'.

Verse 6 begins Eliphaz's general conclusion about human misery and its cause. But there is a radical difference among the commentators concerning the meaning of this verse. The Hebrew text as vocalized in the standard edition of the text has 'For misery does not [*lō'*] come from the dust, nor [*lō'*] is it from the ground that trouble sprouts'; but it has been proposed that in both lines *lû'*, 'surely', should be read instead of *lō'*, giving the verse the opposite meaning. However, there do not appear to be adequate grounds for such an interpretation. Eliphaz is saying that although human beings were made from the earth (Gen. 3.19), that is not the root cause of their troubles. Verse 7 then states that the fault lies in themselves. Trouble falls on each individual from his birth. Alternatively, a proposal to revocalize the passive 'is born' to yield the active 'begets' is a possibility: human beings create their own misery by the way in which they live their lives. Whichever interpretation is correct, this is a realistic if pessimistic view of human nature; it is clearly intended to console Job, but as has been noted above it hardly meets his case, which by any standards is an exceptional one.

There is also uncertainty about the meaning of the second line of v. 7, 'and the sons of *rešep* fly up high'. In view of the fact that *rešep* in Hebrew—a fairly rare word—means 'flame' or 'flash of lightning' in the majority of occurrences, the line has been generally taken to refer to sparks of light or flame rising into the sky. But the connection between the line so interpreted and the thought of the human lot in the first line is not obvious: the imagery does not seem appropriate. It makes more sense to take the word *rešep* in its other sense (Deut. 32.24; Hab. 3.5) of plague or pestilence. It is now known that in north-west Semitic mythology there was a god called Resheph who spread pestilence among human beings; and there is good reason to suppose that this verse makes a poetical allusion to this god—or more precisely to demonic figures associated with him: the 'sons of Resheph', who are envisaged as released on to the earth to bring trouble on humanity.

Verse 8 is a transitional verse. It introduces the doxology that follows in vv. 9-16, but is also directly related to v. 7 in that Eliphaz here states what response he himself is accustomed to make to the sombre state of human existence referred to there. As in 4.7-21 he makes no direct reference to Job's situation, though these verses are still part of his address to Job, and he clearly intends that Job should pay attention and take his own practice as a model. Thus in v. 8 Eliphaz does not give advice as such to Job, but only states what is his own practice: 'But I myself seek God [that is, in prayer], and to God I submit my cause.' He is not here denying what he has just affirmed—namely that trouble (*'āmāl*) is the lot of human beings from which there is no escape. He does not appeal to God to make an exception for him, but 'rests his case', so to speak. He restricted himself to a general act of praise of God, implying, however, that God if he so decides can overrule any particular human destiny. In other words, it is God who rules, not an impersonal fate.

The list of God's attributes begins, like other hymns of praise in the Old Testament, with a participle (*'ōśe*, 'he does' [v. 9]), a stylistic feature that is repeated in vv. 10 and 13, though not in the final verses. Verse 9 is a general statement that God's actions are not only great and numerous but, more to the point, 'unsearchable' and 'marvellous': that is, that God is unpredictable and his actions miraculous. He has total freedom to do as he pleases with men and women as with the created world as a whole. Then, having reminded his interlocutor of the truism that it is God who sends the rain without which there could be no human life at all (v. 10), Eliphaz proceeds to give examples of God's regular intervention (the regularity is indicated by the participles) in human affairs: rescuing and exalting the lowly and the bereaved (v. 11); defeating and confusing the schemes of the crafty (vv. 12-14); and saving the poor from oppression and injustice and giving them hope. The selection of the 'wise' ($h^a k\bar{a}m\hat{\imath}m$, v. 13) for condemnation has caused surprise, especially since the vocabulary employed in this section ($t\hat{u}\check{s}iyy\hat{a}$, 'success', $\bar{a}r\hat{u}m$, 'clever', v. 12, $'orm\bar{a}h$, 'cleverness', $mah\check{s}\bar{a}b\hat{o}t$, 'plans', v. 13) proclaims it to be a typically 'wisdom' piece of literature. But these terms are ambivalent: they are used in the Old Testament in both positive and negative senses according to the contexts in which they occur. Eliphaz appears here to recognize that 'wise' persons may use their wisdom for evil as well as for good purposes; he is not attacking wisdom itself. But as before he has allowed himself to stray outside his original intention to give good advice to Job.

Eliphaz now qualifies his statement about leaving everything in God's hands (v. 8) by introducing the notion of divine *discipline*. It is important to note that at no time in this speech has he said that he believed Job to be a great sinner who has deserved his fate; rather, he has tried to console him by finding some other explanation of his situation, arguing that since human beings are never completely guiltless (4.17), they are all subject to suffering misfortune (5.7). He then (5.8-16) pointed to God as the one who is able to overrule such misfortunes by his sovereign will. Now (vv. 17-27) he explains to Job how this reversal of his fate can come about: Job has only to recognize that his sufferings are not intended by God to crush him, as is the case with the really wicked, but are God's way of exercising discipline over his imperfect human creatures: a temporary affliction, imposed as a warning to amend his life. If he accepts this reproof and discipline, God will restore him to his former prosperity and happiness.

In v. 17, after a preliminary 'Behold!' ($hinn\bar{e}$) that calls attention to a new argument or development (cf. also 4.3), Eliphaz very obviously resumes the role of the wisdom teacher. Not only does he express his thought in wisdom's technical language—$h\hat{o}k\hat{\imath}ah$, 'to reprove'; $m\hat{u}s\bar{a}r$, 'discipline'—each line of the verse is a variant of an extant line of Old Testament wisdom literature, viz. 'Happy [$'a\check{s}r\hat{e}$] are those whom you discipline, O Yahweh' (Ps. 94.12a) and 'My son, do not despise Yahweh's discipline' ($m\hat{u}s\bar{a}r$, Prov. 3.11a). The term $'a\check{s}r\hat{e}$, 'Happy!', also occurs frequently in the wisdom literature (Ps. 1.1; 119.1, 2; Prov. 3.13; 8.32, 34; 16.20), mainly in contexts referring to those who love, trust or obey Yahweh or his wisdom. The application of the phrase to Job was hardly appropriate for him in his present situation, but Eliphaz was confident that Job would in the future be able once more to consider himself happy.

It is part of the unconscious irony of Eliphaz's speech that the good things that he assures Job will be restored to him if he accepts God's reproof—principally the restoration of his health, freedom from anxiety, sudden death and hunger, a new and numerous family and long life— were, in fact, finally restored to him by God (42.10-17), but not at all for the reasons that Eliphaz envisaged. The reader knows, though neither Job nor his friends know, that Job is not being reproved or punished for sins that he has committed but that it is a trial of his innocence that is taking place and that he will be restored to fortune and happiness because he will have successfully passed that test.

The theology of v. 18 echoes that of Deut. 32.39. It is a rejection of theological dualism: it affirms that there are not two gods, of whom one confers wellbeing and the other brings evil on human beings. It is assumed throughout the book of Job that there is only one supreme deity (the Satan of the Prologue is not an exception: his attacks on Job were carried out with Yahweh's permission). Verse 19 is an example of a device used elsewhere in the Old Testament (e.g. Amos 1-2; Prov. 30) and also in Ugaritic and other Semitic literature, in which one numeral is immediately followed by another greater by one. Its purpose here is probably to emphasize that Job will be delivered from every kind of evil however many there may be. Attempts to find exactly seven (or six) such examples in the list that follows are probably not appropriate and have not commanded general assent.

The first line of v. 21 probably refers to calumny or malicious gossip that can disturb social harmony; this is frequently condemned in Proverbs. In the second line it has been proposed to read šēd, 'demon', instead of šôd, 'devastation', but that is not necessary. The statement in v. 23a that Job will live in a covenant relationship with the stones of the field has been regarded by many as so improbable that various proposals have been made to emend 'stones' ('abᵉnê) to 'sons' (bᵉnê) or in some other way. But although this is obviously a very bold assertion, the Hebrew text may be correct; if so, the use of the term here is metaphorical, conveying the notion that the soil will 'co-operate' with Job the landowner. Similarly in vv. 22b and 23a Eliphaz confidently envisages for Job a state of harmony with the wild animals that recalls the eschatological prophecies of Isa. 11.6-9 and Hos. 2.18-22. Verses 24-26 complete the irony by promising Job the restoration of all that he has lost: the security of his home and property ('tent' in v. 24 does not imply a nomadic life but, as in v. 3, is an archaism for 'home' that occurs frequently in Old Testament poetical texts), numerous descendants and a ripe and prosperous old age.

In the closing verse of a speech that began in 4.2 Eliphaz asserts the truth of everything that he has said; but he does not claim that it has come from his own head. He speaks as a representative of a whole tradition of wise men to whom he significantly refers as 'we'. He thus takes his stand on the consensus of this tradition that is older than his own generation (in 8.8 and 16.18 the former sages are known as 'the fathers'), claims that these matters have been thoroughly investigated (*ḥāqar*) and proved true, and now offers the conclusions to Job ('know it for yourself' are the final words of the speech). Eliphaz is thus claiming that Job's problem is non-existent: traditional wisdom has provided a completely satisfactory answer to his predicament, and all that he has to do now is to accept its truth without attempting further investigation on his own account and rather than indulging in self-pity, as he has done in ch. 3.

Although Eliphaz's intention in this speech was to sympathize with Job and to give him encouragement, it was profound disagreement with Job's attitude towards his trials that provoked him to break his silence. He wanted to reassert the traditional wisdom teaching that divided humanity into two groups, the righteous and the wicked, of whom the former enjoy divine blessing while the latter suffer the consequences of their evil deeds. However, he found himself unable to apply this principle to Job's case, since he did not believe him to be a wicked person who deserved his fate; and he was forced, for Job's sake, to make concessions that effectually weakened his position. His arguments—that humanity is inevitably born to trouble, that God in his sovereign power can overrule the 'automatic' rule of fate and exercise his grace towards those who turn to him—obliged him to admit that between the two opposites of righteous and wicked there is a third category to which Job belongs: that of the person who is neither wholly innocent nor irredeemably wicked, but whose faults are redeemable. But there is an underlying irony in all this. Eliphaz was quite unaware that he had shifted his position: he ended his speech in utter confidence that he had faithfully represented the voice of traditional wisdom. There is also a more profound irony in that the mysterious voice that declared that no human being is absolutely pure missed the whole issue that is the principal concern of the book: that it is not human innocence that is being questioned, but divine justice.

Job 6

In this second speech (chs. 6–7) Job does not make a direct reply to Eliphaz, though in the first verses (6.2-13) he picks up a number of key words from his speech: *ka'aś*, 'anguish', v. 2 (cf. 5.2); *tiqwâ*, 'hope', v. 8 (cf. 4.6; 5.16); *tûšiyyâ*, 'success', v. 13 (cf. 5.12); *dikkā'*, 'crush', v. 9 (cf. 4.19). These are here all used in a negative sense: Job is anguished, he hopes in vain, success is banished from him, he wishes that God would crush him. Job has clearly not been persuaded by Eliphaz's arguments; on the contrary, he begins by resuming his earlier lament; and in ch. 6 he denounces his friends as having failed in their friendship—this is somewhat surprising as only one of them has yet uttered a word, but perhaps Job at this point regards Eliphaz as a spokesman for them all and in his sombre mood sees them all as enemies.

Job begins with an attempt to convey to his friends some idea of the immense burden of anger and misery under which he is labouring, and refers, perhaps in self-justification, to his earlier speech (the meaning of the verb in v. 3b is uncertain; it may mean 'have been unrestrained' or 'impetuous'). But the tone of this second speech is no less violent. Job now for the first time (v. 4) directly attributes his sufferings to the deliberate action of God, comparing him to an archer, who, like the Canaanite god of pestilence, Resheph, has shot him with poisoned arrows (this is probably a reference to the disease that has felled him). He also pictures God as threatening him with an array of unnamed 'terrors'. It is the thought that God has become his enemy that is the principal cause of his anguish.

Although Job does not know the circumstances of God's decision described in the Prologue, his knowledge that he is innocent has driven him to conclude that God is responsible for his situation because he knows of no other possible source of it. He has rejected Eliphaz's arguments that misfortune is caused by some innate human weakness or that, alternatively, it is God's way of disciplining those that have erred: his misfortunes are too great for such explanations to be applicable to his own case. He has not, however, rejected Eliphaz's other point, that God who is all-powerful can do anything he pleases with regard to his human creatures; but he turns this belief on its head. The request that he has to make from God is not the restoration of his fortunes; it is, as before, that God should complete his destructive work by putting an end to him (vv. 8-9). The Job of the dialogues has frequently been represented as utterly different from the compliant Job of the Prologue; but is the difference in this speech as great as has been supposed? Job not only does not curse God; it cannot even be said that he reverses his previous admission that God, who will in any case eventually take back all that he has given, has also the right to take it back here and now, before the expiry of the normal span of life. What Job finds inexplicable and hard to accept is that God should be doing this *as an enemy*.

In vv. 5-6 Job takes a leaf out of Eliphaz's book by quoting two proverbs, both in the form of questions, presumably in order to add force to his remarks; unfortunately the purport of these proverbs is not clear. Verse 5 points out that animals do not complain when they have a sufficiency of palatable food, while v. 6 speaks of food that is too insipid to be edible (the meaning of *ḥallāmût*, conventionally rendered by 'mallows', is uncertain). Thus literally interpreted the two proverbs are about two kinds of food, the satisfying and the disgusting; but as is the way of proverbs they are intended to be interpreted analogically. They were probably open to more than one application from the first; in this case it is not easy to see how they were intended to be applied. Verse 7, where Job purports to provide the explanation, is unfortunately obscure. He states that 'they' (unspecified) are loathsome food that he refuses to touch. This has been interpreted in two main ways; that Job is alluding to his present state and pronouncing it unacceptable, or that he is expressing his disgust at the arguments offered by Eliphaz in the two previous chapters.

Job now expounds the reason why he wishes that God would grant his request and take his life (vv. 8-13). In ch. 3 he had said that he would have welcomed death or non-existence because he would thus have avoided the turmoil of life; now he expresses impatience for death because he is not sure how long he will be able to endure his present situation without sinning against the God who has so grievously afflicted him. So he is even able to think of death positively, in terms of hope (*tiqwâ*, v. 8), the word used by Eliphaz in 4.6 and 5.16 in more conventional senses. He even calls it a 'consolation' (v. 10). It is not physical pain that makes him long for it, for that he can endure and even exult in! Rather, the consolation of death will be that he will not have 'concealed', that is, failed to honour, the laws (literally 'words') by which God governs the universe and determines the fates of human beings, as he might have done if his life had been prolonged further (v. 10c). Despite everything, God is still the 'Holy One'. In vv. 11-12 he develops this theme further: he doubts whether he would have the strength to face such a prolongation of his life without committing this error, since as yet he has received no help from God, and has even been deprived by him of his ability to control his fate (*tūšiyyâ*, 'success').

In the remainder of the chapter (vv. 14-30) Job turns his anger against his friends, charging them with failure to act towards him in true friendship. First, in vv. 14-20, he speaks of them (they are the 'brothers' of v. 15) in the third person; but in vv. 22-30 he addresses them directly.

It is difficult not to see this violent attack as being due to his feelings of frustration and hopelessness, for which, in fact, he knows God to be responsible: in the earlier verses he has identified God as the agent of his troubles (v. 4), who even now does not respond to this despairing plea for a quick death. So he rounds on the friends, who had left their homes and businesses to travel great distances in order to be with him and to mourn with him. Eliphaz, the only one who had addressed him in an attempt to console him and offer him advice, was probably mainly in Job's mind here: but Job had no cause to find fault with Bildad and Zophar, who so far had neither spoken a word nor taken any action. This behaviour, however, is psychologically very credible.

The first line of v. 14 is unfortunately untranslatable as it stands, though it seems clear that friends and loyalty (*ḥesed*) are mentioned. One possible emendation of the Hebrew text would yield the following: 'A friend does not refuse his loyalty, so abandoning the fear of the Almighty': in other words, loyalty to friends, which Job finds lacking in his three visitors, is an essential characteristic of true religion. This general statement about friendship is followed in v. 15 by a direct indictment of Job's friends as treacherous. They are compared to the seasonal streams or 'wadis' (*neḥālîm*) of Palestine which are swollen with ice and snow in winter but dry up completely when summer heat comes. Verses 18-20 then develop the simile in an imaginative way: v. 18 pictures desert caravans (reading *'ōreḥôt*, 'travellers', for *'orḥôt*, 'paths') turning aside from their regular routes to look for water and dying in the trackless desert—there is a slight change of topic here from that of unreliability to that of disappointment; both are relevant to Job's claim against the friends. The theme of disappointment is pursued further in vv. 19 and 20, which emphasize expectations dashed. The references to desert caravans and to Teman in Edom—Eliphaz's home (2.11; he is referred to throughout the book as 'Eliphaz the Temanite')—and to Sheba in southwest Arabia, the home of the 'Sabaeans' of 1.15, provide a kind of false 'local colour' common to both Prologue and dialogues, suggesting a desert-dwelling background to the book.

From v. 21 Job turns to address the friends directly. The first line of this verse, however, presents textual and grammatical problems. A literal rendering, 'for now you have become not', is hardly possible; one of several proposals for emendation would yield the translation 'Thus you have now become to me', so bringing the similes of the previous verses to a conclusion and clarifying them. The second line adds emphasis to Job's feeling of disillusionment with a wordplay: 'you have seen (*tir e'û*) a horrible sight and have taken fright (*wattîrā'û*). The friends have been repelled and frightened by the sight of Job (cf. 2.12, where it is said that they at first found him unrecognizable) and have recoiled—a natural reaction perhaps; though the only one of the friends who has so far spoken to Job, Eliphaz, has given no sign of such a reaction. Their fear, if it is not simply imagined by Job, is clearly not the fear of infection or contagion, since the friends are presumably still sitting on the ground in close proximity to him. But Job appears now to have abandoned rational thought about the friends and to have fallen into a state of paranoia.

Job now finds new reasons for what he sees as the friends' hostility towards him, asking in what way he has offended them (vv. 22-24). Knowing that he is not at fault, he asks rhetorically and perhaps ironically whether he has made excessive demands on their friendship by asking them for gifts or to help him out of a dangerous situation when he was under attack from a ruthless personal enemy. There is certainly a touch of irony in his request to them to tell him how he has offended (*hôrûnî*, literally 'instruct me', v. 24). Verses 25-26 probably allude to Eliphaz's remarks in chs. 4 and 5. In v. 2 Job had—perhaps ironically—asked for criticism of his behaviour; but now he rejects the advice that he has actually been given. He admits that fair criticism (*'imrê yōšer*, literally 'right words') would have been painful (*nimrᵉṣû*), but holds the advice that he has received to be valueless, inappropriate to a person in despair (v. 26). In v. 27 he preposterously likens his treatment by the friends to the indignities suffered by slaves: to the casting of lots for the ownership of an orphan sold as a slave because of an unpaid debt, or the purchase of a person's friend to be his personal slave. This extraordinary allegation would be to some degree accounted for if the verse were based, as it may have been, on some current proverbial saying and also if it is a rhetorical question rather than an outright accusation.

Job now turns to the friends whom he has just abused and treats them in a quite different manner, appealing to them as though he can rely on them to understand the depths of his feelings and to recognize the justice of his cause (vv. 28-30). He swears that he has not told them lies (*'im-'ăkazzēb*) and that he is not guilty of wrong (*'awlâ*): his integrity (*ṣedeq*) remains unimpaired. Verse 30b is a rhetorical question; its meaning is not certain, however: in asking whether his palate cannot discern *hawwôt*, he may be speaking of his misfortune (that is the meaning of the word in 6.2), or of wickedness, of which he claims to be innocent.

Job 7

In this second part of his speech Job is no longer addressing his friends but God. In parts of ch. 6 he had spoken *about* God, wishing that he would act to put an end to his life; now he makes his complaint to him directly. The first verses have the form of a general complaint about his wretchedness; but they are a kind of preface to the direct address to God, beginning with v. 7, when he appeals to him to 'remember', that is, to show awareness, of the hopelessness of his existence.

In vv. 1-2, by means of rhetorical questions, Job reflects, not yet specifically about his own state of misery, but about the state of human existence in general. Until his recent trouble he would not have spoken in this way since he had never known hardship or had any direct experience of the sense of frustration of which he now speaks so feelingly; but his new experience had taught him to question whether life had any positive meaning at all. It had given him a new sympathy with his fellow-creatures. For him this scepticism was a new experience, though it had long been a commonplace of the pessimistic literature of the ancient Near East, which gave literary expression to what still remains the feeling of the unknown oppressed and victimized throughout the ages. Job describes it in terms of hard service (*ṣābā'*), a word frequently used in the Old Testament of military service or of the hired labourer (*śākîr*), who was bound to his master for a fixed number of years and who was frequently treated harshly in Israel (Mal. 3.5), despite the existence of laws intended to mitigate his lot (Deut. 15.18; Lev. 25.53), and the slave (*'ebed*). The slave longs for the evening ('shadow') when he can at least rest temporarily from his labours, and the labourer for his wages, which were sometimes not always paid regularly or at the proper time (Lev. 19.13; Deut. 24.14-15). But the harsh 'service' to which Job refers was that of simply being human, and was for life.

Job now (vv. 3-5) applies these general reflections to his own case, which is a particular example of a life that has been emptied of all meaning. Not only has a long period of suffering been allotted to him (that is, presumably, by divine decree); he has been made to endure nights of misery (*'āmāl*): in other words, his wretchedness has made him unable to sleep in the long nights—a common additional misery for those who are in continual pain. In v. 5 he seeks to elicit even greater pity by describing his physical symptoms in repellent but clinical terms: his flesh is covered with *rimmâ*, a word usually rendered by 'worms', but here possibly pus, which hardens to form scabs but then breaks out again (compare 2.7).

In vv. 7-10 Job addresses God directly. In v. 6 he had compared his life (literally, his 'days') to the shuttle used in the process of weaving, which flashes to and fro to make the woven garment, but which carries a limited quantity of thread that soon runs out; he makes a grim pun also on the word *tiqwâ*, 'thread', which also has the meaning 'hope'. This is a commonplace reflection on the ephemeral nature of *all* human lives; but Job here applies it in a particularly poignant manner to his own situation, implying that his own life is now almost over and is swiftly drawing to a conclusion. That he who has just expressed the wish that God would quickly bring his life to an end should complain in this way may seem strange; but in reality this is not so when it is seen in the context of what God has done to him; he is by implication complaining that God should have placed him, who had formerly been enjoying the fullness of life, in a situation in which he is constrained to wish for death.

This becomes clear when in v. 7 he adds to the reflection that his life is a mere breath (*rûaḥ*) the conviction that he personally will never again 'see good', that is, experience happiness. This is what he asks God to 'remember' (*zᵉkōr*, imperative). The appeal to God to 'remember' something as if he might have forgotten something or had not been concentrating on the complainant's plight is a regular formula in the psalms of complaint in the Psalter, where the petitioner asks God to remember his past mercies or the attacks and taunts of enemies (e.g. Pss. 25.6; 74.2; 89.50) or his past promises (Ps. 119.49). Here it is used to suggest that God might even have forgotten the very mortality of those whom he had created mortal. Such an appeal is a mark of a desperate man. It also has an ironical undertone. The topic is continued in v. 8, where Job reminds God that once he is dead he will no longer be able to have him under his eye. There is no possibility of return for those who have gone down to the underworld (vv. 9-10).

Finally in vv. 11-21 Job addresses his first direct anguished complaint to God himself, accusing him of even now continuing to persecute him for no reason. This aggressive Job, a far cry from the meek and compliant Job of the Prologue, now inaugurates his battle to win recognition of his innocence from the silent and unresponsive God, which is a crucial motif of the ensuing dialogue with the friends, who constantly spring to God's defence. This passionate insistence by Job on his integrity will have shown the readers that the author did not regard his earlier acquiescence in his fate as a satisfactory response to God's actions, and that it was essential that God should act to justify himself. This had the effect of creating an unbearable tension to whose resolution the readers would now impatiently look forward. God's response, however, was to be interminably delayed.

In v. 12 Job's complaint is not that God ignores him; on the contrary, he keeps continuous watch over him so that he cannot escape from him, and he feels himself to be imprisoned. He asks ironically whether he is one of the mythological monsters of Western Semitic tradition: the Sea (Yam; see on 3.8) or the Dragon (*tannîn*) whom Yahweh was supposed to have defeated (Ps. 74.13; Isa. 27.1; 51.9-10) but whom he nevertheless continued to restrict and keep under guard (cf. 38.8-11), lest they break out again. That God should so treat him, a mere human being, as if he were a powerful and dangerous beast was for Job a matter of bitter irony. In vv. 13-14 he explains his meaning more clearly: he had hoped to obtain relief (literally, 'comfort'—an ironical allusion to the friends who had come to comfort him but had failed in their mission) through sleep; but even when he was in his bed God was constantly terrifying him by giving him nightmares and making him see frightening visions. Once more he makes it plain, but now directly to God himself, that he would prefer death, even strangling, to his present life; he has rejected his life and now calls on God to 'let him alone' (v. 16). The point of his saying 'I shall not [or do not wish to] live for ever' (*le'ōlām*) is not clear: *'ōlām* when used with regard to the future usually has the sense of eternity or at least of an indefinitely extended period of time. Some commentators take it here in a much more restricted sense, rendering the line by 'I shall not live long', perhaps meaning that as he is already near death it is pointless for God to pay such close attention to a doomed man. This would make an appropriate parallel to the final words of the verse: 'my life [literally, days'] is a [mere] breath' (*hebel*).

Verses 17-18 are a striking example of an ironical allusion to an earlier biblical text; they are a parody of Psalm 8, especially vv. 3-4 of that psalm. Each passage poses the same question 'What is mankind?' (*māh-'enôš*). Both purport to enquire what it is about human beings that has caused God to pay so much attention to them. But the contexts in which this apparently general question is asked are totally unlike, and have opposite intentions. Psalm 8, a psalm dedicated to the praise and glory of God, expresses amazement that the God who has created the heavens with their heavenly bodies should deign to assign to his lowly human creatures a status only slightly below his own (or alternatively, of his angels) and to give them control over all his other creatures. Job, however, uses the topos to charge God with a tyrannical and relentless control over them, shown in daily inquisitions and unremitting examinations. There is heavy irony in the opening words of v. 17, where Job asserts that God has 'made much of' (*higdîl*) his human creatures. This word, literally 'to make great', is frequently used in the positive and laudatory sense of treating a person with great respect or promoting him to an elevated position (a notion that would eminently fit the theme of Psalm 8, though in fact it does not occur there); but here in Job it evidently means to pay attention to someone in a pejorative sense of paying *excessive* and oppressive attention to a person's discomfort or detriment. In this context these two verses, though ostensibly they refer to God's treatment of humanity in general, serve as a personal indictment of God by Job.

In v. 19 Job applies the ostensibly general comment of the previous verses to his own case, repeating his appeal to be let alone and asking why (*kammâ*) God persists in spying on him. The inelegant 'let me alone to swallow my spittle' is probably a colloquialism for 'let me get my breath for a moment'. The first words of v. 20 have been taken by some commentators to be an admission of sin; but, especially in view of Job's consistent claim to be innocent, it is probably best taken as a conditional clause lacking the initial 'if'. Job is saying that even if he had sinned it could make no difference to God as the 'watcher of mankind' to persist with his over-vigilant activity as he will soon be dead. He regards himself as having been made God's special target (a metaphor from archery), and ironically asks why God has taken on himself such a 'burden'. In the final verse of his speech, still speaking hypothetically of 'my [supposed] sin', he (again ironically) tells God that he might as well pardon it now, as he will soon lie in the dust and so be where even God cannot find and persecute him. In addressing God directly in this way Job is clearly seeking to provoke him to answer his complaint. In his anguish and in his disappointment with the inadequate 'comfort' offered by the friends, he can see no other way.

Job 8

It cannot be denied that particularly in the dialogue chapters proper (3–26) the author has to a considerable extent allowed form to predominate over content: that is, the rigid formula by which each of Job's speeches is followed by a speech of one of the friends, and the three friends speak each three times in a regular sequence (even though the scheme remains uncompleted) makes for a degree of artificiality and of repetition of a relatively small number of topics. This thematic artificiality is, however, redeemed by the ingenuity and variety of the imagery employed: each of the friends, in particular, expresses his thoughts in a variety of ways. If the variety, originality and beauty of the imagery are recognized and savoured by the reader, and not mentally reduced to a series of prosaic interpretations, any feeling of irritation at the repetitiveness of the themes will be transcended by admiration of the poetic genius of the author. It is not possible in this commentary adequately to bring out this feature of the poem, though it can to a large extent be appreciated even by the reader of a good translation.

This first speech by Bildad exemplifies the above remarks. In addition, it exemplifies another feature of the dialogue: that the speeches are to a large extent isolated literary pieces, in which the speakers rarely attempt to answer the points made by the previous speakers but pursue their own thoughts. In this way the reader is presented with a variety of ways of looking at the problems raised by Job's situation and his demand for justice from God, but there is little development in the arguments. In this chapter Bildad, like Eliphaz, utterly fails to understand Job's trouble. Although he knows that Job has suffered so severely, he is content to defend God's justice and his equitable treatment of both righteous and innocent in general terms without taking this particular case into account except, like Eliphaz (5.8), to urge Job to commit himself to God, who will give him prosperity and happiness if he is innocent. Bildad also follows Eliphaz in citing the wise men of old as teaching that God is never unjust. Never does he come to terms with Job's protestations that he is an innocent sufferer who has been wrongly attacked by God.

Bildad begins by dismissing Job's speech as a 'big wind (v. 2). But he does not explain why he so disparages it; and the fact that he makes no further direct allusion to it in the course of his speech suggests that he thinks it not worth discussion. To him it is simply rubbish, and Job would be better not to go on talking such nonsense. It would almost seem that he had not paid attention to it. Bildad's first contribution, put in the form of rhetorical questions (v. 3), is an expression of incredulity at the very thought that *God* should twist or bend justice (*mišpāṭ, ṣedeq*). To him such a notion is utterly unthinkable; that God is *ex hypothesi* a God who, unlike human beings, never behaves unjustly is clearly a basic principle on which his understanding of life is based.

Bildad does not accuse Job of having denied this principle, though he may have seen his very protests as constituting a denial of it. In v. 4 he somewhat tactlessly takes Job's children—now dead—as an example of the operation of the universal principle of divine retribution. He does not state categorically that they had sinned and so were handed over by God into the fatal power of their guilt; he makes his question hypothetical: '*If* your children sinned.' But it is difficult not to see this verse as a hidden allusion to their actual fate, which Bildad saw as the consequence of their evildoing.

From Job's children Bildad turns to the case of Job himself (vv. 5-7). Unlike his family, he is still alive, and Bildad holds out hope for his future. But he has completely misunderstood Job's situation. He assures him that God will yet restore him to his former home, though only if he now turns to God in prayer and on the assumption that his former life was pure and upright. Bildad was thus able to maintain his belief that God cannot behave unjustly; it is implied that if Job has *not* been pure and upright he would deserve to be destroyed as his children had been. In fact the reader knows that Job's conduct had been exemplary, and that instead of continuing to be the recipient of God's favour as the doctrine of retribution demanded, he had been subjected to treatment supposedly reserved exclusively for the wicked. Bildad's bland assurance that Job could even now be restored to his former home was, as it turned out, a correct prediction of what as actually to occur (ch. 42), but at this point it was quite unrealistic as a foreseeable prospect; moreover, as far as could then be known it was an impossibility, since Job's family, without whom there could be no real 'home', had been annihilated. Bildad's intention was no doubt intended to offer comfort; but he was grossly insensitive in supposing that Job could again achieve happiness without his family. To one who had experienced God as hostile and malevolent his advice was merely a painful mockery. The characterization of Job's former state as 'small' (v. 7a) is strange; this may be a deliberate exaggeration to emphasize the unimaginable prosperity that could be his in the future.

The remainder of the speech is a general exposition of the doctrine of divine retribution, ending in vv. 20-22 with a renewed reassurance to Job, still on the condition that he is blameless (*tām*, a word used to describe him in 1.1). This passage begins (vv. 8-10) with an appeal to the authority of the ancestors (*dôr rîšôn*, literally 'a former generation') also known as the 'fathers'. These are the sages or wise men of old who by their studies (*ḥēqer*, literally 'investigation') established and caused to be universally accepted the principle of exact retribution that Job (and

so also the author) is questioning. Here Bildad is appealing to a different
source of authority from those cited by Eliphaz, that is, personal experience and direct divine revelation. This appeal rests on the wisdom lore
transmitted from generation to generation (Prov. 4.1-4, where the father
hands on to his sons what he has learned from his own father, is an
example of this). He speaks in the manner of a professor, lecturing Job
on what he is in fact already familiar with (but disputes). Bildad then
(v. 9) justifies his reliance on this traditional teaching by pointing out
that human life is too short for the acquisition of true wisdom: in such a
short span it is impossible to know anything of one's own knowledge
(*wᵉlō' nēda'*). Only a tradition built up over many generations of thinkers
can be relied on. This is a characteristic topos of wisdom literature.
Verse 10, in the form of a negative rhetorical question, asserts that it is
from such teachers, who spoke out of their deep understanding, that
Job ought to learn. Bildad treats Job as if he were a particularly obtuse
pupil, ignoring what he ought to have learned through experience.

A further pair of negative rhetorical questions in v. 11 are examples of
a rhetorical style sometimes said to be characteristic of wisdom speech
but which is in fact found not infrequently elsewhere in the Old
Testament, notably in Amos 3.3-6. Metaphors drawn from the natural
world are employed to make a point which is then repeated in plain
language. These metaphors speak of an impossibility: plants—here the
papyrus and the reed or sedge, of which this is particularly the case—
cannot flourish without an adequate supply of water. Verse 12 repeats
the point: these plants, even though still in full growth and as yet uncut,
will wither for lack of water more quickly than others. The metaphor is
explained in v. 13: the waterless plant stands for the godless, who,
because of their alienation from God, will have no future. An obvious
fact about the natural world is thus used to make a point about the fate
of the ungodly. Bildad then proceeds in vv. 14-15 to press home his
point with another series of metaphors. The metaphor of the spider's
web suggests that, as in 7.6-7, the word *tiqwâ* (v. 13) is used with a
double meaning, 'hope' and 'thread', the latter denoting insubstantiality.
There is another example of this in 27.8. The godless are stupidly confident of their impunity, but their confidence is utterly fragile (the word
commonly rendered by 'gossamer' in v. 14a is of uncertain meaning)
and is pictured as a house that will collapse if someone leans against it
or attempts to put his weight on it, so precipitating his own fall from
which he will not recover.

With vv. 16-18 there is a return to plant imagery; but there is some
doubt whether these verses are a continuation of the topic of the fate of
the ungodly or whether they refer by contrast to the righteous person:
v. 16 begins simply with the word 'he' (*hû'*), which suggests that there
has been no change of subject. Although the picture of wellbeing in vv.
16-17 by itself would be appropriate to the righteous, the implication of

v. 18 is that this will be of short duration—a sequence hardly in accordance with the conventional presentation of the fate of the righteous. Thus it makes better sense to interpret the passage as referring to the wicked. The new metaphor for the fate of the ungodly is that of a well-watered plant (perhaps a vine) thriving in the warmth of the sun, solidly rooted and with spreading branches, to all appearance impossible to dislodge, which can nevertheless be uprooted and destroyed and replaced with other plants, with its very existence no longer remembered. This kind of imagery is frequently found in the Old Testament (compare 18.16; Prov. 24.30-31; Isa. 5.4-6; Ezek. 17.7-10).

In the final verses of his speech (vv. 20-22) Bildad summarizes his view of retribution and again misses the point. Job seems now to be fully recognized as belonging to the category of the blameless (for Bildad there are only two human types). This is the conventional language of the Psalms (Pss. 35.26; 126; 132.18); it even speaks of Job's 'enemies', as though his misfortunes were attributable to human agency. Probably no specific allusion is intended: Bildad is simply the victim of his own eloquence.

Job 9

In this speech, which continues to the end of ch. 10, Job does not attempt to reply to Bildad's lecture, even though his opening words may seem to do so: 'Truly I know that this is so.' His main point is that he is unable to obtain a chance to vindicate himself—to obtain an answer to his complaint from a God who, although he has created him and constantly keeps him under observation, nevertheless ignores his pleas. Much of these two chapters is couched in legal language: Job desperately wants to dispute with God as with a legal opponent, but fails to find him. In his frustration he voices a growing conviction of God's hostility. In this chapter he refers to God mainly in the third person. Although formally the chapter is a reply to Bildad, vv. 1-24 give the impression of being a soliloquy, like ch. 3.

While appearing to assent to Bildad's assertion that God never acts unjustly, Job immediately raises a difficulty (v. 2b). His question is a general one, but one that is of particular relevance to his own case: if it is granted that God always acquits the righteous, how is it possible for any human being to know whether he is righteous or not? How can anyone be sure that he deserves a favourable verdict from God? Eliphaz elsewhere (4.17) had asked the same question and concluded, on the basis of the mysterious message that he had received, that *no one* is truly pure; Job, however, is here making a somewhat different point: while refusing to give up his claim to be innocent he finds himself unable to prove his innocence because it is God who makes the rules and refuses to reveal the standard on the basis of which he makes his judgments. In other words, the question of guilt or innocence before God is not as simple as Bildad maintains. It is therefore impossible for any person to undertake a legal accusation (*rîb*) disputing the correctness of God's judgment: if God put forward a thousand questions in his defence one would never be able to give a satisfactory answer even to one of them (this was later to prove to be the case when in chs. 38–41 God asked Job a great number of unanswerable ironical questions that overwhelmed Job and left him speechless). In v. 4 Job gives his reason for supposing that such an attempt would be bound to fail (though in fact he continues to attempt this in his subsequent speeches): God possesses absolute wisdom (which human beings can never possess) and absolute power.

In vv. 5-10 Job elaborates this statement with illustrations of both God's power and his wisdom. With regard to the former he makes use of the characteristic literary form of the hymnic doxology in which each item in a list of God's works begins in participial form ('he who...'), a form that gives them an enduring and not merely a temporal significance (compare, e.g., Pss. 147.2-6, 8-19; Isa. 40.22-23; 42.5; 43.16-17; Amos 9.5-6). Verses 5-7 assert God's power to destroy the world that he has created. According to the accepted cosmology of the ancient Near Eastern world the earth rested on pillars (Ps. 75.3), and the mountains also formed the foundations that gave it its stability (Ps. 46.2-3). Ps. 93.1 confidently asserts that the world that Yahweh has established will never be moved by hostile forces. Other texts, however, like these verses, affirm God's power to destabilize and so destroy his created world. An additional feature of this destructive power is included in the catalogue of negative divine power: forbidding the sun to rise and preventing the stars from shining. These thoughts, though no doubt derived from actual knowledge or experience of such temporary, partial and local phenomena as earthquakes, eclipses, sandstorms and the like, add up to a picture of a return to the chaos that existed before the world was created—a topic that was by no means rare in Hebrew thought, as is shown by the story of the Flood in Genesis—and are a forcible reminder that the cosmos with all that it contains, including the human race, is finite and, from God's perspective, ephemeral and even dispensable.

That the negative or destructive side of God's activity precedes the positive and creative in these verses is rhetorically effective. In a passage designed to give the greatest possible emphasis to human insignificance before God, the prospect of total destruction would act more powerfully on the mind than a description of the creation of the actual world with which all were familiar, even though the latter commanded unrestrained admiration. In vv. 8-10, however, the praise of God's power is accompanied by praise of his perfect wisdom. (Compare the account of creation in Prov. 8.22-31, where it was *by wisdom* that Yahweh created the universe.) This brief account is mainly confined to the creation of the heaven and the heavenly bodies apart from an allusion in v. 8 to God's defeat of Yam (cf. 7.12). In the same verse cosmology is again to the fore with the reference to God's stretching out the heavens—a phrase echoed almost exactly in Ps. 104.2; Isa. 40.22; 44.24. The identification of the constellations named in v. 9 is not entirely certain; but these stars evidently made a particularly strong impression on ancient observers: all three are singled out by Yahweh in his catalogue of creative acts in 38.31-32, and two appear again in a doxology in Amos 5.8. The 'chambers of the south' may be a reference to yet another constellation. Verse 10 sums up the passage, again emphasizing both God's wisdom ('beyond understanding') and limitless skill.

In vv. 11-13 Job applies these general thoughts about human helplessness in the face of God's absolute power and wisdom to his own case. God can see him (and indeed keeps a strict watch over his actions, which amounts to oppression [cf. 6.12-14]) but makes himself inaccessible so that Job, although he *feels* this oppressive presence, cannot *see* him. God can snatch away whatever he wills—human lives, happiness and reputation, as he has done with Job and his family—and no one can stop him or even attempt to take action against him. Job now sees God as an implacable enemy, giving vent to his fury as he did when he crushed the sea monster Rahab, another mythological image comparable with the references to Leviathan, Yam and the Dragon in 3.8; 7.12.

The theme is further pursued in vv. 14-24. Verses 14-16 are couched entirely in forensic terms: 'answer', 'choose one's words', 'to be innocent', 'opponent', 'appeal for clemency'. Job is convinced that even if he were able to bring his case, as it were to court, God would not listen to his defence. His supreme advantage as the divine bully who has crushed and wounded Job would be deployed in a refusal to submit himself to questioning (v. 19); and even if he did permit this he would be able to twist Job's words and to confuse him, making him condemn himself though he was, in fact, innocent (v. 20). In v. 21 he makes his claim to innocence absolutely plain, stating categorically 'I am innocent' (*tām*, the word used of him by the narrator in 1.1). It is not clear, however, what is meant by 'I do not know myself' in this verse. One suggestion is that it is an expression of rage or despair, meaning 'I am beside myself'. The same phrase occurs in Song of Songs 6.12a, where the meaning may be 'I am beside myself [with joy]'. This interpretation would fit the mood of rejection of life with which the verse ends.

In vv. 24-26 Job reverts, as he has done before, from his own situation to make a general indictment of God's treatment of his human creatures. These verses contain some of the most categorical denials in the book of the traditional belief in God's justice. The statement that 'it is one' in v. 22 is probably a summing up of his reflection on his own fate: the fact that he should be blameless yet driven by God to despair shows that whether he is innocent or not is a matter of indifference to God. He therefore draws the conclusion that this is how God always behaves: he is implacable in his hatred of the whole human race, dealing death to them irrespective of their deserts, even mocking when the innocent are overwhelmed by some calamity and conniving at the moral blindness of corrupt human magistrates, allowing the wicked to rule the earth with impunity. In the final phrase of v. 24 he holds God responsible for all the wickedness that is perpetrated: if he is the real ruler of the world, he alone must be responsible for everything that happens in it.

In vv. 25-31 Job once again (as in ch. 7) addresses God directly; but now he does so without hope, in the knowledge that God regards him as guilty and that there is no possibility that he will change his mind. Job's reflection on the brevity of his life (vv. 25-26) may seem strange in the mouth of one who longs for death, but the point of his reflection is expressed in the line 'they see no good'. It is not the brevity of his life as such of which he complains, but the fact that there is no improvement in his condition. His days flash by like a fragile boat in the rapids or an eagle suddenly swooping on its prey, but he derives no relief. In vv. 27-31 he rejects as impossible two conceivable ways in which he might escape from his misery: first, even if he made an effort to forget his trouble and be cheerful, he would not succeed because there is no way out from suffering in the face of God's condemnation of him; and secondly, any attempt to exculpate himself by admitting that he is guilty (literally, by cleansing himself thoroughly) will be useless because God will plunge him again into his (supposed) uncleanness.

In view of his conviction that God is not going to abandon his determination to hold him guilty, Job reverts in vv. 32-35 to his earlier wish that he could summon him to a trial (*mišpāṭ*) in which he could defend himself, only to conclude that the cards are stacked against him. These verses, which refer to God in the third person, are in the nature of a reflection. First, Job reflects that such an unequal conflict between the all-powerful God and a mortal man would be a travesty of justice. Moreover, in such a case there could obviously be no arbiter to mediate between the two parties or to judge between them. Only if God would first free him from the torture that he was inflicting on him ('his rod') would he be able, like any litigant in an ordinary case, to speak his mind without fear. The final phrase, literally 'for not so am I with me', is obscure: it may mean 'for I am not so in myself'.

Job 10

Deprived of the possibility of a formal trial and having now nothing to lose, Job in this chapter determines to dare to address God again in the strongest possible terms, though now in the certainty that he cannot expect an answer. In even more violent language than before (cf. 7.16; 9.21) he states that he finds his life disgusting. From v. 2 to the end of the chapter he makes the speech that he would make to God if he could be sure—which he is not—that God will be listening. Using forensic language again he asks God not to persist in holding him guilty, and boldly enquires into God's motives in doing so. In a rhetorical question he ironically enquires whether he enjoys oppressing the human beings whom he has created, but also why he appears to exempt the wicked from this treatment, giving approval to their doings. In vv. 4-7 he dismisses, again with a rhetorical question, any excuse that God might have to offer: after all, God's vision is not limited like human vision, nor, being immortal, can he claim that he must put intense pressure on human beings for lack of time. Furthermore, being omniscient (as well as omnipotent) he knows perfectly well that Job is innocent, yet he pretends an urgency to discover and punish his supposed sin.

The verses that follow (8-13) contain one of the most remarkable descriptions in the Old Testament of human conception and growth in the womb, a passage that has frequently been seen as a model of ancient 'science'. Its purpose, however, is a polemical one: Job lays stress on the loving care with which he as an individual had been fashioned by God, only to express bitter astonishment that this same God should now have determined to destroy him. As in 7.7, where he had asked God to 'remember' the brevity of his life, he now ironically draws God's attention to something that might have slipped his mind. Like all human beings he had been fashioned by God from clay (compare, e.g., 4.19; Isa. 45.9; also Gen. 2.7), But God is now turning him back prematurely to dust. From the first he had taken care of him, supervising his impregnation with semen and his gradual formation in the womb, clothing him with flesh and bones. Yet although he had thus given him life and appeared to treat him with kindness, Job now realizes that all this apparent benevolence was false. God had concealed from him his true purpose, which had from the first been far removed from what it had appeared to be.

Verses 14-17 expound God's intentions towards Job more fully. God had carefully preserved Job's life in the past only in order to catch him in the act of sinning; but whether he had, in fact, been wicked or righteous would be all the same to God: though he is innocent, God has overwhelmed him with disgrace and misery, ruthlessly hunting him down like a lion and still constantly adding to his troubles. Even so, in the conclusion of his speech Job shows himself to be still clinging to the faint hope that God might after all be capable of mercy—a thought that somewhat mitigates his picture of him as utterly pitiless. In a final pathetic passage (vv. 18-22) he appeals to him once more to put an end to his misery. After repeating the wish that he had already expressed in 3.11-16 that he had never been born—though this time putting the responsibility for his birth squarely on God (compare vv. 8-12)—he refers once more to the shortness of his life and begs God to withdraw his presence so that he may enjoy just a little respite. He knows that the land of death to which he is going is one of perpetual and total darkness like the chaos that reigned before the creation of the world, and that from it there can be no return; yet even that would be preferable to his present life.

Job 11

It can hardly be said that Zophar, the third of the friends, has a great deal to say in his first speech that advances the discussion, except that he introduces the question of wisdom into the debate. Job's inability to recognize that he is not wholly innocent, maintains Zophar, is the source of his trouble. Once he recognizes that, his guilt will be removed and his life will be transformed. Like Bildad (8.2), Zophar begins by expressing his contempt for what Job has said. Job, he says, has prattled on at great length, and must be answered; but—the language of the law court appears again here—he must be made to understand that he cannot vindicate himself simply by making interminable speeches (compare Bildad's dismissal of his words as a 'great wind'). In v. 3 Zophar accuses Job of unfairness in debate by trying to silence his opponents and even of mocking their arguments; he must be put to shame, and Zophar is the man to do this, as Eliphaz and Bildad have failed. Zophar's tone is clearly more acerbic, even hostile, than that of the previous speakers, who have shown more sympathy with Job; and this speech marks the beginning of a deterioration in the relationship between Job and the friends.

Zophar, in the role of accuser or hostile witness in a legal trial, now purports to cite Job's own words as evidence against him. In fact this is not a verbatim report: these are not Job's actual words, though Zophar is accurate enough in reporting Job's claim to be innocent. But Zophar has misrepresented him in an important respect: he accuses him of intellectual arrogance, claiming 'my doctrine [*leqaḥ*] is pure' (this word does not mean 'conduct' as it is often rendered). In other words, Zophar is saying that Job has claimed to be superior to the friends not only in virtue but in orthodoxy—a claim that, as a self-proclaimed sage, Zophar is not prepared to accept. The reality, that Job's speeches have been those of a desperate man seeking to defend himself rather than of a censorious tutor is lost on Zophar. His case is that Job cannot be a sage since he does not understand the nature of God: he lacks wisdom. With these words Zophar unleashes a series of issues that will be much debated in the rest of the book: that is, what is wisdom? Where does it come from? In what degree, if any, can human beings attain to it? In vv. 4-5 Zophar expresses the pious wish that God himself, as the source of all wisdom, would appear to Job and reveal the secrets of wisdom to him. Such an appearance was, of course, precisely what Job wanted; however, Zophar's wish is clearly no more than a pious exclamation: he himself claims to have all the answers, and now arrogates to himself the role of God's spokesman.

Zophar's next statements are not easy to understand. In v. 6b, elaborating on the phrase 'the secrets of wisdom', he states either that these are two-sided (*kip^elayim*, not 'many-sided' as in some translations) or that they are mysterious. The next line is even more problematic. It may mean 'Know that God exacts from you less than you deserve' or 'Know that God overlooks part of your guilt.' The first of these statements would be harsh, even for Zophar; the latter is more in accordance with Zophar's admission later in his speech that Job is not beyond redemption. That God's wisdom is mysterious is affirmed in vv. 7-12.

The rhetorical questions in vv. 7-8 asking whether Job can discover the mysteries of God's wisdom are reminiscent of the questions put to Job by Yahweh himself in chs. 38-41. Zophar speaks more truly than he knows; but in fact there is no disagreement among the friends or Job on this point. Job is here not learning anything new. The heights of heaven, the underworld of Sheol, the earth, the sea (vv. 8-9)—these mark the limitless extent of God's wisdom, which infinitely exceeds human ability to grasp it. But Zophar uses this familiar topos to instruct Job as if he were unaware of it. He points out that God knows and recognizes worthlessness or evil in an individual and has unlimited power to judge and condemn him accordingly. The accent has now shifted from God's wisdom to his power and to a reassertion of the doctrine of retribution. Verse 12 is evidently a proverb stating by means of a question that a worthless person can no more acquire wisdom than a wild ass can be born as a human being. This appears to mean that there is no hope for such a person. But Zophar has not said that Job is utterly worthless; and the verses that follow make it clear that he does not in fact think so. His point has been that because God is both all-wise and all-powerful nothing will prevent him from exercising judgment on human shortcomings.

In vv. 13-20 Zophar holds out the possibility that Job can be restored to his former happiness and security; but the conditions that he imposes are not only harsher than those imposed by either Eliphaz (5.8-26) or Bildad (8.5-6), but also irrelevant to Job's case. Zophar assumes Job's guilt: he urges him to set his heart towards God (compare the same phrase in 1 Sam. 7.3, where it means to serve him wholeheartedly), to stretch out his hands in prayer and to renounce wicked conduct. He appears to be unaware that Job had in fact always been such a person, both exceptionally devout and exceptionally righteous, and that this had not saved him from his present plight; but he goes on to assure him that he has only to fulfil these conditions for all to go well with him. He is 'preaching to the converted'. His rigid beliefs do not permit him to believe that a person suffering as Job is suffering could possibly be genuinely religious and innocent. The terrifying nightmares of which Job has complained will be a thing of the past if Job follows his prescriptions, and all his fears will be forgotten. In the final verse, in referring to 'the wicked', Zophar is not denying that he puts Job in his present

presumed state into that category; rather, he is setting out the fate that
will be his if he does not reform. Zophar is here employing a standard
device of the wisdom literature (compare, e.g., 8.21-22; Prov. 2.21-22;
10.16) that balances a statement about the positive future of the righteous with one about the fate of the wicked.

Job 12

Job begins his long reply, which continues to the end of ch. 14, on a new note (vv. 2-3): he now addresses himself to all the friends as a group; and for the first time he goes beyond mere dismissal of their arguments and contemptuously attacks their pretensions to wisdom. With heavy irony he attributes to them the arrogant claim that no one can be in the right except themselves: wisdom will 'die' with them because even in the future no one will ever surpass their discernment of truth about God and his treatment of human beings. This attack, which is hardly fair, reveals an exasperated Job, even an offensive Job who has lost patience. The friends, though they have sometimes spoken arrogantly, have never claimed that their convictions were the outcome of their personal experience or their wit: on the contrary, they have been doing no more than to repeat traditional teaching about retribution, and they have admitted this (Eliphaz, 4.12-21; Bildad, 8.8-10). Certainly they have not claimed that there is no more to be said on the subject. Job's resentment here is probably to be understood as directed principally against Zophar, who has treated him as a stupid babbler. He asserts that his brains are the equal of those of the friends, and that all their learned talk is no more than common knowledge.

Verses 4-6 are particularly obscure, and the Hebrew text may well be in disorder. But they appear to have the character of a lament in which Job complains that the truth about human life is, in his recent experience, precisely the opposite of what the friends have asserted: he, who is blameless and a faithful worshipper of God, has become a laughing stock and a butt for ridicule while the violent and brutal are left in peace.

It is not clear whether vv. 7-10 are an expression of Job's own sentiments or are intended as a parody of the opinions of the friends. The latter view is perhaps supported by the use of the second person ('you') in vv. 7-8. Using a topos of the wisdom literature to the effect that human beings can learn from nature—animals, birds, plants, fish (cf. Prov. 6.6-8; 30.24-31)—Job states that the fact of God's universal power is known to all: that this is something about which he needs no instruction. If the 'this' of v. 9 refers to what has happened to him, this is a point on which he and the friends can all agree: it is the question *why* God has afflicted him that is disputed between them. The proverb quoted in v. 11 is used to make the point that Job, like anyone else, is capable of assessing the truth or otherwise of what is said to him. Verse 12, also a proverb, rejects the view that only the aged, with their long experience and knowledge of traditional lore, possess wisdom and so can dismiss Job's own knowledge and interpretation of what has just happened to him.

Verses 13-25 are a *hymn*, not *to* God but *about* him (we should note that many of the verbs describing God's activities, as in many of the hymns in the Old Testament, are participles). The subject is God's possession of perfect *wisdom*, but this is accompanied, as in other such passages, by the notion of his absolute *power*. (Cf. Prov. 8.22-31, where Yahweh first creates Wisdom and then performs his creative acts in Wisdom's presence and the briefer statement in Prov. 3.19 that he founded the earth *by* Wisdom.) This association of God's power with his wisdom has an analogy in the Old Testament concept of *human* wisdom: wisdom is not conceived abstractly or philosophically but concretely. To acquire wisdom is always to acquire power—the practical power to get things done. So here wisdom is God's skill, both in creating the world and in managing it and controlling human society.

This is not the first time that the author of the book has made use of the hymnic form. The hymn put into Job's mouth in 9.5-10 is concerned wholly with God as creator. The hymn in the present chapter more closely resembles that spoken by Eliphaz in 5.9-16, which speaks, *inter alia*, of God's power over his human creatures. The perceptive reader will, however, ask *why* Job introduces this hymn into his speech and what part it plays in the speech as a whole. Neither he nor his friends needed to be reminded of God's unlimited power: and pure praise of the God who is responsible for Job's misery is hardly to be looked for in this embittered Job. What can be his motive, and what is the function of this passage in the speech as a whole? The answer to this question is perhaps to be found in the particular activities of God to which Job has chosen to refer. It is important to notice that the emphasis lies on God's *destructive* power, and on his capriciousness. Job is speaking from personal experience when he describes how God interferes with human lives, choosing to dishonour and depose distinguished and powerful leaders from the positions of honour to which he had himself presumably promoted them, without being answerable to anyone for his actions. In other words, under the cover, as it were, of a hymn of praise, Job is hinting that God exercises his admitted absolute power irresponsibly.

Significantly, the first of God's activities mentioned in this list is his power to destroy: no human being can rebuild what God has pulled down or free those whom he has imprisoned (v. 14—it is interesting to note that the second line of this verse is a clear echo of what Zophar had said in 11.10, but with a very different intention.) Verse 15 hints at God's indifference to human needs: in contrast with the common view that the sending of rain is one of the greatest blessings that God bestows (cf. Eliphaz in 5.10; Pss. 72.6; 135.7; 147.8), Job here mentions in this connection only the two evils of drought and disastrous floods; then in

v. 17, after ironically repeating from v. 13 the slogan that God is all-wise and all-powerful, he proceeds to an account of God's treatment of distinguished human beings—counsellors, judges, kings, priests, nobles and other notable persons, stripping them of their dignity, making fools of them, depriving them of their authority and their powers of judgment (vv. 17-21).

The relevance of the statements in v. 22 that God brings light out of the depths of darkness is not certain; but the verse should probably be taken together with vv. 23-25, which turn from individuals to nations: by depriving them of their leaders' capability to govern and leaving them, so to speak, to wander in a pathless desert, groping in the darkness like drunkards, God destroys whole peoples on whom he had previously conferred power and prosperity. Verse 22 may thus mean that in further extending his destructive work he reveals his hidden mysterious powers. The impression left with the reader of this passage is that despite God's unlimited power and 'wisdom' there is no meaning or purpose in his world.

Job 13

In this chapter Job has clearly reached a turning-point in his struggle. He
no longer has any hope: God may well kill him for his audacity, but he is
determined nevertheless to put his case before him, even though he has
no faith in his justice (v. 13). It is as if he is appealing, so to speak, over
the head of the God whom he knows to a higher truth. He is more insis-
tent than ever on bringing his case to trial in a direct confrontation with
God. Once more the forensic mode is to the fore. Job insists on knowing
what charges God is bringing against him (v. 23). Meanwhile he rounds
on the friends even more fiercely than before, accusing them not only of
being useless but of bolstering their arguments with lies.

He begins with an assertion that he has seen and heard 'everything'
and understood it. In 'everything' he presumably includes what he has
learned about God's destructiveness as related in the previous chapter.
In v. 2 he repeats the claim that he had made in 12.3 that he is no less
intelligent than the friends; but the knowledge to which he refers is not
the same. In 12.3 he was referring at least partly to Zophar's dubious
assurance made in 11.13-19 that he can rely on God's mercy; here it is
his own experience of God's unpredictable behaviour to which he
refers. The friends, who should have been 'healing' him—that is, giving
him comfort—have not only proved worthless but have covered up the
truth with lies. In v. 5, perhaps alluding to their initial silent sympathy
(2.13), he sarcastically tells them that in their case the only possible
'wisdom' would be to say nothing at all—perhaps an allusion to the
proverb in Prov. 17.28 to the effect that it is when fools shut their
mouths that they may acquire a reputation for wisdom. He then, despite
the fact that they had already dismissed what he has had to say as mere
stupid vapourings, demands again that they listen to him.

Job, as has been said, sees himself as about to institute legal proceedings against God. But first he voices his objections against those—
namely, the friends—who will be the witnesses in the case, on the
grounds of their partiality: they are, in fact, *false* witnesses. But he is
confident that, although they will be speaking in God's defence, God
will find them out and silence them with a display of his terrifying power.
These verses (7-12) well illustrate the paradoxical character of Job's
attitude towards God: on the one hand his case is that God ignores the
principle of justice with regard to himself, yet on the other he does not
doubt that God will uphold the principle of justice in rejecting out of

hand those who give false testimony in his (God's) defence. These witnesses will not succeed in their attacks on him because their arguments are, in fact, empty of truth.

Still addressing the friends (vv. 13-19) Job emphatically demands to be heard (there is a strong emphasis on the pronoun 'I'). The friends are peremptorily told to keep silent. He emphasizes the danger of what he is about to do: he is taking his life in his hands, and he recognizes that God may strike him dead. He has no hope (a more probable rendering than 'yet will I trust in him' as in some versions). He is about to defend his conduct in a face-to-face encounter. He has nothing to lose; the only thing from which he can derive a slight consolation (literally 'salvation', v. 16) is that he is not godless: if he were he would never be able even to approach God, who would not tolerate this. He now makes a formal declaration in strictly legal terms that he has prepared his case (*'araktî mišpāṭ*) and is ready to plead. His assertion in the second line of this verse (18) means not that he knows that he will win his case against God but that he knows that he is in the right or that he is innocent. His rhetorical question in v. 19, 'Who is there that can make out a case against me?' implies that no one, not even God, can prove that he is guilty; if such an outcome were a possibility he would say no more and would expire.

In vv. 20-28 Job now addresses God directly. First, he asks for two concessions that he believes to be essential if he is to receive a fair trial. He does not after all, however, actually proceed to the formal defence that he has announced, and indeed never does so; in fact the legal metaphor ceases to be consistently employed soon after this. The statement in v. 20 that if these two things are granted Job will not hide from God is somewhat surprising, as up to now he has never tried to do so: rather the contrary. The meaning may be that if they are not granted he will have to acknowledge defeat and so will have to retreat from God in terror for ever. Unfortunately it is not clear what are the two things for which he asks. One of them, certainly, is stated in v. 21. There Job repeats the request that he has so often made before, that God should cease to oppress him and to terrify him.

In vv. 22 and 23 Job is still calling for a legal contest. He offers God two alternatives: either that God should begin by summoning him to court, when he would answer the charges against him, or that he should be allowed to initiate the proceedings and await God's reply. (It may be noted that the offering of these alternatives appears to imply that the roles of accuser and defender are interchangeable, or that each of the protagonists is prosecuting the other; or, equally, that each has a case to answer. This ambiguity runs through much of the book. Ultimately it represents two facets of the same issue and so does not affect the course of the debate.) In fact the two alternatives proposed by Job are illusory, since God makes no move to speak but reserves his reply. Job is thus obliged to make his case without further delay.

Job's challenge to God in v. 23 to provide him with a list of sins of which he is accused is tantamount to a formal repetition of his previous claims to be innocent. The appeal is to what may be called 'natural justice': it is wrong for a defendant not to be told of what crimes he is charged; and Job makes it clear that this is precisely his situation. That being established, he proceeds to his indictment. God, he maintains, 'hides his face' from him—not in the sense in which the psalmists in the complaint psalms use the phrase, that God withholds his favour from the complainant, but that like a careless or indifferent judge he refuses to consider Job's case. Here Job is viewing God in a dual and immoral role as acting at the same time both as prosecutor and judge in his own cause; a judge who has already decided that Job is guilty without first giving him a hearing, and who is implacably hostile to him.

The indictment in vv. 25-28 follows a course that is already familiar to the reader. Job begins by stressing his utter helplessness: he vividly compares his terror at God's persecution with the situation of a fallen leaf or a bit of dry chaff driven willy-nilly by the wind; then, changing the metaphor, he accuses God of having already decreed (literally, 'written down') his punishment (literally, 'bitter things'), bringing up against him sins committed in his youth. What these were is not explained; but Job, whether they were inadvertent or because they lie in the distant past, evidently does not consider that they affect his basic claim to innocence or that they can be the cause of his present persecution. Using fresh metaphors whose precise meaning is not entirely clear, he complains that he is treated like a closely guarded prisoner whose every action is noted, and concludes by wondering how God can take such trouble to persecute such a worthless person as himself. This final verse makes a kind of inclusio or frame for his words in v. 25.

Job 14

This final section of Job's speech is principally a sombre reflection on human impermanence and the finality of death. It is mainly expressed in general terms, but Job's intention is obviously to apply these thoughts to himself; from time to time he breaks off to address God directly as the one wholly responsible for this deplorable state of affairs and for his, Job's, situation in particular. The chapter has been described as an elegy; but it is not an independent poem. Its thought is closely connected with what has preceded, and especially with the final verse of ch. 13, which can be interpreted in an impersonal sense (its initial words, literally translated, are '*He* wastes away', which may refer to humanity in general). The present chapter, then, should be seen as part of Job's indictment of the God who has appointed death for his human creatures.

In vv. 1-6 Job expresses astonishment at God's perversity in concentrating his attack on a person whom he has already inexorably doomed to death and at the turmoil that inevitably characterizes human life. The comparisons of human beings with a flower that quickly fades and with a passing shadow is a commonplace of Hebrew poetry (cf., e.g., Ps. 103.15-16; Isa. 40.6-8 and, with an individual reference, Pss. 102.11; 109.23). But he argues that it is unreasonable that in addition God should single out an individual to be the object of his particular surveillance and persecution. Job admits—without changing his plea of (comparative) innocence—that all human beings are by nature 'unclean' in God's sight: he would not disagree with Eliphaz's statement in 4.17; but since God already knows when they will die, he appeals to him to desist from persecution and to allow them to live out their lives in peace. They should at least be allowed to derive some enjoyment, even if it is as little as a master allows to his hired labourers. This appeal is not in contradiction with Job's persistent plea for a swift death for himself: at this point he is speaking on behalf of mankind generally—this is part of his indictment that God is unfair not only to him but to all.

The 'little poem' of vv. 7-12, though poetically complete in itself, does not stand in isolation. It elaborates the thought of v. 5 about the inescapability of death for human beings, and leads on to Job's forlorn wish in vv. 13-17 that God might have ordained things differently. It reflects the universal longing for immortality that is a prominent theme in ancient Near Eastern mythology. Job wonders why God has given the possibility of new life to the vegetable kingdom yet has denied it to human beings. Even a tree after being felled may have 'hope'—this is an evocative word used by Eliphaz (4.6) and Zophar (11.18) to encourage Job; but they are thinking only of the present life, when a pleasant and prosperous state will be available to him if he trusts and fears God. Here Job goes deeper: for him it is precisely the knowledge of mortality that is the cause of human misery. Human beings lack the inherent vitality of plant life; their powers fail, and they simply cease to exist (there is a poignancy in 'where are they?', v. 10). 'Until the heavens are no more' (v. 12) does not imply that they will revive at the end of the world; this phrase is a common image of perpetuity (cf., e.g., Deut. 11.21; Ps. 72.17; 89.29).

The meaning of part of the following verses (13-17) has been disputed, and there is also a textual problem in v. 16. But it is clear that Job, now reverting to the personal, here indulges in a fanciful dream of a highly improbable situation in which God might after all behave kindly towards him. He imagines God's protecting him by hiding him temporarily in the underworld—an extraordinary notion, since Sheol was the place from which no one ever returned—until his anger subsided. In other words, he envisages the notion of God's protecting him from himself (i.e. from God). This appears to be a paradoxical concept: of a God as it were beyond God—a God of mercy set against a God of wrath. Here, even if we conclude that Job is guilty of confusion, Job's theological notions are undoubtedly more complex than the narrow and rigid views of the friends. In this fantasy God would fix a time for releasing him from Sheol and would 'remember' him—that is, would resume his former benevolent attitude towards him.

There is some uncertainty about the first line of v. 14, which is frequently rendered as a question: 'If a man dies, can he live again?' This seems to be inappropriate to the context, and the line may in fact mean '*If* a man could die and live again...' If so, Job is affirming that he would endure the hardship ('service') of that sojourn in Sheol until he was released from it. In vv. 15-17 he imagines what his life would be like. 'Call' and 'answer' in v. 15 are no longer used in the legal sense but, as elsewhere in the Old Testament, to describe a friendly relationship. This thought is pursued in v. 16; but there the Hebrew text of the first line has been called into question. The Syriac translation there has a negative ('not') absent from the Hebrew, matching the 'not' of the second line. An emendation is probably not justified: Job appears to be saying that while God *will* continue to scrutinize his conduct he will no longer be on the watch to catch him in the act of sinning. Any sins that he might commit would be, as it were, locked away and sealed so as to be forgotten.

All this, however, was only a dream. In the closing verses of his speech Job returns to reality. God destroys human hopes: they decay and perish as time passes just as does the fabric of the world itself. Even mountains suffer gradual erosion; rocks, usually regarded as symbols of stability and permanence, are dislodged and crash down; stones are washed away by floods and soil is swept away by torrents. This imagery of change and decay in the structure of the world as metaphor for the destruction of human hopes is powerful and sombre, and at the same time realistic. The speech ends (vv. 20-22) with a vivid picture of dying and death. Death is not seen as a 'natural' happening but as the action of God who overwhelms human beings with his infinite power: he 'sends them away' and they cease to exist (literally, 'they go'). It is not clear whether vv. 21-22 refer to the physical and mental decay that often precedes death or to the state of death itself. God 'alters the face', that is, changes the appearance of those whom he consigns to death, and deprives them of memory, so that they no longer know what is happening around them—whether their own children are successful in life or not. If v. 22 refers to the dead, it is unusual in its attempt to describe their feelings; for the author, death is not a state of total oblivion (contrast 3.13, where it is a happy release) but rather one of pain and mourning.

Job 15

In this second speech Eliphaz matches Job's increasing hostility towards the friends. He no longer holds out for Job the prospect of an end to his troubles provided that he fulfils certain conditions, but asserts that he has condemned himself with his own lips (vv. 5-6); and on the assumption of his guilt he simply repeats in somewhat different words, as having the unimpeachable authority of tradition, the old tale of the inevitable downfall of the wicked (v. 20) and the ungodly (v. 34). At this point, the beginning of the second 'cycle' of speeches, the reader may well ask what purpose is being served by the introduction of a second, and even a third, round of speeches. Have the friends not already said all that they have to say? It must be acknowledged that from this point onwards they have little to add that is essentially new. The new things that are said are said by Job, whose speeches enliven the dialogue and so forestall the *ennui* that might otherwise be produced by the friends' repetitiveness. Not only does Job have new things to say; it is he who, humanly speaking, is the hero of the book, whose story is the centre of attention. In relation to him there is constant movement and progression, both in external events (from prosperity to misery and back again) and in his thoughts and arguments, whereas the friends' situation is static, manifesting only a growing increase in impatience with Job. It is not *their* story. Likewise, although it is possible to a limited extent to distinguish between their traits of character, these differences are hardly enough to form a focus of interest for the reader. Nevertheless, their speeches—all of them—serve an important purpose; indeed, they are indispensable to the progress of the book. It is not only that they provide a clear account of the traditional beliefs against which Job is contending and that the tenacity of these beliefs among the author's contemporaries is underlined by their unanimity; the friends also act as necessary foils to Job, inciting him to ever fresh tirades and also providing relief by breaking up what could have been a single, lengthy and tedious diatribe.

Eliphaz begins, as have Bildad (8.2) and Zophar (11.2-3) by disparaging Job's words but also accusing him of deviousness. Job has claimed in 12.2-3 and 13.2 to be the equal of the friends in knowledge— that is, wisdom; and indeed, in asserting his views as against the teaching of the friends, he has by implication claimed to be wiser than they. Eliphaz rejects this claim with his very first word. Like the others, he begins with a question: 'Does a wise man [ḥākām] ...' speak the way Job has spoken? Job's self-proclaimed knowledge is 'windy knowledge':

that is, his words have been dictated by his feelings rather than by reason, so (v. 3) they serve no purpose and are useless. This, says Eliphaz, is not the way a truly wise man argues. Indeed, Job's words are positively harmful: they are irreligious. By his disrespectful speech about God he has undermined the practice of meditation on God's deeds and teaching that characterizes the truly pious (compare Ps. 119.97, 99 and *passim*). It is not certain which of Job's words Eliphaz has in mind; it may be his questioning of God's justice, or his depiction of God's destructiveness in 12.13-25. Eliphaz then goes further: he claims to have detected the cause of Job's impious words. No one could speak as he had spoken whose mind had not been corrupted by sin; Job must therefore be guilty of sins that he had concealed, and it is these sins that have dictated his words and made him speak with guile, intent on leading others astray (vv. 5-6).

Verses 7-10 are ironical and still concerned with Job's claim to superior wisdom. Eliphaz mockingly suggests that the profundity of wisdom to which he lays claim could be possessed by no ordinary human being, and asks whether he is the mythological 'primal man' who existed before the creation of the world. The reference is clearly not to the first man Adam of Genesis 1-3, who was not pre-existent, nor was he born: rather he was *created* by God. The myth in question is not directly recorded in the Old Testament, but there seems to be a hint of it in Ezek. 28.12-19, where the king of Tyre is portrayed in terms of a primal being full of wisdom who was later found to be sinful and was cast out of Eden. There is perhaps a further allusion to this myth in Job 38.4, 21, where Yahweh ironically enquires whether Job was present at the creation of the world and so acquired knowledge of its workings. Another form of the myth appears in Prov. 8.22-31, where it is not a human being but personified Wisdom who claims to have been created by Yahweh as the first of his acts of creation, 'before the hills' (cf. Job 15.7b). The question of the origin of wisdom is also raised in Job 28, where it is concluded that only God knows where it is to be found.

Eliphaz asks in v. 8 whether Job has listened in God's council. This recalls certain passages in Jeremiah that seem to suggest that this is a special privilege of Yahweh's prophets. But here the allusion is clearly not to the prophets. To have heard what is said in God's 'council' (see on 1.6) and so to acquire God's own wisdom would be the privilege of the 'primal man' of v. 7. Job is asked whether he alone possesses that wisdom. In vv. 9-10 Eliphaz makes a somewhat more modest claim for himself and his friends—probably for himself in particular: they must be wiser than Job because they—or at least one of them—are much older. This is an argument that Job had already rejected in 12.12. The question will be raised again in 32.6-10, when Elihu also rejects it.

In v. 11 Eliphaz refers to his own earlier speech, which Job has unreasonably rejected although it was, in Eliphaz's own opinion, both consolatory and gentle. (He refers to it as 'the consolations of God', presumably claiming to be God's authorized spokesman.) In calling it consolatory or comforting he is presumably alluding to his statement in 4.17-21 that no human being is righteous in God's sight, repeated here in vv. 14-16, and to his encouraging assertion that God is ready to pardon and restore those who accept his discipline. He cannot understand why Job should not accept this sound doctrine, but presumes that he judges it to be too feeble or irrelevant to his situation. He finds Job's reaction to it senseless, showing that he has lost control of his judgment (literally, 'heart'), so that he has turned against God with angry words (vv. 12-13). Job's claim to be righteous Eliphaz regards as overstated; in a rhetorical question in v. 14 he points out that perfect righteousness is an impossibility for human beings, contrary to their nature. He repeats his earlier statement in 4.18, that even God's angelic servants, here called 'holy ones' as in 5.1, are imperfect: God cannot wholly trust them. The 'heavens' in v. 15b may refer to the heavenly bodies, here also regarded as God's servants (cf. 38.7). This is a clear statement that although he is surrounded by a host of such celestial servants, the supreme God (El) has no rivals who might dispute his absolute power. The present argument is an *a fortiori* one: if even these are untrustworthy (the author may here have had the mysterious incident of Gen. 6.1-4 in mind), mankind is obviously far more imperfect. In order to press his point home Eliphaz here in turn overstates his case, describing human nature (including, of course, himself) in the most extreme terms as abominable, corrupt and, in a particularly vivid phrase, drinking wickedness like water.

Eliphaz ends his speech (vv. 20-35) with a description of the misfortunes that will be the lot of the wicked (though he does not say *when* this will happen). The theme is basically the same as that of a passage in Eliphaz's first speech (5.12-14) and one of Bildad (8.18-19), but is here expressed in much greater detail. Eliphaz does not claim originality for it; he explicitly states, as had Bildad in 8.8-10, that it is the teaching of the sages of old, though he also claims that it corresponds to his own experience—'what I have seen', v. 17. The first of these claims makes good sense. This is a 'set piece' of traditional wisdom teaching. It does not mention Job, nor does it identify him with the 'wicked' (v. 20) who are its subject, nor does it balance its assertions with a corresponding statement about the fate of the righteous. But it implies, despite Eliphaz's earlier statement of vv. 14-16 that *all* human beings are steeped in sin, that the 'wicked' are a definable class of irredeemable persons for whom there is no escape from the consequences of their wickedness. Here Eliphaz is making a different point. The passage is intended as a warning to Job to avoid falling into such a trap. However, it falls on deaf ears, because Job knows from his own experience, and will state plainly, especially in his later speeches, that the facts are precisely the opposite of what Eliphaz asserts (e.g. 21.7-13, 30.32).

In vv. 17-19 Eliphaz states his intention to tell Job what he knows about the wicked, and insists that it is now Job's turn to listen. He equates his own observations with the teaching of the sages—perhaps because the latter have so coloured his outlook that he sees everything from their standpoint. He stresses the antiquity of this tradition, handed on through many generations. In v. 19 he is clearly concerned to emphasize its purity: it has not been corrupted by alien notions. However, it is not clear what is the 'land' to which he refers, which had been given exclusively to the early sages. The context in which the book is set—the non-Israelite provenance of Job and the friends—rules out any possibility that Eliphaz has in mind the occupation of Canaan by Israel (described in the book of Joshua); and in any case it could not be said that Israel at that time had no contact with foreigners! For this reason some critics have regarded v. 19 as a gloss expressing Jewish orthodoxy. But Eliphaz may be referring to some otherwise unknown episode in the history of his own people.

Verses 20-26 do not purport to describe the final fate of the wicked. Rather, they are intended, somewhat unrealistically, to represent them as perpetually terrified of the fate that might be theirs. They know that they will not be able to escape the darkness of premature death but will surely be destroyed (v. 22), because they have impiously dared to oppose God. In a series of vivid images v. 27 now moves to a description of the actual fate whose anticipation has been tormenting them. Though they have become sleek and fat with self-indulgence (v. 27), they are destined to lose all their wealth, to be driven to live in degrading circumstances and to wither away like a dried up plant, unable to bring their plans to fruition, and perhaps (vv. 33-34) to remain childless. Only in v. 34 does Eliphaz give a specific instance of their crimes: bribery here means corruption of judges and witnesses in the courts—a practice frequently condemned in the Old Testament laws. But the speech concludes (v. 35) with a much wider though less specific indictment. Is it coincidence that some of what Eliphaz says about the fate of the wicked could be descriptive of what had happened to Job? There is, however, no direct allusion to him, and Eliphaz may not have had him in mind. On the other hand, if Eliphaz had believed Job's claim to be wholly undeserving of his fate he probably would not have spoken in this way.

Job 16

Of this speech of Job's, which continues through ch. 17, it cannot be said that he has any essentially new arguments to put forward. It consists mainly of a renewed bitter complaint, sometimes expressed in extreme metaphorical terms, about God's treatment of him, stressing his utter helplessness in the face of God's attacks. Ironically, the depiction of his sufferings here has affinities with passages in individual complaint psalms in the Psalter in which the psalmist complains to God of attacks by his human enemies; but the enemy is now God himself. The friends are only occasionally mentioned after the first few verses. Only occasionally also is God addressed. The main impression is of a monologue; nevertheless the *effect* of the speech is that of a cry to God for pity.

Job's opening words (vv. 2-6) contain the only allusion in the speech to the previous speeches of the friends, mainly to them as a group but in v. 3 to a single person, presumably Eliphaz who has just spoken. Continuing the disputants' by now regular practice of mutual contempt for opposing arguments, Job points out that he has heard it all before and not only from them but from others: their words have thus been a waste of breath. They have claimed to bring comfort to him, but all that they have done is to make things worse for him: they are all 'comforters who have brought trouble' (*'āmāl*). If he were in their place, he tells them, he could give the same advice and shake his head over them (in exasperation, or perhaps in derision). If they were in pain he could speak comfortingly to them to relieve their pain (v. 5). Here he is speaking ironically: if words could put things right, as the friends seem to think, he would use them; but Job is now contemptuous of mere words: he knows that for such a purpose words are ineffective. He points out that all the friends' speeches have made no difference at all to his own suffering. On the other hand, to keep silent (as in 2.13) has not helped either; in other words, nothing can help him.

In vv. 7-17 Job tries to express his conviction of God's unrelenting antagonism to him in a lament in which he evokes a series of pictures of violent assault and humiliation. The meaning of vv. 7-8 is not clear: they probably refer to Job's sickness. In vv. 7b and 8a Job accuses God directly (this has been ignored in modern translations, though not in AV and RV). In v. 9 he views God as an enemy who falls on him like a wild beast. 'They' in v. 10 are Job's human enemies, who, seeing that Job is a victim of God's anger, insult and abuse him. In v. 11 he laments that God has deliberately subjected him to their malice. These verses are reminiscent of passages in complaint psalms, such as Psalms 22, 31 and 35, and are not to be taken literally: no one has in fact behaved in such ways.

In vv. 12-14 Job dramatically depicts the suddenness of God's attacks on him, using the imagery of the battlefield. He remembers his former state of carefree prosperity that was so rudely shattered by a brutal physical attack; then, slightly changing the metaphor, he speaks of himself as the victim of an ambush or a concerted attack in which he had found himself surrounded by God's troops of bowmen (not to be distinguished from God himself) who used him as a target, shooting him with their arrows and destroying his kidneys and liver. This latter image is not far from the literal truth, as Job is in fact suffering from a loathsome disease (2.7) whose external symptoms point to an internal disorder; but the imagery is also symbolic: the kidneys were associated in Hebrew thought with the affections, and the word 'gall' ($m^e r\bar{e}r\hat{a}$) is derived from a root meaning 'bitterness'. In v. 14 these attacks are described as incessant, like the assaults of a determined hand-to-hand fighter as in v. 12, which together with v. 14 marks out the limits of the pericope. In vv. 15-17 Job drops the highly metaphorical language of the previous verses. Despite God's attacks on him he in fact remains alive; but he feels that death is near. The wearing of sackcloth was a conventional sign of mourning for the dead; and although Job would, of course, be mourning the death of his children, v. 15 probably means that he has prepared for his own death. His statement that he has 'laid his horn in the dust' may have a similar meaning, that his life is over. The 'deep darkness' on his eyelids in v. 16 also stands for the approach of death. But he still stoutly maintains his innocence of any crime and the sincerity of his piety.

Much of vv. 18-22 presents great difficulties in the Hebrew, and some lines have been rendered and interpreted in quite different ways by the commentators, as a comparison between various modern versions (e.g. RSV, NRSV, NEB, REB) clearly shows. There can be no certainty about such passages. What is clear, however, is that Job is giving God as it were a last chance to recognize the validity of his case before he dies. Having accused him in vv. 7-17 of deliberate brutality he now once more changes his tack and treats him as one who could conceivably be amenable to reason. This ambivalent attitude towards God is a frequent feature of his speeches and is intended to provoke the readers to a serious consideration of the tremendous issues at stake for themselves and ultimately for all human beings. The paragraphs that follow here will present a selection of possible readings of the text that seem to the present writer to have the greatest probability.

The meaning of v. 18 at least is plain. Job, who has pointed out in 7.21 that it is the earth (that is, the soil) that will receive his body when he is dead, so putting him beyond the sphere where God could find him whether to pardon or to persecute him, now makes an appeal to the earth not to cover his blood. This presupposes that Job will die a violent death, like Abel (Gen. 4.10), whose blood cried to God for vengeance. The notion alluded to here (as also, for example, in Isa. 26.21; Ezek. 24.8) is that the murderer will then be found and punished. But here the murderer (when Job's anticipated death occurs) will be God himself! It is with v. 19 that the difficulties of this passage begin. Job maintains that 'even now' there is a witness, not on earth but in heaven, who will testify on his behalf. Who can this witness be? Opinions are divided. Strange though it must seem, the most probable answer to this problem is that it is God himself! Although, as has been seen, the existence of lesser heavenly beings subordinate to God is pre-supposed in the book, it is difficult to suppose that Job could imagine any one of them in this role; indeed, he had already rejected the possibility of a mediator between himself and God in 9.33. An alternative proposal, that Job means that his own lament will be an effective witness in heaven, is equally implausible. The most probable solution is therefore that in these two verses we have another example of Job's ambivalent attitude towards God. In other words, although Job believes that God is the cause of his troubles, he also knows that God knows him to be innocent, and he still cannot wholly believe that he will not acknowledge this to be so.

If the above interpretation of v. 19 is correct, vv. 20-21, though difficult, are best understood as continuing to refer to the 'witness in heaven'. The ambivalent attitude towards God as implacable adversary and yet just judge is still maintained. Verse 20 thus expresses a hope that the 'witness' will act as Job's friend and interpreter when he weeps before God, and v. 21 that he will plead on Job's behalf, although Job is a mere human being, just as on the purely human level a man might plead for his neighbour. (It should be noted that some of the modern versions render v. 20 quite differently). The point of v. 22 is to draw attention to the urgency of the matter: when Job is dead it will be too late. The 'way of no return' is of course the path to the abode of the dead (compare 10.21-22). The mention of 'a few years' may seem to detract from the sense of urgency that Job intends to convey; but the word 'year' in Hebrew is often used imprecisely, and it is the word 'few' that conveys the essential point.

Job 17

This chapter is a continuation of Job's monologue, with occasional verses addressed to God (vv. 3-4) and to the friends (v. 10). It is mainly concerned with Job's thoughts about his coming death, together with the abandonment of all hope. He feels himself to be already in the grip of death (v. 1), and proceeds to enumerate the causes of this feeling. He has become the object of mockery and antagonism when he might have expected sympathy (v. 2). Here he does not specify the friends, though he probably interprets the tone of their speeches in this way. Verses 3-5 are difficult. In v. 3, apparently addressing God directly and speaking metaphorically, he refers to a pledge made to God that God must honour because there is no one else to do this. This is the technical language of security for loans: in Israelite law and practice a debtor who could not discharge his debt promptly was obliged to deposit some object in his possession as a guarantee of later payment. Job sees himself as being in the position of a debtor who has offered a pledge of his integrity; if God does not accept it, he is lost. Since God has made the friends incapable of recognizing Job's innocence (v. 4a), God cannot claim any credit from this situation (this may be the best interpretation of v. 4b). Verse 5 is probably a proverb, whose meaning and relevance, however, are not clear. It may refer to persons who invite their friends to a meal while their children are starving; but who are those persons?

After returning to his previous complaint that he has become an object of mockery and contempt (v. 6) and to his lament that he is near to death (v. 7; compare v. 1), Job makes ironical comments on those who fail to understand the truth about his situation. The righteous and innocent (or does Job mean those who *claim* to be righteous and innocent?) are appalled at 'this'—that is, Job's wretched misery (an allusion to 1.12, 13), but their perturbation is not due to a recognition that he is an innocent sufferer. On the contrary, they regard him in their ignorance as godless, deserving his horrible fate (v. 8). This feeling makes them all the more determined to hold on to their own blameless way of living (v. 9). These verses are an indirect allusion to the friends, whose lack of insight Job now asserts in a direct address, saying that even though they may think that they still have something to say to him, he is now sure that none of them possesses enough wisdom to understand the true facts (v. 10).

The speech concludes (vv. 11-16) with the topic of death and the consequent loss of hope. Verses 11-12 speak of the end of all Job's plans and wishes for the future: his life is over. Verse 12 is not, as some modern translations render it, a citation of an opinion of the friends that Job's fate can be reversed, turning 'darkness' for him into 'light'. Rather, it is a continuation of the sentence begun in v. 11 about Job's former hopes. He had hoped that 'light'—that is, God's favour—would be restored to him, banishing his present state of 'darkness'; but that hope is now abandoned. Like the closing verses of Job's earlier speeches (7.21; 10.21-22; 14.20-22), vv. 13-16 re-emphasize these thoughts. Sheol and 'the Pit' are synonyms for the underworld, the abode of the dead; the worm obviously signifies bodily corruption in death. These verses, with their references to 'house' (cf., e.g., Ps. 49.14), couch and 'family relationships', stress the new and permanent status of the dead, who are cut off from the normal enjoyment of these things by the living: 'house' and 'couch' may also allude to the custom of gathering the bones of the dead in an ossuary. There is a play on the meanings of *qwh*, 'to look for', in v. 13 and *tiqwâ*, 'hope', the noun, in v. 15: to 'look for' or anticipate death is to *lose* all hope, which for Job means hope of vindication. So hope and Job will perish together (v. 16).

Job 18

Bildad in this second speech has absolutely nothing new to contribute to the debate. Apart from some further adverse comments on Job at the beginning (vv. 2-4) it consists entirely of a description of the fate of the wicked. Like other similar descriptions in the book (8.11-15 [also Bildad], 15.20-35 [Eliphaz] and, later, 20.5-29 [Zophar]), this passage does not specifically identify Job with the wicked but is nevertheless extremely pointed, while once again missing the point. It is purely imaginative: Bildad cannot possibly have personally observed what he describes. This is another 'set piece'—an extended expression, albeit in superb poetry, of the traditional doctrine of retribution in its purest form. This time, perhaps ominously, there is no balancing statement about the blessed future of the righteous or about the possible redemption of the penitent.

In vv. 2-4 Bildad first expresses impatience with Job's refusal to desist from making speeches and to concede defeat. He states his opinion that unless he speaks more cogently there is no point in continuing to argue. He accuses him of despising the intelligence of himself and his colleagues. But in v. 4 he goes much further: in his assertion that he is in the right and that the friends with their God-given wisdom are in the wrong, Job has tried to overturn the moral order of the universe, usurping the place of God and attempting to undo his work in peopling the world (cf. Isa. 45.18) and securing its foundations (cf. Pss. 93.1-2; 104.5). Bildad thus appears fearful of the consequences of what he regards as Job's blasphemy. For him, Job is not just a foolish babbler but a potential destroyer of cosmic stability.

Verses 5-21 describe in vivid imagery the calamities that will fall on the wicked, ending with their final destruction. The key images are darkness (vv. 5-6); snares (vv. 7-10); terror and fatal disease (vv. 11-14); and finally total extermination of the wicked together with their families (vv. 15-19). The chapter closes with a comment on the effect on others of witnessing their horrible fate (v. 20) and a general summary (v. 21). Much of the imagery is conventional; it is their combination in a single passage and their deadly sequence that create the total effect on the reader.

The image of the extinguishing of the light of the wicked is a standard one in the book of Proverbs (e.g. 13.9; 20.20; 24.20). Job will later contradict this notion of Bildad's in its own terms, asserting that on the contrary it is precisely the wicked who in his experience are the ones who are permitted to prosper (21.7). Light as a symbol for life is an obvious image frequently employed in Old Testament poetical texts; it is used by Job himself when he expresses his longing for death (3.20). In vv. 7-10 the symbolism changes to the equally standard one of a journey and of the need to keep to the right path. For the wicked, life will be like walking through a minefield set with hidden snares. Their certain downfall is emphasized by the use in vv. 8-10 of no less than six different words denoting nets, traps, nooses and so on, terms normally used of the hunting and trapping of wild animals. Their fate will correspond to that which they had prepared for others (v. 7b). These verses are an extended example of a topos that occurs frequently in Proverbs (1.17-18; 6.5; 7.22-23; 22.5).

Verses 11-14 describe the panic that will overtake the wicked. But these 'terrors' are not just ordinary fears. They are personified as the agents of death driving the wicked to their dreadful deaths (cf. Job 27.20; Ps. 73.19; Ezek. 26.21; and Job's estimate of his own situation in 30.15): hunger, calamity and disease followed by death itself. Verse 13b depicts 'the firstborn of Death' as consuming the flesh of the wicked. This representation of death (*māwet*) is reminiscent, as probably in a number of other Old Testament texts (e.g. Jer. 9.21; Hos. 13.14; Hab. 2.5), of the Canaanite god Mot, god of plagues and death and ruler of the underworld, who opens his jaws and consumes his victims. (It is not certain whether the reference is to a 'firstborn son of Mot' to be distinguished from 'Death' or whether the phrase should be read as 'Death the firstborn', that is, Mot himself, who is described in the Ugaritic texts as a 'son' of the high god El.) But the 'king of terrors' (v. 14b), before whom the wicked will be dragged by his agents from their supposedly secure homes to his underworld domain, is undoubtedly Death himself.

In vv. 15-20 Bildad depicts—always with a lively imagination—the total obliteration of the wicked, even to the destruction of their very homes, and the effect of this on their horrified contemporaries. First, in v. 15 their houses are destroyed, seemingly by some supernatural means, by fire (this is the probable meaning of v. 15a) and by the scattering of brimstone or sulphur on their ashes. Verses 16-19 extend their fate to include the extinction of their children and descendants (precisely what had happened to Job's family!), first through the imagery of a dead tree and then in plain terms. The lack of progeny to continue the name and memory of the deceased, so important for Israelites and their neighbours, means total annihilation. The wicked do not suffer ordinary death in leaving this world, but are forcibly thrust out of it as if they had never existed. In v. 20 Bildad goes as far as to say that their fate, when it is generally known, will strike all humanity, from west to east, with horror.

In v. 21 he summarizes his conclusions: this is the fate of the wicked who 'do not know God'. This phrase does not signify genuine ignorance of God but rather religious apostasy and moral corruption (cf. Hos. 4.1;

5.4; 8.2; Jer. 2.8; 4.22; 9.3). This verse is generally interpreted as harking back to the topic of former homes of the wicked, now abandoned or destroyed; but it also has a further meaning of the grave or the underworld: 'habitation' and 'place' are used in this sense elsewhere (Isa. 22.16; Ps. 49.11). That is now to be their permanent home, and that is the proper place for them.

Job 19

Job's reply in this chapter differs in several respects from his previous speeches. Reproaches against God occupy the bulk of the chapter, but God is not directly addressed. On the other hand, the friends are addressed, as a group, three times, in vv. 2-6, 21-22 and 28-29. Job refers in greater detail than before to the effect of his situation on his social relationships: he is now estranged from family and friends, no longer master of his own household, physically repulsive even to his wife, despised even by children—all as a consequence of God's hostile action against him. He pleads with his friends to pity him instead of assaulting him with their speeches. As in some of the other speeches in the book much of the detail is imaginary: Job describes scenes that cannot have taken place as there has been no interval in the dialogue with the friends in which they could have occurred, though they would no doubt become reality in the future if Job's misery were to be further prolonged. These scenes are therefore proleptic; but the desperation of Job's words is real enough. The purpose of the description, which in many ways resembles passages in some of the complaint psalms in which the psalmist describes his miserable situation in prayer to God, is rhetorical. It has a twofold aim: it is at the same time an appeal to his friends for sympathy, and evidence to be used in his coming 'legal action' against God, whom he still expects to 'see' and by whom he still expects—or at least, hopes—to be vindicated. There is an irony here in that when Job does in fact 'see' God the encounter will be very different from what he expects. The reader, as well as Job and the friends, is due for a surprise.

Job's complaint that the friends have 'crushed him with words' (v. 1) is a nicely judged repartee to Bildad's similar comment on him in 18.2. These sallies indicate that the tempers of the parties are becoming frayed. The 'ten times' of v. 3 is to be taken as meaning an unspecified but excessive number of times (compare Gen. 31.41); the second line of that verse is probably a statement rather than a question: the friends are quite shameless in their attacks. Verse 4 is not an admission of sin: rather, Job is saying that even if he had committed some kind of misdemeanour he could only have harmed himself. He has done his friends no harm, so their attacks on him are quite unjustified. Their arrogant and self-righteous attitude shows a misunderstanding of the true situation, that it is God who is the culprit: God has twisted the evidence against him and overwhelmed him by deploying his all-powerful 'siege weapons' (rather than 'net') against him (v. 6). God ought to be his protector, not his enemy. But to call on him for help would obviously be futile (v. 7).

The cry of 'Violence!' (*ḥāmās*) was evidently the way in which persons who had been the victims of violent attacks customarily appealed for help and for justice to be meted out to the criminal (Jer. 20.8; Hab. 1.2; cf. Deut. 22.24). Job knows that even if he were to make such an appeal to the heavenly judge he would get no answer: his case (*mišpāṭ*, 'justice') would simply go by default. Here he comes close to accusing God not only of a hostile attack on him but of being a corrupt judge in his own case.

In vv. 8-12 Job deploys a whole battery of metaphors to describe what God has done, and is still doing, to him. First, using the image of life as a journey, he asserts that God has blocked his way and plunged him into darkness. Secondly, God has stripped him of his dignity (-*kābôd*, not here 'glory'). 'Crown', literally 'garland' in the same verse (9), does not imply that Job was a king. Although that is one of its implications, it can mean a kind of tiara as worn by well-dressed women (Ezek. 16.12); a bride could be 'crowned' with it at her wedding; and it is also used metaphorically in Lam. 5.16. Here it is parallel to *kābôd* and denotes Job's honourable and distinguished position in society, now totally lost. Verse 10 contains two images: that of a building that has been demolished and that of an uprooted tree for which, unlike a tree that has merely been felled (14.7-9), there is no hope of revival. Finally in vv. 11-12 Job reverts to the metaphor of an attack by an enemy who has besieged him with his army.

In vv. 13-19 Job suddenly breaks down, abandons his metaphorical language and speaks in plain terms of the breakdown in his relations with family and close friends that is the consequence of God's relentless hostility, of which he had spoken in vv. 6-12. He has become an outcast whom no one wants to know (in 2.12 the friends do not at first recognize him). These verses poignantly reveal the utter isolation that he feels. The list of those who have rejected him is in ascending order of persons on whom his happiness had depended. It begins with the outer circle of his relations (literally, 'brothers'; but the word has a wide range of meanings, and here probably means members of his clan) and others who are merely acquaintances (v. 13). These have abandoned him because he appears to be an outcast from society. He moves on in v. 14 to his more intimate family and close friends and in v. 15a to the 'guests' in his house, that is, the 'resident aliens' who have come to live under his protection, but who have now 'forgotten' him. Even his own servants no longer obey him: they regard him as an outcast from his own house, and he is reduced to pleading with them (vv. 15b, 16). Even more terrible is that his own wife and family (perhaps meaning his brothers) find him physically repulsive (v. 17), and even children are repelled by him (v. 18). Verse 19 is a summarizing conclusion to the list, which marks out these verses as a self-contained literary unit. Verse 20 is a kind of appendix that appears to revert to Job's illness, but its meaning is far from clear. The first line is almost identical with Ps. 102.5b, which suggests that it may be a quotation from a proverb. It has been pointed out that it makes no sense anatomically. The second line is equally obscure and may also have a proverbial origin; teeth, however, have no skin! (The fact that it has become a proverbial expression in English sheds no light on its meaning in Job.) 'I have escaped' may suggest that Job is saying that he feels himself to be close to death.

Between two further addresses to the friends (vv. 21-22, 28-29) is enclosed the celebrated and difficult passage in which Job expresses a wish based on a conviction. There is no specific address to the friends in vv. 23-27, and God is spoken of in the third person. But the fact that these verses occur in the context of address to the friends perhaps suggests that he is still primarily speaking to them.

Job's sudden cry for pity in v. 21 has been seen by some commentators and translators as totally out of character: elsewhere Job never asks for pity, and that he should now ask for it from the friends, who think that he fully deserves God's punishment, is incongruous. But the verse has been widely misunderstood and its significance overestimated. The verb *ḥnn* hardly means 'to pity' in the sense of being sorry for a person in distress. It can simply mean to show kindness or consideration, for example, to the poor (Prov. 14.31; 19.17; 28.8) or to anyone in trouble (Ps. 109.12). It is to friendship that Job is appealing; the first line of this verse should be rendered by 'Show me kindness: you are my friends'. This word 'friends' (*rē'îm*) is that used of the three friends in the Prologue (2.11); it is significant that it is *not* one of those used by Job in vv. 13-19 with reference to those who have deserted him. He is thus recognizing that despite everything these three are his true friends: they alone have not thrown him over. There is at the same time a slightly ironical note here: the 'friendship' for which he is asking is simply that they should give up their verbal attacks on him—it is already more than enough that he should have to bear *God's* attacks (v. 22). The second line of this verse is to be understood as metaphorical: it refers merely to verbal abuse (compare the use of the same expression in Ps. 27.2).

Verses 23-27 are notoriously difficult. The Hebrew text itself makes it very unclear what Job is actually saying—particularly to what extent he is speaking confidently and to what extent he is merely expressing a forlorn wish. Who is the 'redeemer' of v. 25? Does Job expect to be vindicated before he dies, or does he think that this will happen in some way after his death? Here it is not possible to discuss in detail the many solutions that have been proposed to these questions. All that can be done is to put forward what seems to *this* reader to be most probable. One thing, however, should be clear: that to look for total logical consistency in these verses is unrealistic. We have already seen that Job vacillates in his attitude towards God. Although he regards him as his enemy and as the one who has deliberately wrecked his life, there remain moments when he continues illogically to place some kind of hope and trust in him. Indeed, this fluctuation of belief is an essential aspect of the author's presentation of Job. It shows Job to be a human being bewildered by what has happened to him. But this does not exhaust the author's purpose: more important for the theology of the book is that the tension thus created in Job's mind serves to expose the problem of the divine nature.

In vv. 23-24 Job expresses a wish—indeed, a longing. The exclamation 'O that ...!' (*mî-yittēn*) indicates, as elsewhere in Hebrew (e.g. Ps. 55.6; Jer. 9.1), that what is wished for is an impossibility, or at least unlikely to be granted. In this case Job's wish is that his 'words'— probably his 'case' or formal defence—should be engraved on a monument or stele (the word commonly rendered as 'book' may refer to bronze or copper here) as a permanent testimony of his innocence. Neither the reason for this nor the connection between vv. 23-24 and 25-27 is, unfortunately, clear. Verse 25 begins with a confident statement: 'But I know' (not 'For ... '). The disputed question here is the identity of the 'redeemer' (*gō'ēl*). In Israelite law the *gō'ēl* was the person whose duty it was to come to the aid of a distressed kinsman by redeeming family property that he had been forced to sell (Lev. 25.25) or in certain other ways. In Second Isaiah, however, the word is regularly used in a highly theological sense: it is *Yahweh* who is Israel's *gō'ēl*), who will save his exiled people Israel (e.g. Isa. 41.14; 43.14; 44.6). Job, deserted by all his friends, was certainly in the position of one who needed a *gō'ēl* to help him. But to whom does this verse refer? Three main interpretations have been proposed. One view is that this is a metaphorical reference to Job's 'words' in v. 23: in other words, it is Job's 'case' (his plea of innocence) that will speak for him and declare him innocent. Another view is that the word refers to some heavenly being (since no human *gō'ēl* seems to be a possibility) other than God, who will stand between Job and God and plead Job's case. A third view, and that which has long been that most widely held, especially in Christian circles, from early times, is that the 'redeemer' is God himself.

There are difficulties with all three theories. The picturing of Job's 'words' in terms of a living person, a 'near kinsman' who will 'stand up' on the earth may be thought, even in a literature that abounds in personifications of inanimate things, to be excessive and improbable. The problem with the theory of a heavenly advocate who will appear on the earth to defend Job is that it introduces a hitherto unknown element into the situation and disturbs the presupposition elsewhere consistently accepted by the dialogue, that Job's dispute is with God alone. Such heavenly disputants as are mentioned in the book are merely 'supernumeraries' with no active role to play. The third view, that it is God himself who is here said to be Job's *gō'ēl*, is open to the objection that he can hardly be at the same time Job's enemy and legal opponent, and his 'helper'. However, in view of what has been said above about Job's ambivalent attitude towards God, this seems to this reader to be the most probable interpretation of the verse. There is good reason, therefore, to identify the *gōʾēl* with the 'witness in heaven' of 16.19. The contrast between Job's confident attitude towards God in vv. 25-27 and his devastating accusations in vv. 6-12 is indeed striking, all the more so because in ch. 21 he relapses into his earlier disillusionment. It cannot therefore be said that these verses mark a definitive 'conversion' of Job. But they are significant in that they point forward to the final denouement.

Even if this interpretation is correct, serious problems remain. One of the chief of these is the question whether Job expects his vindication to be achieved in his lifetime or after his death. In vv. 26b and 27a he speaks of 'seeing God' in order to present his case face to face with his adversary; but whether this is an expression of confidence or merely a wish is not clear. Verse 27a, 'my eyes will see, and not another', perhaps suggests the physical vision of a still living person ('on my side' in NRSV is misleading; the Hebrew has simply 'for myself'). 'In my flesh' (literally, 'from my flesh') in v. 26b also suggests physical vision—'*without* my flesh' is almost certainly a mistranslation. Similarly *ʾaḥᵃrôn* (v. 25b) probably means 'at last' rather than 'at the last', which would give the word an eschatological sense. Verse 26a is unfortunately almost unintelligible. The balance of probability thus seems to lie with Job's seeing God in his lifetime, though this may be a wish rather than a certainty. The final line of v. 27, 'my heart [literally, 'my kidneys', the source of the emotions] fails in my breast', probably refers to Job's emotional exhaustion.

This interpretation of the passage would rule out the traditional view—improbable in any case because of the rarity of such a belief in the Old Testament and its late date—that it expresses belief in a personal resurrection after death. In view of Job's admission elsewhere in the book that no one can return from the realm of death and that God himself has no power over the underworld, it is out of the question that he should here express such a hope.

Following this expression of his conviction that he has God as his *goʾel*, Job turns in vv. 28-29 on the friends, of whose 'persecution' he has already complained in v. 22, with a warning. They have, he says, justified their persecution on the grounds that he is guilty and so deserves it. But since he is in fact innocent, they are false accusers; and that is a crime deserving severe punishment (see, e.g., Deut. 19.16-21). In fact at the end of the book (42.7-9) it is stated that the three friends incurred Yahweh's anger, which was appeased only when Job prayed for them. The final warning that there is a 'judgment' (v. 29c) for wrongdoers may seem ironical, since Job has all along questioned the integrity of God's justice (e.g. 9.21-24). But it may be the author's intention here to suggest that Job's new-found confidence that God will act as his *go'el* has shaken that belief.

Job 20

In this second and final speech Zophar does not address Job directly at all, except for the single word 'you know' in v. 4. He does, however, regard himself as impelled to answer Job, who, he feels, has insulted his intelligence by presuming to give him instruction (vv. 2-3). The whole of the remainder of his speech (vv. 4-29) is a disquisition on the inevitable discomfiture and ruin of the wicked (r ᵉšā'îm) or godless (ḥānēp, v. 5). This follows the pattern of the preceding speeches by Eliphaz (15.20-35) and Bildad (18.15-21) and is, like them, a 'set piece' of theoretical wisdom that cannot have any base in Zophar's personal experience and is expressed mainly in generalizations and metaphors. The fact that despite his indignation Zophar simply repeats the well-worn theme of the fate that awaits the wicked shows that he has finally made up his mind about Job: he is evidently to be classed as one of the wicked, irrevocably doomed. There is no suggestion that he might still take warning and so avoid that fate. The speech purports to be an 'answer' to Job's questioning of God's retributive justice in passages like 9.22-24.

The poem comprises three fairly clear sections. Verses 4-11 develop the theme of the end of the wicked in a premature death, a frequent wisdom theme (cf., e.g., Ps. 37.10, 20, 35-38; Prov. 10.25, 30; 13.9). Verses 12-23 pursue this theme further with a series of metaphors in which wickedness is described in terms of eating. Only in v. 19 is there an allusion to *concrete* actions attributed to the wicked. Verses 24-28 resume the tale of disasters in store for them; v. 29 sums up the whole matter in a conclusion closely resembling the final verses of chs. 11 (11.20, Zophar) and 18 (18.21, Bildad), which deal with the same theme.

In vv. 2-3 Zophar explains why he feels impelled to speak again: what Job has said has put him in a state of mental agitation. Just as Job has accused the friends of 'insulting' him (19.13), so Zophar in turn complains that Job has insulted *him*, not as a person but in his attempt to destroy the whole basis on which his faith is built, namely God's justice. The 'spirit' that impels him to answer him (v. 3b) is Zophar's own 'spirit', that is, his intellect (the spirit *of* his understanding, not *beyond* it as in some translations).

Zophar begins his declamation with an appeal to ancient tradition similar to those made by Bildad (8.8-10) and Eliphaz (15.8-10). But his rhetorical question 'Do you not know...?' is contemptuous. Job, of course, knows that tradition as well as do the friends. His case against God's injustice is based not on ignorance but on personal experience. Zophar's choice of the word 'know' may be an indirect allusion to Job's

confident 'I know' (19.25): Job has claimed that he has a *gō'ēl*, clearly
for Zophar there is no *gō'ēl* to assist the wicked. He seeks to strengthen
his appeal to tradition by claiming that the impermanence of the rejoicing of the wicked has been universally known and accepted from the
time of the first man. He may also be alluding here to Eliphaz's sarcastic
remark (15.7-9) that Job has behaved as if *he* is that first man and so has
greater knowledge and wisdom than anyone else.

Verses 5-9 speak of the brevity of the triumph of the wicked and assert
that despite their aspiration to godlike heights they will suddenly disappear, to the astonishment of those who knew them, and be forgotten.
Verse 8, which compares their brief life to a dream or a night vision,
echoes the language of a similar passage in Psalm 73 (esp. v. 20), language that was probably conventional. Verse 10 speaks of the destitution of their impoverished children. Verse 11 sums up this passage with
a reference to the burial of the wicked while still in the prime of life.

Verses 12-23 turn to the actual *behaviour* of the wicked, though this
is mainly depicted in metaphorical language. There is a remarkable
concatenation of related metaphors here, all connected with overeating
and its effects on the greedy. The insatiable appetite of the wicked for
riches is portrayed in terms of gluttony and the unfortunate effects of
overeating: food poisoning, vomiting and so on that will not only take
away all enjoyment but will eventually kill those who indulge in it.
Verses 12-13 speak of wickedness as something that the wicked enjoy as
one might enjoy a good meal, savouring it so much that one is reluctant
actually to swallow it. This picture of the wicked as sadistic as well as
predatory is characteristic of wisdom teaching in that there are no half
measures. The division between righteous and wicked is an absolute
one; and the latter have no redeeming features at all.

The effects of this gluttony are perhaps depicted in two different ways
in vv. 14-16. The 'food' in question, here identified as 'riches' (that is,
wealth derived from others, v. 15) turns out to be poisonous. According
to v. 15 it will be vomited up; according to v. 16 it will cause the deaths
of the wicked, who will never again 'see'—that is, enjoy—the abun-
dance of wholesome food that is generally available. The eventual consequences for those whom they have cheated are set out in v. 18. The
first half of this verse still retains the original metaphor: the wicked will
be forced to vomit up ('give back') the criminal profits that they have
made—or, perhaps, they have not succeeded in actually 'swallowing'
them. The second half of the verse provides the key to the metaphor.
The activities of the wicked are described as 'exchange' (*tᵉmûrāh*),
evidently some kind of commercial enterprise from which they would
have made a profit. That of course was not in itself a criminal activity;
but v. 19 states in plainer language how these particular profits have
been obtained: by 'crushing the poor' and dispossessing them of their
homes (compare Amos 4.1, which also speaks of 'crushing the poor',

referring to the unscrupulous seizure of property by creditors from poor debtors).

Verses 20-23 employ the 'eating' metaphor in a somewhat different way. The insatiable greed of the wicked (v. 20) will cause a general shortage and so put an end to their prosperity. The 'nothing left' of v. 21 seems to mean that they will have reached the limit of what they can extort from others and will be left without further resources. The irony of these verses is evident; but it seems to be implied here that the wicked, if left unchecked, would have consumed all the available sources of wealth. This may be a reference to those whose aim was to 'corner' the agricultural resources of the country (compare Prov. 11.26; Amos 5.11). But, says Zophar with grim humour, they will get their fill after all: God will fill their bellies not with food but with his wrath.

The speech concludes with a series of other violent images. The first of these (vv. 24-25) is of a battle scene in which the wicked are pictured as a defeated warrior who avoids one weapon directed at him only to succumb to another—a bronze-tipped arrow that enters his body and pierces a vital organ, the gall bladder. This double attack symbolizes the inevitability of his fate (compare the use of the same device in Amos 5.19). When he draws out the arrow he realizes that the wound is fatal and is overcome with terror of death. The imagery of v. 26 is more obviously supernatural: darkness, a frequent symbol of death in this book and elsewhere in the Old Testament, will fall on the wicked and their 'treasures'—the ill-gotten gains that they have set aside for future use; and a fire kindled by no human hand (perhaps Zophar was thinking of lightning, but we may compare the 'fire that will not be quenched' of Isa. 66.24 and the destructive fire sent by Yahweh [Lev. 10.2; Num. 11.1]) will consume them and their homes. These are signs that even heaven and earth have rejected them (v. 27). Verse 28 is now recognized as referring to floods and torrents of water that will be sent by God—perhaps a reminiscence of the Flood (Gen. 6-8) sent to destroy the irrevocably wicked inhabitants of the earth. The final words of the poem, apart from the general conclusion in v. 29, are significantly 'the day of God's wrath'. Verse 29 declares plainly that there is no escape for the wicked because God has irrevocably decreed their fate.

Much of this speech picks up Job's own words and uses them against him. Job had pictured his treatment by God in terms that Zophar now uses to describe the fate of the wicked. For example, Job had described himself as pierced by God with poisoned arrows (6.4), and as having his gall spilt on the ground by God's archers (16.13). He had spoken of his advocate in heaven (16.19); Zophar now declares that heaven itself turns against the wicked. It cannot be doubted that he has Job in mind throughout this speech, although he never addresses him directly.

Job 21

In this speech, which, like his immediately preceding one (ch. 19), is addressed to all the friends as a group, Job turns the tables on them. He picks up and comprehensively rejects the assertions that they have made about the fate of the wicked. Almost the whole of this speech (vv. 7-33) is a direct contradiction of what they have said. The friends, if only by implication, have included Job among the wicked, whose inevitable ruin they, especially Zophar in the immediately preceding speech (20.5-29), had proclaimed. In answer to this Job could have simply pointed out that their warnings were irrelevant to his own case since he was not wicked. Instead, he chooses to ignore the hidden reference to himself and to keep the discourse impersonal and so universal in scope. He asserts the exact contrary to their claims. He asserts that far from suffering the terrible fate envisaged for them, the wicked as a group enjoy the happiness and prosperity that, on the friends' submission, is reserved for the righteous. What he is claiming is not just that God fails through indifference to reward human beings as they deserve, but that he deliberately flouts the principles of justice—and not just in isolated instances but consistently and universally.

The chapter begins (vv. 2-3), like the earlier speeches both by Job and the friends (cf. 8.2; 11.2-3; 12.2; 15.2-3; 16.3; 18.1; 19.1) with a mocking reference to the worthlessness of the words that have been spoken 'on the other side'. Emphasizing the importance of what he is about to say, Job taunts the friends (who have, in fact, not offered him any comfort despite their intentions [2.11]). by saying that the only 'comfort' that they can now offer him is to keep their mouths shut (as they had done when they arrived; 2.13) while he speaks. After that they can, if they dare to do so, sneer at him. But whether they do so or not is irrelevant: it is not to them, who as mere mortals can neither harm nor heal him, that his complaint is addressed. It is against God; and he has had good reason to lose patience with God, because he has not deigned to answer his charge. Job's friends, on the other hand, ought to be appalled and awestruck at the sight of his misery (v. 5); indeed, he himself is utterly horrified when he contemplates it.

Verses 7-16 are a direct denial of the assertions of Zophar in ch. 20 and of Eliphaz in ch. 15 about the fate of the wicked. Job depicts the wicked in vv. 7-13 as enjoying a life of ideal happiness, prosperity and contentment: a long life marked by undiminished and even increasing vitality, domestic security and freedom from the fear of divine retribution, material success, numerous and cheerful families and finally a peaceful end. This picture of wealth and prosperity, which was precisely what Job had once possessed and had expected to continue to enjoy, but of which he had been deprived by an unjust God, is given the form of a bitter lament by the opening word 'Why?' in v. 7. It is a picture of what *should* still be Job's; yet (vv. 14-15) these are the people who have abandoned all regard for the God who has given them these things. (The point of v. 16 is unfortunately not clear. Though sometimes taken to be a question, the first line may be a comment that the prosperity of the wicked is not due to their own efforts; the second line could be seen as a sanctimonious reflection by Job. But none of the proposed interpretations is satisfactory, and it may be best to regard the verse as a not very apposite addition by a reader.)

Verses 17-21 may be seen as a reply to Bildad's speech in 18.5-21 as well as to that of Zophar in ch. 20. They present the obverse of the picture in vv. 7-15 of the prosperity of the wicked, picking up and elaborating the topic of their immunity from anxiety and from divine punishment that had been touched on in v. 9. Using the device of the rhetorical question Job rejects the assertion of Bildad (18.6), also expressed in other words by Zophar in 20.5-9, that the 'lamp' of the wicked will be extinguished, challenging them to tell him how often this occurs. Then in vv. 19 and 20 he takes up and rejects a possible objection to his position, namely, that even though the wicked themselves may escape punishment, that punishment will fall on their children, who will suffer for the sins of their fathers. He neither confirms nor denies this view, which was current in the time of Ezekiel but rejected by that prophet (Ezek. 18.1-4), but argues that this would be equally immoral. It is the wicked themselves, who callously give no thought to what may happen to their children after their death, who ought to bear the brunt of God's anger; but that simply does not happen in God's world.

In vv. 22-26 Job is concerned to make the point that there is no moral law governing the fate of individuals: some enjoy prosperity, some not. The implication is that God is indifferent to their fate. The only thing of which one can be certain is that all will die and will moulder in the grave. There is thus no special judgment reserved for the wicked. This directly contradicts the assertion of Zophar (20.11) who seems to specify this fate for the wicked only. The paragraph begins (v. 22) with another rhetorical question. The notion expressed in this verse, that God, who judges even the heavenly beings (*rāmîm*, literally 'exalted ones') is omniscient and not to be instructed by mere human beings, would not of course have been denied by the friends; but here it is used ironically, and the irony is directed against both the friends and God. On the one hand, the friends, with their confident claim that they know more about human reward and punishment than God himself, have presumed to teach him his own business. On the other hand, God, who is the undisputed supreme judge, fails to exercise his authority equitably.

The remainder of Job's speech (vv. 27-34) is addressed to the friends. They have tried to put him in the wrong by identifying him with the wicked and so concluded that he has deserved the fate that they take to be normal in such a case. Several passages in the earlier speeches of the friends are in Job's mind in his summary (v. 28) of what they have said, for example, 15.34 (Eliphaz); 18.14-15, 21 (Bildad; 20.26-28) (Zophar); but in the reference to the 'prince' (*nādîb*, meaning a potentate with perhaps the nuance of 'tyrant') Job may be making a direct ironical allusion to his own former status. He now (v. 29) rhetorically appeals to the witness of those who have travelled and had experience of the world, any of whom could testify that the wicked frequently go unpunished even in the 'day of wrath' when others suffer. No one dares to accuse them of their misdeeds or to bring them to account; and when they die they are buried with great ceremony, surrounded at their funeral by numerous mourners in a choice location and with people appointed to guard their tombs (vv. 32-33; cf. Eccl. 8.10). Job concludes (v. 34) as he had begun, by once again scornfully dismissing the so-called 'comfort' offered by his friends as meaningless and even as deceitful—an abandonment of friendship.

Job 22

In this third speech Eliphaz adopts a much harsher tone than before. He has no new arguments to put forward, but he is now clearly hostile. Although in his conclusion (vv. 21-30) he repeats (ironically?) his appeal to Job (cf. 5.17-26) to be reconciled with God and again assures him that if he does so he will be restored to his favour, he now goes beyond his earlier contention that Job *must* have been wicked, and purports to list specific crimes that he *has actually* committed. Of these he can, of course, offer no proof at all: the reader knows that he has simply invented them. The author no doubt intended this to be seen as a consequence of Eliphaz's strong resentment at Job's equally harsh indictment of the friends as false friends (21.34). But Eliphaz relies for his 'proof' on the fundamental principle of God's justice: since God is just, only a life of exceptional wickedness can account for his harsh treatment of Job. This is a monstrous theory: it turns on its head the traditional principle of divine retribution. The belief that God punishes the wicked has become in Eliphaz's mind a belief that anyone who suffers in this way must *ipso facto* be very wicked. That is, Eliphaz manufactures 'facts' to fit his theory.

He begins (vv. 2-4) from God's transcendence. God cannot be affected by or derive any advantage from human behaviour: he is self-sufficient and entirely impartial, utterly unmoved by earthbound motives. Therefore, if he has rebuked Job and become his adversary, Job cannot, as he has maintained, be innocent. Job's treatment by God proves his guilt (v. 5).

The crimes that Job is supposed to have committed (vv. 6-9) are to a large extent the very crmes that Job will specifically deny on oath when he comes to make his so-called 'negative confession' in ch. 31. They are social crimes and are forbidden in the Old Testament laws. Eliphaz has picked them because they are precisely the kind of crime that might plausibly be attributed to the powerful landowner that Job had once been. But Eliphaz gives way to a wild imagination in his accusations, even asserting that Job has 'crushed the arm of the orphan', an unheard-of act of gratuitous violence (though see below for an alternative explanation). The taking of pledges from one's poorer neighbours (v. 6, 'brothers') was a common practice that eventually led to the expropriation of a debtor's possessions by a creditor who seized the land for himself; it was condemned in the laws (e.g. Exod. 22.25-27; Deut. 24.6, 10, 17) and denounced by the prophets (e.g. Amos 2.8; Ezek. 18.16). Verse 8, though ostensibly a general statement, implies that Job has been such a person, seizing the land of the poor by unscrupulous methods and so establishing himself in sole possession (cf. Isa. 5.8). In this verse such people are called 'men of the [strong] arm' (*'îš z^erôa‘*); this word (*z^erôa‘*) is, significantly, used again in the following verse, where Job is accused of crushing the 'arm'—that is, the ability to lead an independent life—of the orphan.

After this list of Job's crimes, which he expresses in quite precise, matter-of-fact terms, Eliphaz reverts to conventional poetic language: snares, sudden panic, blindness, drowning are symbols expressive of Job's present suffering, and they are, claims Eliphaz, the consequence of his sinful life. The whole passage, which in Eliphaz's mind constitutes proof of Job's guilt, resembles the denunciations of the prophets: first the indictment; then, preceded by the word 'therefore', the punishment. Only a sinful life can have produced such suffering.

Each of the three sections into which Eliphaz's speech is divided (vv. 1-11, 12-20, 21-30) begins with a reflection on the nature of God. The first of these refers to God's transcendence, with the implication that his judgment of the wicked, such as Job, would be impartial; the second stresses his omniscience: God sees the deeds of the wicked and will surely deal with them as they deserve. It ought to be common ground that God dwells in heaven even above the stars (v. 12; cf. Deut. 5.22; 2 Sam. 22.10; Ps. 97.2); but Eliphaz accuses Job of twisting this belief for his own purposes: of concluding that God is *unable to see* through the darkness and clouds that envelop him: he 'walks about on the vault of heaven', not on the earth, and there is therefore nothing to restrain Job from behaving as the wicked have always behaved (v. 15). Needless to say, the words attributed to Job in vv. 13-14 were never spoken by him; on the contrary, he has even complained that God will not leave him alone but is the 'watcher of humanity' and observes all that he does (7.17-20; 18.14-15). Once again, Eliphaz takes refuge in falsehood and misrepresentation to prove Job's guilt.

In vv. 16-18, after repeating his earlier statements that the wicked will be duly punished by overwhelming disaster and premature death, Eliphaz purports to cite yet another example of blasphemy. This time he does not attribute it directly to Job but to the wicked in general: nevertheless this is a warning to Job not to imitate them. There are, in fact, two distinct 'quotations' here. First, the wicked are supposed to have addressed God, telling him not to interfere with them. Secondly, they scornfully claim that he will not, or cannot, interfere. This second quotation, like that attributed to Job in vv. 13-14,, is reminiscent of the thoughts conventionally attributed to the wicked in psalms of lamentation, for example Pss. 10.4-13; 64.5-6; 73.11; 94.7. This would not be an outright declaration of atheism, which is never envisaged in the Old Testament, but a declaration of independence from all moral restraint on the blasphemous grounds that God is powerless and so irrelevant to human behaviour. In v. 18a, having now raised himself to a pitch of furious indignation at what he claims to have observed, Eliphaz adds a further point to his indictment: namely, that it is the One to whom alone in reality they all owe their prosperity that the wicked think they can safely ignore. In the second line of this verse he asserts, in words identical with those spoken by Job himself in 21.16b (though on this see above), his hatred of them. But in vv. 19-20 he takes comfort from his conviction that the righteous will triumph over the wicked after all, and will exult in their discomfiture.

Even now, in this final speech, it seems that Eliphaz does not despair of Job's rehabilitation: in vv. 21-30, resuming the role of teacher of wisdom, he makes a final appeal to him. It is God, he tells Job, who is the true teacher: even now if Job will resume his communion with him he may be able to save not only himself but others. How God's instruction is to be conveyed to him and by what means is not specified; but, as with the instruction of the human teacher in Proverbs 1-9, it undoubtedly corresponds to Eliphaz's own theology based on tradition—in particular, to the belief that God will reward the righteous and those who turn to him. Eliphaz makes it clear that Job must begin by renouncing his wickedness (*'awlâ*) and his wealth and recognize that true wealth is to be found in God alone (vv. 23-25). That God-given wisdom is more precious than gold, silver and precious stones it is a commonplace of the wisdom literature (so, e.g., Prov. 3.14-15; 8.10, 19; Job 28.15-19); but in repeating these commonplaces Eliphaz has clearly forgotten that they are totally inappropriate to Job's present situation.

In v. 27 Eliphaz speaks of a resumption of friendly relations between Job and God: when the penitent Job makes a request to God he will grant his prayer. There will be virtually no limit to what God will do for Job: whatever he decides on will be successful (v. 28—the irony is that of the author, not of Eliphaz!). The meaning of v. 29 is unfortunately not clear: it seems to have something to do with the punishment of pride and the rewarding of humility. The interpretation of v. 30 is also uncertain; it perhaps contains a promise that the 'new' Job, whose hands will now be clean, will be able to achieve reconciliation with God even for other guilty persons.

All this Job has heard before; it makes no impact on him at all; and in his following speech he ignores Eliphaz's words altogether. His own problem remains unsolved, and God seems, as ever, remote. In ch. 23 Job concentrates on his present situation and takes no heed of the friends' specious promises.

Job 23

As there is no indication in the text of a change of speaker between 23.1, which announces the beginning of this speech of Job, and 25.1, which announces Bildad's reply, it is natural to suppose that Job continues to speak throughout chs. 23 and 24. However, interpreters have noted that much of what is attributed to him in ch. 24 appears to be out of character: that in those parts of that chapter he seems to be taking the view of the friends with regard to the fate of the wicked rather than his own view. This kind of problem is, in fact, not confined to ch. 24. Bildad's reply in ch. 25 is unaccountably brief; further, in this third cycle of speeches, which began with Eliphaz in ch. 22 there is no speech by Zophar at all as would have been expected. Again, parts of Job's speech in ch. 27 also appear to follow the views of the friends rather than his own; and it has also been suggested that part of ch. 26 may originally have been the continuation of Bildad's speech. These anomalies have given rise to the opinion expressed by some scholars that in the early course of transmission there occurred at this point in the text some accidental disruption in which the order of the verses has become muddled, some material may have disappeared altogether and the identities of the speakers have become confused; and that the text that we have is the result of a not very successful attempt to reconstruct its original order. Other attempts have been made to account for these phenomena, and these will be discussed as the commentary proceeds. But the immediate task is to comment on ch. 23, which is unaffected except that it remains uncertain whether it comprises the whole of this speech by Job or not.

Job begins (vv. 2-7) by expressing even more passionately than before his intense desire to find the elusive God and argue his case with him; the language is once again that of the law court. Such a direct encounter, he is sure, is the only way in which he will be able to justify himself; his arguments with the friends have proved useless, and his situation is no better than it was before (v. 2.). He does not now expect that God will come down to him, but toys with the possibility that he might be enabled to approach God in his dwelling place in heaven. Then he would be able to do what he had not been able to do: to argue his case and listen to God's reply. If only this were possible, Job feels that despite his earlier feeling that God had become his enemy God would not crush him with his overwhelming power but would accept his claim of innocence and acquit him. It is evidently this vindication that Job wants even more than the restoration of his health and prosperity. This confidence exemplifies one side of Job's oscillation between the extremes of hope and despair that reflects the author's own thoughts about the human predicament and which we have already encountered in the book.

After this burst of confidence Job falls prey again to misgivings (vv. 8-17). First, he is still frustrated by his inability to establish contact with God. He remains confident that God knows everything about him and that if he were to put him to the test (the metaphor is that of the refining of metals in a furnace) he would emerge as pure gold (vv. 10-12). But God has hidden himself from him; and wherever he looks for him (in vv. 8-9 'forward', 'backward', 'left' and 'right' should be read as 'east', 'west', 'north' and 'south') he cannot 'see' him. But this thought is then succeeded by a more frightening one: that God may, after all, prove not to be amenable to persuasion, but may have already made up his mind about him. 'He is One' (or 'He is alone') in v. 13 is not a formal statement of monotheistic faith, though Job clearly takes it for granted that God is the one and only arbiter of human destiny and that he does whatever he wishes and cannot be dissuaded. So in Job's own case God will carry out what he has determined for him, as he does in all other cases. This thought leads Job in vv. 15-16 into a state of abject terror. Gone (for the moment) is all his confidence in a just God who will certainly acquit him when he hears his case; and Job, who a moment ago desired so passionately to be brought face to face with him, is now desperately afraid of what will happen to him if this occurs. The final verse (17) is probably not a wish but a further expression of his terror; he feels himself to be already engulfed by a deep darkness from which he will never escape (cf. 10.22 where also he speaks of such a darkness).

Job 24

The interpretation of this chapter is particularly difficult in that the persons referred to are not named, and their identity can only be surmised from the ways in which they are pictured. Thus v. 2 begins with a third person verb, but it is not said who 'they' are. ('The wicked', found in some modern translations of this verse, is absent from the Hebrew text; it has been added by the translators to help the reader. In this case, however, the remainder of vv. 2-4 leave no doubt that this guess is correct.) But in vv. 5-12 there is a clear change. It must be presumed that 'they' are now the oppressed 'needy' and 'poor' of v. 4, though this identification is not clearly indicated by the grammar. Again, in the middle of this section (v. 9) 'they' are again the wicked, although from v. 10 'they' are again clearly the poor. There is a further change of subject in vv. 13-17, where 'those who rebel against the light' are once again the wicked. The wicked continue to be the subject of the rest of the chapter, though from v. 18 onwards a new problem arises. As has been noted above, vv. 18-24, which announce their downfall, read strangely as a statement by Job, who has elsewhere complained continually that the wicked are protected and favoured by God. This constant oscillation between one group of persons and another, combined with an apparent alteration in Job's attitude, has made some commentators suspect the chapter's literary unity.

Verse 1 raises the question why God's judgment of the wicked appears to be indefinitely postponed. 'Time' (*ʿēt*) and 'day' (*yôm*) are used together as elsewhere (e.g. Isa. 13.22; Ezek. 7.7, 12) to signify the fate or doom appointed for the wicked; this is Job's reply to the assertions of Eliphaz (15.23) and Zophar (20.28) about the imminence of God's wrath. Posing ironical questions, Job asks for evidence for their assertions, arguing that even those who are in God's confidence never see any evidence of their truth.

As examples of the crimes of the wicked that go unpunished, Job lists in vv. 2-4 some of their characteristic actions. Some of these are specifically condemned in the Old Testament laws; some are the same as are attributed to Job by Eliphaz in 22.6-9. They are all acts of brutality that were regarded with abhorrence not only in Israel but throughout the ancient Near East, where in particular orphans, widows, the poor and disadvantaged generally were seen by universal consensus as being under special divine protection. Encroachment on the property of others by shifting boundary markers is forbidden in Deut. 19.14; 27.17 and is condemned in Prov. 22.28; theft of cattle is an indictable offence according to Exod. 22.1-4. The taking of pledges from widows—in this case of the ox that would probably be the widow's sole source of livelihood—is also forbidden in Deut. 24.17; Job was accused of a similar crime by Eliphaz in Job 22.6. Verse 4 is a general accusation of intolerable intimidation by the arrogant wealthy. These accusations, not being directed at specific persons, are too general to be susceptible of proof, as are Eliphaz's accusations against Job in 22.5-9; but there is no reason to doubt that this kind of tyranny was commonplace in the author's time.

In vv. 5-12 Job turns from the oppressive actions of the wicked to describe the misery of their victims, who are outcasts from society and who even when they find menial employment are treated worse than slaves and left by their employers to starve. In vv. 5-8 some are depicted as literally destitute, forced either to scavenge for food for their children, like wild asses in the desert and waste land, or to enter cultivated fields to glean what is left over of ears of corn and grapes after harvest, as was permitted in the laws (Lev. 19.9-10; 23.22; Deut. 24.19-22)—activities, however, that provided neither clothing nor shelter from the weather. Verse 9 is an interpolation that some scholars believe to be misplaced, perhaps from after v. 3. It refers to an act even more brutal than what is alleged in v. 3: the seizing of members of a family—here even small children—as surety for the payment of debts (cf. Exod. 21.7; Lev. 25.39-40; 2 Kgs 4.1; Neh. 5.4-5). The repetition in v. 10 of the topic of nakedness already mentioned in v. 7 may be an indication that the author's vein of inventiveness is beginning to be exhausted. Verses 10b-11 turn to a description of those who are obliged by reason of non-payment of debts to do agricultural work for others: they carry the sheaves of harvested corn to be stored in the barns, operate the olive presses and tread the grapes, yet they are in a starving condition because they are forbidden to partake of these three staple products, corn, oil and wine (cf. Hos. 2.8). In v. 12 there appears to be a change of scene from countryside to town; but there the situation is no better. The point of this verse lies, however, in the final line, which sums up Job's conclusion about the whole matter: God pays no attention to the cries for help of the poor and oppressed.

In vv. 13-17 Job's (or the author's) imagination takes full flight and enters the realm of the fantastic. The tone of these verses is so markedly different from that of the earlier sections of the chapter that the view of those commentators who see them as an independent poem becomes almost plausible. Whereas vv. 1-12 had been based on the realities of oppressive landowners and of those who suffer from their cruelty, these verses depict a group of people who are completely estranged from normal behaviour: they are those who 'rebel against the light', preferring the darkness for carrying out their evil deeds. The word 'light'

(*'ôr*) has a variety of meanings in Hebrew, some of which are represented in this book. In general it signifies what is good; it had been created by God as a gift to the world. Often it is a synonym for life itself. But it also has the property of bringing to light all that is done in the world, whether good or evil. For this reason it is hated and avoided by the wicked. While some of the deeds alleged here—burglary and adultery—belong to the realm of the everyday, v. 14 best illustrates the lack of specificity in the indictments in this passage: to set out while it is dark with the deliberate intention of killing the poor hardly belongs to the realm of reality.

The preceding verses have not drawn any conclusions from their description of the behaviour of the wicked—whether it is held to be punished or not. The final verses of Job's speech, as has already been noted, constitute—together with 27.13-23—one of the greatest of all the problems of the book. Several different attempts have been offered to account for Job's sudden abandonment of his own position, which he has expressed even in this very chapter (v. 12c), namely, that God does nothing to right the wrongs of those who have suffered injustice. The principal explanations proposed are

(a)   That Job is here 'quoting a version of the view of the friends. It is a fact that in the Old Testament such 'quotations' expressing views contrary to those of the speaker are not infrequently introduced with no formal indication that they are to be understood as such, for example with a formula, such as 'But *you* have said . . . '. The difficulty with this theory in the present case is the improbability that such a lengthy 'quotation' should have been made just at this point, at the climax of Job's speech.

(b)   That these verses were originally intended to be read as a speech, or part of a speech, by one of the friends—that they are the 'missing' speech of Zophar or a section of Bildad's now unsatisfactorily short speech in ch. 25—but that for some reason they have become misplaced, or that a formula, such as 'Then X answered . . . ', has dropped out of the text.

(c)   That they are an addition made to the original text by an editor or glossator who disagreed with Job's views. But if this were the case one would expect such an interpolation to occur earlier in the book.

(d)   That they are a quite separate poem having no connection with the rest of the book.

Whatever may be the correct solution to this problem, I shall interpret these verses as they stand, as part of the book as we have it.

These verses are among the most difficult in the book, and some commentators have found parts of them untranslatable. Any attempt to

comprehend them is bound to be partially conjectural. But it is clear
that vv. 18-20 confidently assert the sudden ruin of the wicked, ending
with their death and obliteration from human memory, while vv. 21-24
draw a picture of how their apparent power and prosperity prove illusory. Verse 18 speaks first of the instability of the wicked—like flotsam
(*qal*) on the face of the waters—and then proceeds from water to land
and from metaphor to sober reality: their 'portion'—that is, their landed
estates—will be reckoned accursed (*qll*), so that even those who were
formerly compelled to tread their grapes (as in v. 11) will no longer be
willing to do so. Verse 19 picks up the reference to water, whose evap-
oration in the intense heat is a symbol of the disappearance of the
wicked into the underworld. Even their own mothers (*reḥem*, 'womb')
will forget their existence, and only the worm that feeds on their
corpses will find them delicious (literally, 'sweet')!

Verse 21 reverts to the topic of the anti-social crimes of the wicked;
but v. 22 asserts that although they may continue for a time to enjoy
their power, there will come a time when they will lose confidence
even in their own survival: however much they may appear to have
achieved security, God has their deeds under his eye (v. 23), and they
will suddenly disappear from the world of the living (v. 24). Of the two
similes in this verse the meaning of the first is not clear. Some translators
have had recourse to the Greek, which reads 'he withers like mallows in
the heat'; but this is quite uncertain. The chapter ends with a pug-
nacious challenge to whoever has been listening to dismiss the preceding speech as deliberate falsehood or simply as worthless. This kind
of ending is exactly what we might expect either from Job himself (cf.
19.28-29; 21.34) or from the friends (Eliphaz, 5.27); but here it is
completely incongruous in the mouth of Job, as the view expressed in
vv. 13-24 is precisely the opposite of his own.

Job 25

As has been suggested above, part of Bildad's final speech may be missing, or may have been preserved elsewhere in the book. What remains—a reflection on God's absolute majesty and the impossibility for sinful and puny human beings to sustain a claim to be judged righteous by him—brings nothing new to the discussion. Others have made the same point, notably Eliphaz (4.17-21; 15.14-16) and Job himself (9.2-3; 14.1-4). There ought, therefore, to be no dispute between Job and the friends on this matter. Yet although Bildad does not address Job or refer to him by name in these verses, it is true that Job has in fact frequently claimed to be righteous (9.15, 20; 12.4; 13.18; 22.3), pure (16.17) and blameless (*tām*, 9.20, 21). Bildad has a point, therefore; however, righteousness is a concept not easy to define. God's righteousness and human righteousness are not the same thing. The righteousness (*ṣdq*) to which Job lays claim is basically a legal one and akin to innocence; it is not absolute moral perfection. What Job is maintaining throughout the book is that he is undeserving of the exceptional punishment that has been inflicted on him, and innocent of the crimes of which the friends have accused him. He has conformed to the standard of righteousness (*ṣedeq*, *ṣᵉdāqâ*) that, according to Old Testament teaching, God demands of human beings. This is not remotely comparable with the righteousness, or justice, of God that the friends have loudly proclaimed but which Job has questioned. In this sense, therefore, this speech of Bildad's, if directed against Job, is beside the point.

Bildad begins his speech with a consideration that is common ground for all the contestants: the infinite majesty and power of God. Job has already spoken (13.11; 23.15) of the terror that God inspires. Bildad here speaks first of God's undisputed power over the heavenly sphere, where he permits no rebellion but 'makes peace', and then of the numberless heavenly 'squadrons' whom he employs to enforce his will on earth (cf. 19.12, where Job complains of the attacks of these *gᵉdûdîm* on him). The verse in which Bildad moves to his conclusion that in the face of this terrifying God no human being can claim to be pure or righteous (v. 4) is simply a quotation of a rhetorical question already posed twice by Eliphaz (4.17; 15.14).

There seems to be a leap in thought from the idea of God's power to that of human moral unworthiness; the implication is probably that such an all-powerful God cannot be ignorant of the behaviour of his human creatures. The thought is reinforced by an *a fortiori* argument (vv. 5-6) that also has been already used by Eliphaz in similar contexts (15.15-16).

If even the moon and the stars cannot match the purity of their creator, much less can a human being. The rare word *rimmāh*, 'worm', in v. 6 is used elsewhere as an image of the decomposition of corpses after their burial; but it also occurs in the present sense of degradation or humiliation of human beings in Ps. 22.6 and Isa. 41.14.

Job 26

In the first verses of this chapter (vv. 2-4) Job addresses the previous speaker (Bildad) in a heavily ironic spirit not unlike that of the opening verses of earlier speeches in the book. But the remainder of the chapter makes no reference to Bildad's arguments. It is an ostensibly non-controversial statement about the creation of the universe by God. It has therefore been concluded by many commentators that it cannot be the continuation of Job's speech, though there is nothing here that is in any way inconsistent with Job's position or that would be more appropriate on the lips of any of the friends. Rather, the problem is simply that these verses are not particularly appropriate at this point: this confession of faith in God as Creator seems to serve no immediate purpose. No polemical use is made of it. The conclusion in v. 14 that God's ways are utterly mysterious and beyond human comprehension is quite uncontroversial, and is in fact in agreement with Bildad's own comments in ch. 25 about the infinite distance between God and his human creatures. It is probable, therefore, that these verses are not the continuation of Job's reply to Bildad (which may no longer be extant). It is not clear at what point, if any, they can be fitted into the book.

Verses 2-4 consist entirely of ironical questions in which Job mocks Bildad's speech—and, it would seem, those of the other friends as well—as being utterly useless. He, Job, is the helpless one who needs help; but they have given him none. He represents himself as the one who lacks wisdom and needs advice (there is a double irony here, as in fact Job does not believe that he needs advice), and although he has received a torrent of advice, it has been worthless. In v. 4 he challenges the friends' claim to supernatural revelation, such as was made by Eliphaz in 4.12-17, when he referred to a supernatural voice that spoken to him. He rejects such claims: their advice has no such supernatural origin.

Before proceeding to speak of God's creation of the heavens and the earth in vv. 5-6, Job asserts his power over the underworld, the abode of the dead. The dead ($r^e p \bar{a}$'$\hat{\imath} m$) are conceived, in terms of the cosmology current in the ancient Near East, as located in the nether waters (cf. 2 Sam. 22.5; Ps. 88.7; Jon. 2.3). Abaddon, a word related to '$\bar{a} b a d$, 'to perish', is synonymous with Sheol as a name for the place of the dead. These verses state that even the dead are not beyond God's control: his omniscience extends to the underworld and strikes terror into its inhabitants (cf. Amos 9.2). In other speeches, however (7.9; 10.21-22; 14.14; 16.22), Job seems to imply that God's power over the dead is limited in that their fate is irrevocable: there cannot be any return from the grave.

Verses 7-9 have a distinct literary form: that of the participial hymn. Each of these verses begins with a participle with God as the implied subject, and they form a list of God's creative acts (the list is continued in vv. 10-13 but in a different grammatical form). The participial form is characteristic of hymns of praise and comparable passages in larger contexts in which Yahweh's great deeds, whether creative (e.g. Pss. 104; 147; Isa. 40.22-23; 51.9-20) or redemptive (e.g. Pss. 103.3-5; 146.6-9) are celebrated. The form also occurs elsewhere in this book. Some of the items listed here have close affinities with 9.6-10; 36.27-32; 37.14-24 and parts of Yahweh's speeches in chs. 38–41, making the creation hymn in various forms a major theme of the book.

Verses 7-13 can only be properly understood on the basis of contemporary cosmological beliefs. In the Old Testament references to cosmology there is considerable variation as to the details, a fact that makes precise understanding difficult. Elsewhere in similar passages the verb 'to stretch out' (*nāṭâ*, v. 7) has 'the heavens' as its object. Here what God stretches out is called *ṣāpōn*, which usually means 'the north'. This may refer to God's dwelling place in the heavens, although this is not certain. 'Hanging the earth on nothing' is probably an allusion to cosmological speculations: it seems to contradict statements that it rests on 'pillars' or 'foundations' (e.g. Job 9.6; Prov. 8.29). Verse 8 marvels at the way in which God made the clouds a receptacle for the rainwater, whose weight, however, did not burst their receptacle and descend to flood the earth as had occurred during the Great Flood, when 'the windows of heaven opened' at God's command to destroy mankind (Gen. 7.11). Verse 9 may simply refer to God's control of the clouds so that they can hide even the brightness of the full moon from view; alternatively the reference may be not to the moon but to God's using the clouds to conceal his throne—an interpretation that may support the supposed reference to God's dwelling place (rather than 'the north') in v. 7.

The 'circle' that God marked out by decree according to v. 10 is somewhat different from the circular vault of heaven on which God is said to walk in 22.14. Here, as in Prov. 8.27, it denotes the horizon, which to the ancients marked the outer edge of the world conceived as a flat disc. Beyond that was the darkness of the hostile waters surrounding the world. What is being said here is that when he created the world God set a boundary round the earth, preventing those waters from encroaching on it and overwhelming it (cf. 38.8-11). Only within those limits was there light, supplied by sun, moon and stars (cf. Prov. 8.27-29). Verses 11-12 confirm this in different words. God's action in v. 10 was a rebuke to the threatening waters that caused even the 'pillars' that supported the heavens and kept them in place to tremble and gasp with astonishment. Verse 12 employs the language of myth. The myth in question is that of God's victory at the time of the creation of the world over the hostile sea and over the chaos monster Rahab (see the comments on 7.12 and 9.8, 13 above). Another version of the myth is alluded to in v. 13b, where the 'fleeing serpent', mentioned in Isa. 27.1 (cf. Isa. 51.9) also represents the forces of chaos destroyed by God at the creation. Similar myths are found in both Babylonian and Canaanite (Ugaritic) literature.

Just as vv. 5-13 foreshadow Yahweh's speeches (chs. 38-41) in their catalogue of God's great deeds in creation, so does v. 14, with which Job concludes this speech, foreshadow Job's reaction to Yahweh's self-revelation in 42.2-6. In both passages there is an expression of total humility: a confession of the immense gulf that exists between God and man. However much learned discourse has taken place in the speeches of the friends and however much they have professed to understand God, they in fact, like all human beings, know nothing at all about him. They may think that they know his 'ways'—that is, his deeds (for the meaning of 'ways' here see Prov. 8.22) and his nature—but that knowledge is in reality insignificant. It does not begin to comprehend the reality of God, or his tremendous power, which is like thunder in comparison with the mere 'whisper' that has been vouchsafed to them. Paradoxically it is Job who, in confessing his utter ignorance, has already begun to 'speak of God what is right', for which God will commend him in 42.7-8. It is because he achieved that perception even before Yahweh appeared to him and addressed him directly, while the friends have arrogantly claimed superior knowledge of God, that Job finally receives God's approbation.

Job 27

As the text is now arranged, the speech of Job that began in ch. 26 is continued; and in fact Job speaks continuously until the end of ch. 31. But this long speech has been broken up by new headings, one in 27.1 and the other (verbally identical) in 29.1. The heading in 27.1 seems to have been intended to indicate a change of direction. The debate with the friends is now complete, and the friends do not speak again. Although he addresses them briefly in vv. 5, 11 and 12, Job is no longer primarily concerned with them. Some commentators have suggested that the heading in v. 1 may have been added for another reason: that, as in 24.18-24, there is reason to suppose some dislocation in the text in that a large part of this chapter expresses sentiments that are difficult to attribute to Job. At least vv. 13-23 and possibly also vv. 7-12 would, it is supposed, be more appropriate in the mouth of one of the friends, and once again it has been supposed that these verses are part of the 'lost' third speech of Zophar. As with 24.18-24 they will be interpreted here for what they contain, no particular attribution being proposed. It is difficult to see why the dislocation, if that is what it is, should have been the occasion for the heading in v. 1, which can be explained satisfactorily as purely editorial.

Job begins (vv. 2-6) with a pair of formal oaths in which he stakes everything on the truth of his claim to be innocent of the wickedness that has been alleged against him. (The heading of v. 1, whether editorial or not, is in fact singularly appropriate here in view of the solemn nature of what follows.) Once more the language is that of the court of law: Job is making a formal defence. With supreme irony he draws God into the affair: the same God whom he holds responsible for his misery is now summoned as a witness to his veracity. To swear by God's life (elsewhere in the Old Testament *Yahweh*'s life) was the most solemn kind of oath possible, bringing severe retribution on a person who swore falsely (cf. Lev. 19.12; Num. 5.20-22). Job does not deny that it was God who gave him life (v. 3); but he still maintained that he had deprived him of justice and embittered his life (v. 2). In vv. 5 and 6 he turns almost for the last time to address the friends, and affirms with another oath that he will never give up his claim to integrity (*tummâ*, which God had attributed to him in 2.3 and which his wife had urged him to abandon, ch. 2.9), so admitting that the friends are in the right. He thus gives formal notice that he is now ready to defend himself, come what may.

The interpreter of vv. 7-10 faces two major difficulties: (1) Can the statements in these verses about the fate of the wicked be reconciled with Job's general position? (2) Who is 'my enemy' (*'ōy^{e}bî*) in v. 7? Is it God, of whom Job has earlier complained in 13.24 that he treats him as an enemy? This is hardly possible in view of vv. 8 and 9. But it is also difficult to take it as referring to the 'friends', since despite their some- times acrimonious debate, nothing has been said that would justify Job's use of such a strong expression. But is Job the speaker here? These verses are equally improbable in the mouth of the friends. There is no consensus of opinion among the commentators. It may be best to take the verses as an interpolation into the original book by someone who misunderstood Job's position and placed them inappropriately in his mouth. The sentiment that they express is one familiar from such psalms as Psalm 35.

If vv. 7-10 are an interpolation, vv. 11-12 can be seen as the contin- uation—and, it seems, the conclusion—of Job's speech. He addresses the friends for the last time. The verbs in v. 11 are to be taken as refer- ring to the past rather than the future: 'I have been teaching...', and so on. Job claims that all through the debate it is he and not the friends who have told the truth about the way in which God exercises his power (literally, his 'hand') and about his mode of operation ('that which is with' him). Verse 12a is a conditional clause: '*If* you have seen this': that is, the friends have had an equal opportunity of understanding it. But they have made a nonsense (*hebel*) of it, that is, they have com- pletely misunderstood it.

Verses 13-23 speak of the fate of the wicked in terms strongly rem- iniscent of similar speeches by Eliphaz and Bildad, of Zophar's descrip- tion in 20.5-29 and of that wrongly attributed to Job in 24.18-24. They have been identified as part of Zophar's 'lost' third speech; but all that can be said with certainty is that the view that they express is not that of Job but of the friends.

Verse 13, which introduces the passage, is fundamentally the same as the verse that concludes Zophar's speech in 20.29. In using the words 'portion' (*ḥēleq*) and 'inheritance' (*naḥ^{a}lâ*) the verse assumes that the destiny of all human beings is irrevocably determined by God and is part of his universal design. The particular destiny reserved for wicked oppressors is then described. Verses 14-15, perhaps with a grim allusion to the fate of Job's own family, speak of the children of the wicked who suffer for the sins of their fathers in being destroyed by a succession of disasters that figure frequently in both Old Testament and Near Eastern writing: sword, starvation, plague. These are represented in personal terms that point to their widespread devastation: pestilence 'buries' its victims in the absence of survivors. So frequently will these disasters follow one upon the other that the victims' widows will be incapable of mourning.

Verses 16-17 refer to the wealth accumulated by the wicked, which they will not live to enjoy but which will become the property of the righteous. The verb 'divide' or 'share' ($yah^al\bar{o}q$) in v. 17b corresponds to the noun $h\bar{e}leq$, 'portion', in v. 13: if disaster is the 'lot' of the wicked, it is the 'lot' of the righteous that they should succeed to the wealth of the wicked. That wealth is represented as consisting of silver and luxurious clothes, which they 'pile up' as if they were no more valuable than dust or clay. The righteous will inherit their silver and wear their clothes.

Verses 18-19 continue the theme of the ephemeral nature of the wealth of the wicked under different imagery. The houses that they build will be 'like the moth' ($k\bar{a}'a\check{s}$), not 'nests', a symbol of fragility (cf. 4.19) and will be no more solid than the temporary huts of those who guard vineyards. Verse 19 expresses the matter with yet another image: the wicked will go to bed wealthy, but when they wake up in the morning their wealth will be gone. Verses 20-23 picture the suddenness of their destruction in terms of natural disasters: first floods and then violent storms. But the use of the rare word $ball\bar{a}h\hat{o}t$, 'terrors', in v. 20, shows that the author is thinking of demonic forces behind these natural phenomena (cf. 'the king of terrors', 18.14). This picture picks up the confident statements of Zophar in ch. 20, which had been categorically rebutted by Job in 21.18. The reference to the $s\hat{u}p\hat{a}$, 'storm-wind', in v. 20 has been associated by some commentators with the wind (not necessarily a whirlwind) from which Yahweh appeared to Job in 38.1; but there a different word ($s^e'\bar{a}r\hat{a}$) is used. In Elihu's speech in 37.9 $s\hat{u}p\hat{a}$ does occur again, where it is said to be an example of God's marvellous works of creation.

Job 28

The questions of the authorship of this chapter and of its place in the book have been considered in the Introduction. There is nothing in the text—not even an introductory verse like 27.1 or 29.1—to suggest a break in continuity; it will therefore be assumed here that Job is understood still to be speaking. The chapter purports to constitute a reply to a question posed in vv. 12 and 20 about the 'location' of wisdom, asserting that this is known to no one but God himself. Wisdom is here depicted as if it were a 'commodity' of enormous value that human beings strive to find (cf. Prov. 3.15); it is not personified as in other parts of Proverbs 1–9, especially in Proverbs 1 and 8, where Wisdom herself is represented as speaking. The search for wisdom is, of course, a universal one; it is the foundation of all the philosophies. The spatial language used here ('where?', 'place' and other such terms) probably owes something to mythical concepts; but it is used symbolically. The underlying questions are 'Who possesses wisdom?' and 'How (if at all) is it possible to acquire it?'

The chapter asserts that only God is truly 'wise'; only he fully possesses wisdom. It was through this wisdom that he performed the acts by which the universe was created and which no human being can emulate (vv. 23-27; cf. Prov. 3.19). Nevertheless according to v. 28 there is a possibility for human beings to obtain wisdom by fearing God and rejecting evil. This statement does not contradict what has been said in the preceding verses as some commentators have maintained. The wisdom that is stated to be attainable by human beings is of a different order from God's wisdom; by fearing God and rejecting evil—of which Job was a pre-eminent exemplar according to the Prologue (1.1, 8; 2.3)—men and women are able to acquire, as a special gift from God, a kind of wisdom scaled down, as it were, to their capabilities.

As a final statement by Job (before he moves on to make his formal defence in chs. 29-31) the chapter is a self-contained and well-structured poem. Its literary skill is shown in its oblique approach to its topic. It begins not with wisdom but with an account of what human beings can achieve without wisdom: their remarkable ability to discover gold and precious stones and the great effort that they expend to this end (vv. 1-11). Every precious thing, it seems, is within their grasp. But not wisdom. The question where it is to be found (v. 12) is answered negatively in vv. 12-22. Wisdom is inaccessible not only to human beings but also to other living creatures and even to death, the ruler of the underworld (v. 22). The human preoccupation with gold and precious stones with which the chapter begins is shown to be nugatory, as wisdom is infinitely more precious than those things (vv. 15-19). The negative conclusions of vv. 12-14 and 21 are balanced by vv. 23-27, which assert that God alone understands and possesses wisdom, and the whole poem is balanced by v. 28 with its alternative answer to the question where wisdom is to be found.

Verses 1-11 offer a fascinating glimpse of mining activity in the ancient world for gold, silver, iron and precious stones. The author was evidently a learned person familiar with the technology of his time beyond the confines of his own country; the land of Israel did not produce these things, at any rate in sufficient quantities to justify mining operations. The author, however, knew of deep underground mines in which it was necessary for the workers to swing suspended from ropes (v. 4). Unfortunately our knowledge of ancient mining is too limited to make it possible to understand the details. Verse 6 adds lapis lazuli (*sappîr*—not sapphires), a precious stone much valued by the ancients, to the list. The meaning of v. 5 is not clear; it probably draws a contrast between the tranquil surface of the earth, which continues to produce the common necessities of life, and the upheavals envisaged by the author as occurring underground, whether as the result of mining operations or, as some have conjectured, of volcanic activity. Verses 7-11 are concerned to stress the thoroughness of human ingenuity in penetrating to the most inaccessible of places and overcoming all obstacles in a determination to prise hidden treasures from their place of concealment. Even the eagles and other birds of prey, noted for their acute vision, which enables them to spot their prey while still in flight, are unable to see these activities; and the lions and other wild beasts passing by on the ground are no less ignorant of them. These engineers employ every possible means in their search: smashing through the hardest of rocks, shifting soil on a massive scale (the hyperbole of v. 9b may be an ironical allusion to 9.5-6, where Job lists 'overthrowing mountains' as an example of activity proper to God alone), sometimes boring tunnels in the rocks and at other times damming streams (v. 11a—rather than 'probing' as in some modern translations) and so successfully bringing hidden treasures to light. This verse (11) leads up to the crucial question of v. 12: but where is *wisdom* to be found? Human beings have looked everywhere and nothing, one would suppose, ought to be inaccessible to them. Everything is within their grasp, except one thing: wisdom.

The author answers the question negatively by first stressing, in terms that ironically recall the successful discovery by human beings of all the *other* most valuable objects in creation (vv. 13-14), the utter inaccessibility of wisdom, and then pointing out that they have missed the most valuable thing of all, which even this accumulated wealth cannot purchase (vv. 15-19). Verse 13 recalls vv. 7-8: just as the animals cannot see the 'path' to human mining operations, so human beings do not know the 'way' to wisdom. Even the sea affirms that it would be useless for them to pursue their search for it, for it is not to be found there.

Verses 15-19 are an elaborate development of the topic of the infinite value of wisdom, a topic that is expressed more succinctly in Prov. 3.14-15; 8.10-11. Here it is developed with great skill by means of a kaleidoscopic series of changing images. There are here no less than five words and phrases denoting different kinds of gold, and a whole series of precious stones and objects is listed to demonstrate the incomparability of wisdom. Literary skill is also shown in the variation of the sentence structures and the variety of the vocabulary. Thus wisdom's *price* is above that of corals; it cannot be *equalled* by gold or glass objects; it cannot be *compared* with chrysolite; it cannot be *purchased* with gold or *exchanged* for objects of fine gold; coral and crystal are not even to be *mentioned* as comparable with it; and so on. The list contains items of great rarity, such as crystal, chrysolite and glass. Such items as these and the different kinds of gold of differing value mentioned must have been so rare as to be almost fabulous in the eyes of the readers—an Aladdin's cave of treasures or a multi-millionaire's hoard. The imagination is intended to boggle. So a list of negative items again leads up to the question of wisdom's provenance. Wisdom is more desirable and more valuable than anything in the world; but where does it come from, and where is to be be found? The repetition of the question is like the tolling of a bell. Wisdom's inaccessibility is further confirmed by v. 21, a verse taken partly from v. 7 and partly from v. 13b, and by v. 22. In the latter verse wisdom's 'hiddenness' is accentuated by a reference to the underworld, the only remaining part of the universe, whose great depth below the earth is proverbial (cf. 11.8). In the Old Testament the word 'death' (*māwet*) sometimes retains mythical overtones of Mot, the ruler of the underworld and of the dead (Jer. 9.21; Hos. 13.14; Hab. 2.5); so here Death, together with Abaddon (see 26.6) is represented like the sea (*tᵉhôm*, 'deep'; *yām*, 'sea', also words with mythical overtones) as speaking. The two speak in chorus to deny all knowledge of the whereabouts of wisdom—they have only heard a report of it! Evidently the dead are no more able to find wisdom than are the living.

Verse 23 at last gives the positive answer to the repeated question of vv. 12 and 16. Only God knows the 'way' to wisdom (picking up on v. 13a); he alone knows its 'place' (answering v. 20b). He has this knowledge because he alone is able, unlike human beings, however skilful, and with sharper vision even than the sharp-eyed birds of prey (v. 7), to see everything that exists in the world (v. 24). However deeply wisdom might be hidden, God knows where it is to be found. This ability to observe everything was frequently attributed to deity in the ancient Near Eastern world, and the Old Testament was no exception (cf. Ps. 33.13; Prov. 15.3; Zech. 4.10). Here this knowledge is closely connected with God's creation of the world. In describing this the author has singled out for mention those actions that emphasize the skill with which God ordered the meteorological phenomena whose ordering made the world a habitable place: adjusting the weight of the wind to limit its force; limiting the extent of the waters which could threaten human life (cf. Prov. 8.29); setting a limit to the rain and to the thunder that accompanies the rainstorm and appears to threaten the human race. It was precisely in the process of creation, says the author, that God 'saw' wisdom (v. 27). Wisdom is thus the fundamental principle of order in the universe (see Prov. 8.22-31 for a comparable statement). These verses make it clear that God's wisdom is utterly different from any 'wisdom' that human beings might claim to possess.

The word 'then' in v. 27 is used in a temporal sense: it was in the moment when he created the world that God encountered wisdom. This way of expressing the matter is similar to that of Prov. 8.22-31. In Prov. 8.22 a personified Wisdom speaks of her association with Yahweh as having existed before he began to create the world; whether she claims that he created her or 'acquired' her at that time depends on the meaning of the ambiguous verb *qānāh*, which is disputed. Here this association is stated to be contemporary with God's acts of creation. It is described in four verbs the precise meaning of some of which is not clear. First, God 'saw' wisdom; this may mean that he then became aware of wisdom for the first time: he 'discovered' her—perhaps implying wisdom's pre-existence. The most common meaning of the second verb (*sippar*) is to 'tell, inform, declare to' someone, but in this case it almost certainly means something like 'assess, appraise' (literally 'number, count' as in 38.37; Ps. 22.17). The third, *hēkîn*, sometimes comes close to meaning 'create' (cf. Ps. 65.9; 74.16; Prov. 8.27), though it can also mean 'establish', 'appoint'. The fourth, *ḥāqar*, 'search', 'explore', is probably an allusion to v. 3, where it is used of the miners who search for metal ores (but do not find wisdom!). In Jer. 17.10, where Yahweh is said to 'search the human heart', it clearly means to have a complete knowledge of something, and that is the most probable meaning here. In sum, this verse does not necessarily state that God created wisdom but states that it is his peculiar possession, and implies that it was the instrument that he used when he created the world (cf. Prov. 3.19-20). It is not confined to any specific location but pervades the whole universe. Verse 28, as has been explained above, speaks of a quite different and inferior kind of wisdom that God has made available to human beings.

Job 29

Chapters 29–31 form a closely knit triad. In ch. 29 Job laments the loss of his former status when he 'lived like a king among his troops' (v. 25); in ch. 30 he describes in pathetic language his present miserable and degraded state, which he claims is due to God's persecution; in ch. 31 he defends his conduct, swearing with an oath that it has been exemplary and citing a long list of sins of which he has been innocent.

To whom are these chapters addressed? There is no longer any reference to the friends: the debate is over. Nor, apart from a short passage in 30.20-23, is God specifically addressed. Nevertheless these chapters should be seen as constituting at last the formal charge against God that Job has all along wanted to be allowed to make. Admittedly God has still not appeared; at the close of this section (31.35-37) Job is still demanding an answer. Although the speeches of Elihu in chs. 32–37 interrupt the sequence, chs. 38–41 are to be understood as God's counter-charges against Job. Chs. 29–31 and 38–41 together thus have the character of a legal process marked by the speeches of accuser and defender respectively.

Job's purpose in chs. 29–31 is to make use of every possible rhetorical device to elicit sympathy for his case and to persuade God—who, being in a position of absolute power, is in a sense judge as well as litigant—that his case is a convincing one. Chapters 29–30 are a diptych: they describe the two contrasting periods of Job's life—his former idyllic existence and his present condition as an outcast rejected even by the dregs of society—in extreme terms reminiscent of mediaeval paintings of heaven and hell. Together they form an impressive lament. Job's description of his former life in ch. 29, which begins with the regretful words 'Oh, that I were...', while it has its own interest at least for the modern reader as an account of the prosperous and blissful existence of a patriarchal chief, is in fact as much a lament over past glory as ch. 30 is a lament over the misery of the present. In both chapters the author has made use of a literary convention found in some of the psalms of lamentation and more particularly the book of Lamentations.

In 29.2-6 Job recalls the time when God had been his friend and had lavished his blessings on him, and expresses a longing for a return of the past. In those days God had 'watched' him (*šāmar*) (v. 2). Here this word denotes God's protective care, very different from the surveillance (*šāmar*) of which he had complained when he had felt that God was waiting to detect him in sin (10.14; 13.27; 14.16). The 'lamp' and 'light' (v. 3) symbolize godly blessing (cf. Pss. 18.28; 119.105). Verse 5 alludes to the loss of Job's family that had occurred as a consequence of the withdrawal of God's favour (1.12, 18-19). Verse 6 is expressed in hyperbolical language, but the reference to unlimited milk and oil describes accurately enough Job's actual prosperity in the past, presupposing vast herds of cattle and olive groves.

In vv. 7-10 Job describes his former standing as leader of his community. He seems again to be indulging in hyperbole: he represents himself as having had virtually royal status (cf. 'like a king', v. 25). He depicts his arrival at the square before the city gate, where justice was traditionally administered, to take his official seat there as judge (cf. 1 Kgs 22.10; 2 Chron. 32.6). He presented an awe-inspiring figure. The young men (or boys) were afraid to face him, the old men stood out of respect, and even the chief citizens broke off their conversations and dared no longer speak. The words *śārîm* (often translated as 'princes') and *nĕgîdîm* ('nobles'), though they can have a more generalized meaning, suggest that Job had had a very high status indeed. This is a somewhat different picture from that of the Prologue, which, though it represents Job as an extremely wealthy man and the greatest of all the people of the east, says nothing about his being a political ruler or judge.

Verses 11-17 elaborate the reason (*kî*, 'because', vv. 11, 12) why Job was treated with such respect by his people. It was not just fear that motivated them as would have been the case with a tyrannical ruler, but reverence and respect for his policies. Both the judgments that he pronounced and the actions that they saw him perform met with their approbation (v. 11). The actions described in vv. 12-17 are those of a righteous ruler, such as are set out for example in Psalm 72, and which were recognized generally in the ancient Near East. They are those of a king who administers justly with special concern for those who are particularly vulnerable to oppression and unable to defend themselves against inferior judges who take bribes from wealthy litigants (cf., e.g., Exod. 23.2, 6-9; Amos 5.12; Prov. 17.23). The poor, orphans, widows and foreign workers traditionally fell into this class; also the disabled (blind and lame) who were natural victims of injustice. Job's equitable policy (*ṣedeq*) and just decisions (*mišpāṭ*) were so characteristic of his rule that they might be said to fit him like a cloak (v. 14). Verses 16 and 17 portray him as actively investigating cases of alleged tyranny and rescuing victims from the clutches of their persecutors. Job thus refutes in detail the unfounded allegations of Eliphaz in 22.5-9.

From his account of his exemplary life Job turns in vv. 18-20 to the hopes for his future that he had entertained in the days of his prosperity. Like the friends, he had then expected that a blameless life would be blessed by God: that he would live to a great and honoured age (v. 18). 'Die in my nest' is an unusual expression; if the text is correct it probably means to die surrounded by one's family: a 'good death' like those of the patriarchs Abraham (Gen. 25.8-9); Isaac (Gen. 35.29), Jacob (Gen. 49.33; 50.1-14) and Joseph (Gen. 50.24-26). The simile of the phoenix, the fabulous bird that was supposed constantly to renew its life after its death, is another colourful hyperbole.

Verses 21-25 resume the theme of vv. 7-17; this discontinuity may be due to an unintentional displacement of the material within the chapter. This group of verses probably originally followed v. 10, though v. 25 reads like a summarizing conclusion. Verses 21, 22a elaborate the theme of vv. 9-10: the silence of the assembled citizens was in order to listen to Job's words of wisdom. In vv. 22b-23 the precious quality of what Job had to say is expressed in terms of the dropping of the dew and the coming of the rain. The verb *ntp*, 'drop, drip', is a fairly frequently metaphor for human speech (cf., e.g., Prov. 5.3; Amos 7.16); waiting hopefully for the relief of the arrival of the rain after a dry, hot summer was a common experience in Palestine (cf. Jer. 8.20). The meaning of v. 24 is uncertain. The first line may refer to Job's contemptuous laughter rather than to his smile: this seemed so out of character that those who heard it were unwilling to believe it. On the other hand, when he showed them his other, favourable side (cf. Prov. 16.15 on the light of the king's countenance), they accepted it gladly and treasured it in their memories. Verse 25 presents Job as a masterful ruler, regulating the conduct of his subjects and yet, as the pastor of his people, deigning to comfort the bereaved like God's servant in Isa. 61.2.

Job 30

In ch. 29 Job described his former life lived under God's blessing when he was the revered leader and ruler of his community. In that chapter there was also a note of self-justification: he was anxious to emphasize, in line with the Prologue (1.1), that he had always behaved justly and with kindness towards his subordinates. Job was never slow to lay stress on these qualities; in the dialogue with the friends, with whom he was on terms of social equality, he had always spoken proudly, and he had even refused to bow before God himself when the question of his personal integrity was concerned. In ch. 30 he takes a further step in his defence. The dramatic contrast between 'then' and 'now'—between what God had done *for* him in the past and what he had now done *against* him—constituted in itself a powerful indictment against God that hardly needed to be spelled out, though in vv. 20-23 Job does spell it out in a direct address to God. He begins, however, with a pathetic description of his present humiliation at the hands of the very outcasts from society.

The significant initial word of the chapter, w^{e}'*attāh*, 'But now', v. 1), is repeated twice more in vv. 9 and 16. Verses 1-16 describe in pathetic language how Job is now treated by the rabble. However, doubts have been expressed by some commentators whether vv. 2-8 belong to the original text. They speak not of the malice of these people but of their situation as outcasts of society who are reduced to living in more or less subhuman conditions, barely scratching a living from the desert and waste places. It has been argued that these verses are inappropriate to their context, not in any way contributing to the point that Job is making; and that they would fit better into one of the descriptions of the fate of the wicked in an earlier chapter. Can these, it is asked, be the same people as those who now surround Job, mocking and spitting at him in vv. 1 and 9-10? (It is perhaps relevant to point out that the passage contains an unusually large number of rare words whose meaning is obscure, and that the text is by no means without difficulties.) On the other hand, it has been pointed out that it is unreasonable to judge ancient poetry by the canons of western logic, and that the passage may simply be intended to express Job's patrician contempt for such low-class ruffians.

In v. 1 Job, who had spoken only a little earlier (29.24) of times when he had expressed contempt of others (*śāḥaq*, literally 'laughed'), complains that the tables have turned with a vengeance. It is now others who despise him (again *śāḥaq*). And the mockers are themselves utterly despicable. They are young men (possibly the young men who had hidden themselves, not daring to appear before Job in former times, ch. 29.8), who now refuse to accord to Job the respect that was normally due to the old. They are also of low extraction: it is not they but their fathers whose social status was so low that Job would not have considered employing them even in menial outside tasks. They clearly take after their fathers. This may suggest that they are outlaws, not recognized as citizens. If so, the description of their way of life in vv. 2-8 may after all make sense. These were people who were outside Job's responsibility as ruler. But it is hard not to detect here a note of social arrogance, which Job retains even though he has himself become virtually an outcast.

This attitude finds expression in vv. 2-8, if it is the same people who are described here. They are useless for work because as outcasts they are unable to live as do ordinary citizens by cultivating the fields and so providing themselves with food and shelter, and so are half-starved and suffer from cold. Job's unsympathetic attitude is characteristic of that of the farmer or town-dweller towards the desert-dwellers: they are stupid (*bᵉnê-nābāl*) and of no account (*bᵉnê bᵉlî-šēm*, v. 8). It is interesting to note that these verses strongly resemble the description of the wicked and their fate in 24.5-8. But now (vv. 9-11) it is Job who is an outcast and subjected to abuse. His tormentors mock him but keep away from him, only approaching him to spit in his face. Although the subject of the verbs in v. 11a is not named in the text, it is generally agreed by the commentators that the reference is to God. Job is saying that the reason for his humiliation is that God has withdrawn his support from him— though it is not clear what is meant by 'he has loosened my cord'. It may mean that God has rendered him unable to defend himself by (metaphorically) loosening his bowstring.

In vv. 12-19 the identity of Job's adversaries becomes even more confusing, partly because of the omission of the subjects of some of the verbs. Verse 12 may refer either to the same people as in the previous verses or to another group of tormentors; in v. 15 there is mention of 'terrors' (*ballāhôt*) as in 18.11 and 27.20; finally the 'he' (with a singular verb) of vv. 18-19 appears again to be God, who is then directly addressed by Job in vv. 20-23. The consequence of this multiplicity of subjects is to enhance the dramatic effect by implying that Job is being attacked from all sides and in more than one way. This effect is further enhanced by the bewildering piling up of images.

It is not clear whether Job's assailants in vv. 12-15 are the same as in the preceding verses: the subject of the first verb of v. 12, sometimes rendered by 'rabble' or 'brood', may suggest that a different group is intended. These are not content simply to insult Job but actually assault him. The metaphors employed in these verses are very mixed and not easy to sort out. The middle line of v. 12 may mean that Job's assailants deliberately trip him up, sending him sprawling; but in the last line of that verse he seems to be depicted as a city under siege, and this image is continued in v. 14 with the breaching of the city walls. In v. 15, however, the author reverts to the topic of apparently supernatural hostile forces, the 'terrors' (*ballāhôt*), together with the imagery of natural phenomena: the wind that 'blows away' Job's dignity and the passing cloud that symbolizes the loss of his prosperity.

Job knows that it is God who is his real adversary and tormentor: it is he who has arbitrarily stripped him of his health, wealth and dignity and permitted him to be harassed by both human and supernatural assailants. He now returns in vv. 16-23 to his complaint against God. Verses 16-17 describe in plain terms the broken state of his health: his strength has gone (v. 16a), and, as he has complained earlier (7.3-5), he is in continual pain, especially at night. Verses 18-19 revert to metaphor: God has put a stranglehold on him and flung him down in the dirt. In 2.8 the author of the Prologue had stated that Job literally seated himself in the ashes as a sign of grief and humiliation. Here, however, the phrase used is 'dust and ashes'. This appears to have been a standard expression signifying self-abasement: Abraham applied it to himself in a self-deprecatory sense (Gen. 18.27), and Job was himself to use it similarly in 42.6. But here Job's use of it is indicative of his arrogance: he is implying that he would not have used it of himself or thought of himself in this way in former times; his doing so now was due solely to God's deliberate humiliation of him.

Job now brings this humiliation and its consequences to God's attention in a direct address (vv. 20-23), in a passage that at this point in the book can hardly be other than the formal indictment of the accused (God) by the plaintiff (Job). In fact, although chs. 29-31 as a whole may be regarded as the 'speech for the prosecution', these four verses are the last in which Job speaks directly to God, and indeed the last words that he speaks at all before God makes his own speech, to which he responds in 40.4-5 and 42.2-6. Verse 20 is a general indictment, the last of many similar ones. The complaint that God does not answer Job's cry for help is one that occurs frequently in the psalms of lamentation in the Psalter. It is a cry of desolation. The second line of this verse is probably defective in the Hebrew in that the negative particle 'not' has been accidentally omitted. It probably means 'I waited, but you did not pay attention to me'. In v. 21 Job accuses God of changing his attitude towards him; he had never been cruel in the past, but now he has become so. 'You lift me up' in v. 22 is probably part of the accusation: Job is 'lifted up' not in exaltation—referring to his former state of blessing— but in order to be buffeted by the storm and wind. Finally Job concludes that it is God's intention to destroy him altogether, handing him over to the realm of death.

Job now sets out his case in summary terms (vv. 24-31). Although there is no textual indication that God is still being addressed, these verses are clearly a continuation of the preceding passage. They consist of two parts, with v. 26 as a transitional verse. In vv. 24-25 Job reiterates his claim to have lived a virtuous life: although now with emphasis on his feelings rather than his actions, he affirms that he had always shown concern for the poor and sympathy for the harshness of their lives. He does not fail, however, to say that he had expected to be rewarded for this compassionate feeling, whereas his recompense had been misfortune rather than prosperity, darkness rather than light (v. 26). Verses 27-31 elaborate the nature of this 'evil' and 'darkness'. These verses well illustrate the subtleties of the Hebrew verbal system. (All the verbs are in the perfect tense or its equivalent, though they are frequently rendered in translation by the present tense. In fact they refer to things that had occurred in the past but whose effects have remained in operation up to the present.) Job's emotions (literally, 'entrails') had 'boiled over' when he had first had to face unpleasant reality, and this agitation had not subsided (v. 27). Life had become dark to him; his unanswered cries for justice had made him like the desert-dwelling jackals and ostriches with their peculiar moaning cries; he still suffers from burning fever and a horrifying skin disease (cf. 2.7; 7.5). All joy in life has ceased and has been turned into weeping (v. 31; compare the similar metaphor in Lam. 5.15).

Job 31

This chapter, the last of the 'trilogy', has the character of a legal defence (but also, in another sense, by implication, of an indictment of God, since Job has the dual role of accuser and defendant). It is made, as it were, to the 'court', and it demands a reply. If God still remained silent and made no reply to Job's challenge, it was to be assumed that he admitted the truth of Job's claim.

The main body of the chapter consists of a long catalogue of offences that has been dubbed a 'negative confession'. This term is employed by Egyptologists to describe the declarations of innocence prescribed in the Book of the Dead and other Egyptian funerary texts, in which the dead person supposedly had to defend himself before the divine judges before he could be admitted to the blessings of eternal life; he declared that during his life he had not committed a prescribed list of sins. The prescribed declaration was made in the words 'I have not committed X'. In the present chapter the dominant form of declaration is a conditional sentence: 'If I have…then let X be done to me', though there is considerable variety in the way in which the various items are formulated.

It is notable that the sins listed are all, with one exception (vv. 26-28 on idolatry) ethical rather than cultic in character, and also that for the most part they are not crimes punishable by human law, yet they are abhorrent to God (as testified, for example, by the prophets). There is an emphasis, as in Job's earlier speeches, on the duty to protect the disadvantaged. These sins were obviously those that Job regarded as particularly heinous.

Job now gathers up his earlier assertions of virtuous behaviour into a comprehensive catalogue. But first he emphasizes the solemnity of his self-imposed obligation: the catalogue that follows in the rest of the chapter is introduced by an emphatic statement (v. 1a) in which he makes it clear that his innocent life was the consequence of a settled, fixed determination to avoid all temptation to evil. At some time in the past—probably while he was still a young man—he had 'made a covenant with his eyes': that is, he had decided to control inordinate desires. Several kinds of covenant (*berît*) were distinguished in Hebrew speech. The word implies some kind of mutual relationship between two or more parties, sometimes between equals and sometimes between a superior and an inferior. The form that is used here (*kārat berît le…*) is that which denotes the imposition of an obligation on another person. Metaphorically it could also be used of a relationship with inanimate objects or with animals (5.23; 41.4) or even with death (Isa. 28.14, 18).

This is the only passage in which it is used in connection with a part of the body of the person who instigated the covenant: Job has placed his *eyes* under an obligation. The metaphor is a bold one. But the eyes are the organs that more than any other part of the body expose a person to temptation; ascetic theology speaks similarly of 'the custody of the eyes'. The most obvious of these temptations is sexual, as Job recognizes in the example that he gives in the second line of this verse; but there are other temptations to which the improper use of the eyes can lead, such as to cupidity or idolatry. In sum, Job had made a promise, and more than a promise, to avoid sin; the word *bĕrît* was closely associated with the swearing of an oath (cf., e.g., Deut. 29.14).

In vv. 2-4 there is a strong element of irony. Job is here stating not his present belief but the belief that he had held and on which he had based his actions before calamity fell on him. Citing 27.13 and 20.29, which express the traditional view, Job asks how he could have sinned without God knowing. But this belief in God's justice has, of course, been shattered (cf. 21.7-15). He now knows that what he ironically affirms in the questions of vv. 2 and 3 is not true: the questions become almost a taunt levelled at a God who does not behave as he is alleged to behave. In v. 4 Job further points out the true implications of God's watch upon him: God's 'numbering his steps' and spying on his actions had been the subject of his complaint (14.16); but now he turns the tables on God: if God has, in fact, been watching him so closely, he must know that Job is innocent; yet (Job implies) he has treated him as if he were guilty.

Verses 5-6 open the list of sins of which Job is claiming to be guiltless with a general disclaimer of falsity (*šāw'*) and dishonesty (*mirmâ*) or deceit. He is defending his integrity (*tummâ*), which Yahweh and even Job's wife had recognized in the Prologue as his inalienable characteristic (2.3, 9) and which he had earlier sworn never to abandon (27.5-6), but of which he now ironically pretends that God, the God who 'numbers his steps' (v. 4) is unaware. He asks that God should have him weighed in the scales to 'discover' whether he is guiltless or not. This notion is reminiscent of the Egyptian idea of the weighing of the heart of the dead person mentioned above; there are, however, some Old Testament verses (Prov. 16.2; 21.2; 24.12) in which Yahweh is said similarly to weigh or assess (a different verb is used) the hearts or the spirits of the living. It is significant that Job here thinks it necessary to specify that the scales used must be accurate (*mō'z⁽e⁾nê-ṣedeq*). The noun *ṣedeq*, here used adjectivally, also means 'honest'; the phrase inevitably recalls the opposite expression *mō'z⁽e⁾nê mirmâ*, 'false (that is, dishonest) scales', scales that were evidently widely used to cheat customers (Amos 8.5; Prov. 11.1). *mirmâ* is precisely conduct of which Job was claiming to be guiltless (v. 5). Job does not directly suggest here that God might be disposed to cheat, though the unexpected use of the word *ṣedeq* can hardly have been without deliberate intent.

The point of vv. 7-8 is to be found in the third line of v. 7. The word *mû'm* (more usually *mûm*), often meaning simply 'spot, blemish', can also mean a wrong done to someone else (so Lev. 24.19); the nature of this wrong is defined by the phrase 'to cling to one's hands'. The reference is to *theft*, probably here the seizure of another person's land, not necessarily illegally but nevertheless immorally. The first line of the verse classes such an action as an example of 'turning from the way', that is, the way of righteousness (cf. 17.9; 23.10, 11). The sequence 'eyes, heart, hands' describes the origin and evolution of acts of wrong-doing: they begin with the eyes (cf. v. 1), are then conceived in the heart and finally express themselves in action. Verse 8 is the first of Job's self-imprecations and is expressed in farmer's language: Job is ready to stake the loss of his land for others to profit by, or the loss of his crops, against his protestation of innocence.

Verses 9-12 are a disclaimer of *adultery*. The language of vv. 9-10— *petaḥ*, 'door'; *ṭāḥan*, 'grind corn'; *kāra'*, 'kneel'—may have sexual connotations beyond its literal meaning. In the literal sense this self-imprecation in v. 10 means that Job envisages a situation of impoverishment when his wife would be obliged to perform menial labour for others; but the verse could mean that she would have punished him for his adultery by taking a lover. Verses 11-12 stress Job's abhorrence of adultery: it is a heinous sin (*zimmâ*) deserving exemplary punishment (cf. Lev. 18.17). The emphasis, however, is on its destructiveness rather than its punishment by the judges; it is a consuming fire (cf. Prov. 6.27-29). The statement that its destructiveness reaches to Abaddon, the realm of the dead (see on 26.6) is probably simply intended for emphasis; there is a similar expression in Deut. 32.22. The statement that the commission of this sin would have destroyed Job's wealth (*t^ebû'â*, not 'harvest') is more strictly to the point. God had, in fact, destroyed Job's wealth; but this was not because he was an adulterer.

In vv. 13-23 Job turns to possible accusations of sins against his dependants. Verses 13-15 concern his treatment of his own *slaves*. In asserting that he had not rejected claims (*mišpāṭ*) made by his slaves when they brought a legal case (*rîb*) against him, he is maintaining that he had shown them much more consideration than was required by the law. Although the Old Testament laws required that slaves should be treated humanely (according to Deut. 24.17-18, 21-22, Israelites were to be motivated in their behaviour towards the disadvantaged by the memory of their own slavery in the past in Egypt), slaves had virtually no legal rights, and certainly not the right to summon their own masters to court in a legal dispute. Job recognizes that God expected more from him than conformity to his purely legal obligations and that he must answer directly to him. In v. 15 he develops this thought further, citing,

as if it were generally acknowledged as a guiding principle in this matter, a saying equalled elsewhere in the Old Testament only in a few passages (Prov. 22.2; 29.13; perhaps also Mal. 2.10), implying an equality
between masters and slaves in view of their common origin as created
by God. In vv. 16-23 he applies the same principles to his other dependants, the *poor*, *widows* and *orphans* whom it was his duty to protect.
He declares that he never allowed the poor to starve, denied orphans a
square meal or left the poor in rags; he never behaved violently to an
orphan when he was sitting as judge 'in the gate', even though he might
have been supported in such conduct by his fellow-judges. On the contrary, he had treated the orphan like a son and looked after the welfare
of the widow, and he had received the blessing of the orphan whom he
had clothed. The self-imprecation in v. 22 is governed by v. 21: the
dislocation of Job's arm would have been an appropriate punishment for
violence against the orphan. In v. 23 Job confesses that if he had
committed such sins he would have been rightly afraid of God's wrath.

In vv. 24-28 Job affirms his avoidance of two sins: *greed* and *idolatry*.
The two are perceived as similar in nature: to *trust* in wealth is a form of
idolatry. Job had indeed been very wealthy; but wealth in itself is never
regarded in the Old Testament as evil; on the contrary, it was regarded
as a proper reward for wisdom (Prov. 3.16; 8.18-21; 1 Kgs 3.3). Solomon's great wealth was regarded with pride by the author of 1 Kings 10.
Job claims here that he has never gloried in his wealth (v. 25) and so
turned from God. The reference to the worship of sun and moon in vv.
26-27 may be an allusion to the propensity of some Judaeans in the late
monarchical period to resort to such worship because Yahweh seemed
to have failed to protect them (so Deut. 4.19; Jer. 8.2; 2 Kgs 21.3-5). Job,
although in the poem he is not represented as a worshipper of Yahweh,
is depicted as a patriarch of ancient times who, like Abraham (e.g. Gen.
14.19-20) worshipped El as the sole God: he was a monotheist to whom
idolatry was anathema. Verse 27 alludes to the practice of 'kissing' a god
(normally his statue) as an act of adoration (1 Kgs 19.18; Hos. 13.2).
Kissing one's hand towards a god would presumably be a symbolical
action performed when the deities concerned were heavenly bodies (cf.
Ezek. 8.16). To Job (v. 28) this would be a betrayal of the true God
'above'. (The absence of the usual self-imprecatory formula in this and
some other passages in this chapter was probably intended to lighten its
otherwise somewhat monotonous tone.)

The sins disclaimed in vv. 29-34 are *Schadenfreude* (rejoicing at the
downfall of an enemy, v. 29), cursing or ill-wishing an enemy (vv. 30-31)
and concealing sin (vv. 33-34). Verse 32, however, is an exception:
there, rather than using the formula 'If I have ...', Job makes a positive
claim to generous conduct: 'has not/have not...' In v. 31 'the men of
my tent' may mean 'my household' or 'my intimates': 'tent' is frequently
used in this book in the sense of 'home' or 'household'. Job is here

seeking to exonerate his companions as well as himself. The blood-thirsty wish in that verse is not to be taken literally. In vv. 33-34 the sin envisaged is that of falsely concealing a sin for fear of possible reprisals or humiliation if the facts were generally known. In v. 33 $k^{e'}\bar{a}d\bar{a}m$ may mean 'like Adam' (cf. Gen. 3.10) rather than 'as others do'. If so, Job is claiming to be more honest than Adam!

Now (vv. 35-37) Job breaks off his defence to demand, for the last time, that his case should be heard and that God, his 'legal opponent', should appear to answer it. Some commentators have suggested that these verses are out of context: they constitute the climax of the chapter—and indeed of Job's whole case—and should be moved to follow vv. 38-40. It is not certain that this is so, however, and here they will be taken in the order in which they stand in the Hebrew text. Job begins in v. 35 by expressing, not for the first time, a wish that there should be a judge or arbiter to hear his case. As in the somewhat similar passages 16.19 and 19.25, the identity of such a person is disputed; the most probable solution is that it is God himself, who somewhat confusingly combines the roles of judge and disputant. Job sets the seal on his testimony by affixing his signature (literally, his 'mark') on it, and calls on God to do the same. He is so confident that that document ($s\bar{e}per$) will vindicate him that he intends to flourish it in triumph. He had been deprived by God of his dignity; but now he will be able to approach God once more in his true dignity 'like a prince' ($n\bar{a}g\hat{i}d$). Whereas he had earlier accused God of 'numbering his steps'—that is, of spying on him to detect his sins (14.16), now he will tell *him* what has really been the 'number of his steps'—that is, he will convince him of the innocence of his life.

Verses 38-40 belong to the same series as vv. 5-8, 9-10 and 16-22, except that the final imprecation in v. 40 is not precisely a self-impre-cation, but is rather a universal one. The personification of the ground ($^{a}d\bar{a}m\hat{a}$) in v. 38 as crying out and weeping is characteristic of the Hebrew way of thinking; it is paralleled in Jer. 12.4, where the earth ($'\bar{a}re\d{s}$) is said to mourn over the wickedness of its inhabitants (there is a similar personification in Job 5.23, which speaks of a covenant supposedly to be made between Job and the stones of the field; compare also Gen. 4.10, where Abel's blood cries out from the ground). In the present case too, the thought is that the ground weeps because a crime has been committed against it. The crime envisaged seems to be that Job has seized land from its proper owners to their detriment. A similar crime is mentioned in 24.2 and perhaps 31.7. The punishment invoked in v. 40—the failure of the yield owing to the rank growth of thorns and weeds—is a standard image in the Old Testament, harking back to Gen. 3.17-18, where it is caused by a universal curse on humanity, and occurring in the denunciations of the prophets (Isa. 34.13; Hos. 9.6) as well as Job 31.8. The absence from v. 40 of a specific reference to Job suggests a universal application here as well: such a heinous crime would have had cosmic consequences. It may be for this reason that the verse has been placed at the conclusion of the chapter.

Whatever may have been the original order of the last six verses of this chapter (see above), all commentators agree that the chapter always ended with the last line of v. 40. That verse may be a subsequent editorial addition like Ps. 72.20 and the final line of Jer. 51.64, though its inclusion in the ancient Greek version attests its antiquity. But it is, in fact, peculiarly appropriate to its context. The verb *tammû* means 'are completed' rather than merely 'are ended'. Job's case is complete; there is nothing more that he can say. He can only await God's reply, which, however, is delayed by the six chapters in which Elihu has his say.

Job 32

The question of the place in the book of the speeches by Elihu (chs. 32–37) has been discussed in the Introduction. These chapters are essentially a single monologue following the lengthy monologue by Job (chs. 27–31), although they have been divided into four by new headings in 34.1, 35.1 and 36.1. It has been suggested that Elihu, who has been present at the discussion between Job and the friends and has listened to their arguments (32.2-5) presents himself (rather inadequately!) as the arbiter whom Job had requested in 31.35. It would appear that he does regard himself somewhat in this light: he is critical both of Job with his assertions that God is unjust and of the friends with their insistence that sin is always punished and that the righteous are always rewarded. He is thus a late participant in the debate, and he attempts to achieve a solution.

Verses 32.1-5 are in prose. They are part of the narrative that began with the Prologue and that continues to introduce each development of the story throughout the book. Verse 1 introduces Elihu's intervention by stating that the friends had come to the end of what they had had to say. Job had made his final speech, and they, at a loss for further things to say in view of Job's stubborn assertion, despite their arguments, that he is innocent (*ṣaddîq*), had for the first time not responded. This gave Elihu the opportunity to have his say. He is introduced formally—more so than the friends—and proves, unlike any of them, to have a name and ancestors with an Israelite flavour, even though he does not specifically mention Yahweh. Nevertheless his name, literally 'He is my God', may be a variant of the name of Elijah ('Yahweh is my God'). The first thing that we learn about him is that he became angry. This is never said about Job or his friends, who had conducted a rational debate even though their exchanges had sometimes been acrimonious. But Elihu is furious with them all. The meaning of v. 4 is probably that he had waited *with* Job (rather than *for* him), that is, he had waited for the friends to reply to Job's latest speech, as they had done on every previous occasion. Their silence provoked him to a further outbreak of anger (v. 5).

Elihu's speech, like all the earlier speeches in the book, is in poetical form. Verses 6-22 of this chapter are a lengthy and elaborate defence of his presumption, as a junior who might be expected to keep quiet in the presence of his elders, in stating his opinion. First (vv. 6-10) he rejects the traditional notion that wisdom is restricted to the aged; then (vv. 11-16) he contemptuously taunts the friends with their failure to answer

Job's arguments. In vv. 17-20 he confesses to an uncontrollable urge to state his opinion, and finally in vv. 21-22 he promises to speak impartially. The reader is clearly intended to see him as a bumptious young man as well as an arrogant and short-tempered one; however, the view of some commentators that he is essentially a comic character, a mere fool, introduced to give light relief to an otherwise over-solemn work, is mistaken, partly because a 'joke' lasting through six chapters would be disproportionate in a work of this length, and partly because Elihu does, in fact, have some serious contribution to make.

'I said' (*'āmarti*) in v. 7 refers not to Elihu's spoken words but to his thoughts. No distinction is intended in v. 8 between spirit (*rûaḥ*) and breath (*nešāmāh*). The two words occur again in parallelism in 27.3, where possession of spirit/breath is synonymous with being alive: in Hebrew thought God, in breathing into the creatures that he had made, has conferred life on them (Gen. 2.7; 7.15). Elihu's point is that because of this, wisdom and knowledge of what is right are not a prerogative of one person rather than another but are available to any living human being (v. 9). Consequently his own understanding (*dēa'*) is as valid as any, and he therefore has an equal right to voice his opinion (v. 10).

In vv. 11-14 Elihu directly addresses the friends. He is determined to present himself to them not as an unreflecting hothead but as a serious person who has followed the debate closely and found their arguments totally inadequate to answer Job and prove him wrong. They therefore have no right to claim, as they have done, that they possess a genuine wisdom: *if* Job is to be proved wrong, this cannot be done by any human being (*'îš*) but only by God himself (*'ēl-*, v. 13b). This powerful statement, expressed with great emphasis in the Hebrew, should not be understood, as it has been by commentators and translators, as part of the friends' supposed opinion; it represents Elihu's own belief. Although he is confident of his own ability, he is not claiming that he can decide the issue; he is merely pointing out (v. 14) that if he had been the recipient of Job's attacks he would not have replied with the same arguments as those of the friends. In vv. 15-16 he alters his stance and now refers to the friends in the third person. They have lost their initiative and show by their silence that they have nothing further to contribute. Elihu does not see why he should wait any longer, and is prepared to speak in his turn.

Verses 17-22 are full of bombastic claims by Elihu, showing that he *is* after all an 'angry young man', full of himself and rather a fool. He uses the expression *'ap- ʿanî*, 'even I', twice in v. 17, and first person singular verbs nine times in six verses. He also claims, like Eliphaz in 4.12-16 and Jeremiah in Jer. 20.8-9, to be under an inner compulsion to speak that he cannot control or deny, perhaps amounting to divine inspiration. There is unconscious irony here. Elihu's claim (v. 18) that it is his 'spirit' (*rûaḥ*) within him that forces him to speak no doubt refers back to his claim in v. 8 that the possession of God's 'spirit' or breath within every person can lead to understanding; yet there is also here an ironical allusion to Eliphaz's contemptuous reference in 15.2 to garrulous persons who are filled with 'wind' (*rûaḥ*). The verb 'find relief' (*rwḥ*) in v. 20 is probably also a somewhat comic play on words. The analogy with wineskins ready to burst in v. 19 is frankly comic. Finally Elihu's undertaking to be impartial and not to give undeserved honour to anyone because he would not know how to do it (vv. 21-22) is disingenuous, since he has already shown prejudice against one class of persons (the elderly) in v. 9.

Job 33

In this chapter Elihu turns from his dismissal of the friends for their inability to establish a case against Job to make what he evidently regards as a conclusive critique of *Job*'s arguments—an evenhandedness that goes some way to justify his earlier promise that he will not favour either side. He now acts as though he had been appointed as arbitrator in the case of Job versus God, calling on Job to prepare (*'ārak*) his case (which he had already done, 13.8; 23.4), to take his place in court (v. 5) and to pay attention to him when he speaks (vv. 31, 33); however, he somewhat patronizingly concedes him the right, if he has anything pertinent to add, to speak again (vv. 5, 33). Whether Job can have any more to contribute, Elihu is not sure; but he assures him that he has his interests in mind and hopes that the result of his examination will be favourable to him (v. 32b). In any case he is sure that he has a monopoly of wisdom from which Job can learn. His arrogance has no bounds: after pretending in 32.6 that he had at first been hesitant to address his elders, he now kindly assures Job that he need not be afraid of him!

In vv. 1-7 Elihu is concerned to establish his superior status. 'Now' in v. 1 indicates a change of the person addressed, specifically named as Job. The combination of the word-pair 'hear' and 'listen' is found elsewhere in forensic discourse; if this is an allusion to Isa. 1.2 it is an indication that Elihu is, as it were, 'playing God'. Verse 2 has been dismissed by some commentators as otiose; but it is in fact the formal announcement of an intention to make an important speech, and it also serves as a claim to impartiality. In v. 4 Elihu harks back to his earlier statement in 32.8, justifying his claim to speak with special knowledge. There may even be a suggestion here that he is the very voice of Wisdom herself (cf. Proverbs 8, especially vv. 7-8). Verse 6 in conjunction with v. 7 is patronizing. Although ostensibly it is a humble admission that Elihu is a mere mortal and not God, it implies that Job might have thought otherwise! It is actually a covert claim that Elihu, though not actually God, is fully authorized to speak for him.

Now (vv. 8-11) Elihu, who can claim to have been present during the debate with the friends and so had actually heard Job speak, purports to quote his actual words in which he had allegedly claimed to be totally without sin. In these 'quotations' there is a mixture of truth and distortion. Job had, in fact, complained (10.6) that God had found pretexts in order to find him guilty as Elihu alleges in v. 10a; and in vv. 10b and 11 Elihu does quote words that Job has spoken virtually word for word (13.24, 27). However, his most damaging accusation (v. 9) that Job had

claimed to be sinless completely distorts the facts. Job had never claimed to be morally 'clean' (*zak*), though he had once said (16.17) that his *prayer* was 'clean'. In making this accusation Elihu is simply joining Zophar, who had *said* that Job claimed to be 'clean' (11.4). Nor had Job claimed to be without sin (*peša'*), pure (*ḥap*) or free from iniquity ('*āwōn*). His words, addressed to God in 10.6, were, 'You seek out my iniquity ['*āwōn*] and hunt down my sin [*ḥaṭṭā'*], although you know that I am not guilty [*raša'*].' But this plea of 'not guilty' was not a claim to be sinless: Job was doing no more than to claim that *in this instance*—that is, with regard to the particular sins of which God appeared to have accused him—he was not guilty. So Elihu begins his 'examination' of Job's conduct by deliberately distorting his words.

In vv. 12-13 Elihu begins his argument. Job is mistaken, and he will put him right. But despite his declared intention to reply to 'this matter' (*zō't*, that is, Job's claim to be guiltless and his complaint that God is hostile to him) he first takes up another complaint of Job's (expressed, for example, in 23.3-5; 30.20) that God refuses to answer him. Citing the undisputed fact that human beings cannot pit their puny strength against an all-powerful God (v. 12b), Elihu declares that the desire to expect a face-to-face encounter with God is futile: no one can expect God to reply to *everything* that human beings choose to say to him (v. 13b is probably Elihu's own opinion, not Job's: the Hebrew text does not indicate otherwise). But in vv. 14-15 he qualifies this statement by saying that God nevertheless has other mysterious ways of addressing human beings of which they may be unaware. Such divine communications, Elihu says, occur in dreams and visions of the night when one is asleep. Elihu does not actually claim to have had such an experience himself, although he does claim some kind of divine inspiration (e.g. 33.4), and he speaks of God as a teacher from whom he had presumably received salutary instruction (36.9-12). Earlier in the book Eliphaz (4.13-17) relates a similar experience; and in v. 15 here Elihu actually quotes 4.13 verbatim. Similar experiences are related of Samuel (1 Sam. 3.4-18) and Solomon (1 Kgs 3.5-15); in those two cases the setting was a temple in which the recipients of the message were spending the night. 'Once... twice' (cf. also 'twice, three times' in v. 29) is an example of a 'numerical saying' in which the higher number is the operative one (cf. Amos 1.3-2.6; Ps. 62.11). Here the intention is to assert that God emphasizes his messages by repeating them or that he is not deterred by the recipient's failure to recognize them in the first instance. In the same verse the verb *šûr*, 'to perceive', probably implies the ability to recognize a divine communication, as in the case of the seer Balaam in Num. 23.9 and 24.17.

In vv. 16-30 Elihu is at pains to comfort Job by assuring him of God's good intentions towards mankind in general. He illustrates this in a number of ways. Verses 16-18 complete the sentence begun in v. 15:

God uses dreams to terrify people in their sleep and so to warn them to change their ways; the sin of arrogance is cited as a notable example of these 'ways'. Such a reformation will spare them from death. The 'Pit' (*šaḥat*, v. 18) is the equivalent of Sheol, the underworld which is the abode of the dead; 'passing through the River' (probably better, 'channel' or 'canal') is an image that occurs only here and in 36.12a in the Old Testament, but as denoting the passage to the underworld it has analogies in other cultures. This notion of being spared from death does not denote immortality but refers to premature, perhaps violent, death occurring as a result of sin (cf., e.g., Prov. 15.10; 19.16).

Verses 19-22 speak of another way in which God warns those who have not understood the message conveyed in dreams. Such people can be chastened by severe sickness, which brings them close to death. They lose their appetite for food and are reduced to mere skeletons, feeling themselves to be close to the 'Pit' and the messengers of death. But God does not allow them to perish (vv. 23-25). In every case (*'im* at the beginning of v. 23 means 'when' or 'whenever'), he employs one of his innumerable angels or heavenly messengers as a mediator (*mēlîṣ*) to rescue them. This mediating angel is precisely opposite in function to the messengers of death of v. 22. Job had longed for such a mediator (9.33; 16.19; 19.25) but without much hope. Elihu now assures Job that God has no less than a thousand (i.e. innumerable) angels ready to perform such tasks. The last line of this verse (23) seems strange until it is realized that the word *yošrô*, which would normally mean 'his righteous conduct', in this case means something like his *duty* to be righteous, which the mediating angel will inculcate ('declare'). In v. 24 the speaker appears to be God himself, who commands his angel to save this person from death at the last moment. Because he has now learned his lesson and abandoned his wicked ways (v. 17), he will be 'ransomed', and his former health will be restored to him (v. 25). These verses are thus a declaration of God's grace, similar to the assurances given to Job by the friends if he will repent (e.g. 5.18-26; 11.13-19; 22.21-30). Like them, Elihu does not accept Job's claim to be righteous, but speaks only of forgiveness for the repentant sinner.

The sinner's restoration to health will be followed by a confession of sin and an act of praise to God, who accepts his supplication and restores him to his favour (vv. 26-28). This confession is evidently conceived as made publicly before a congregation (cf. Ps. 22.22; 40.9-10): the second line of v. 26 is, literally, 'and he [God] reveals his face amid shouts of joy' (*tᵉrû'āh*). To be permitted to see God's face in such a context was to experience divine acceptance (cf. Gen. 33.10). The third line of v. 26 is obscure; it may mean 'and he reports to others his salvation'. Verses 27-28 quote the confession supposedly made by the worshipper to the assembled congregation. The 'light' that he is now confident of seeing is life itself, the light that he would never have seen again if he had 'gone down to the Pit': 'to see the light' means simply to be alive, as in 3.16 and Ps. 49.19, though here it is also the light shining from God's face (cf. Num. 6.26; Ps. 31.16; 80.19; 119.135).

Elihu indicates that he has now completed his exposition of this topic by bringing it to a close with a somewhat superfluous series of remarks in which he mainly repeats his own words. In v. 29 he adds 'three times' to his earlier statement (v. 14) that God shows his concern with errant human beings 'once and twice', and in v. 30 he merely reiterates what he has said in v. 28. In vv. 31-33 he recalls the beginning of the chapter by addressing Job in similar terms: 'listen to me'; 'answer me'. But he also makes it clear that he has not yet finished what he has to say. His final words in this chapter, however, show confusion of thought: in v. 12 he had stated that Job was wrong in his contention that he was innocent, but now he says (v. 32b) that he will be delighted to prove him right! In v. 33 he makes the extraordinarily presumptuous claim that he is fully qualified, presumably on the grounds stated in 32.7-10, to do what his elders had not been able to do: *he* will teach Job wisdom— that is, he claims to possess a knowledge which all have sought and which, as Job had discovered (ch. 28), is the possession of God alone. This presumptuousness is what the book of Proverbs (26.5, 12; 28.11) calls the folly of being 'wise in one's own eyes' and Isaiah (5.21) includes in a list of sins that especially incur God's anger.

Job 34

Despite his assurance to Job in 33.32 that he wished to vindicate him, Elihu in this chapter shows that he sides with the friends in holding him guilty. The matter, he maintains, is simple: by claiming to be innocent Job has accused God of injustice. But since this is manifestly an impossibility, God's condemnation of him must be fully justified, and he must confess his sin and appeal to God's mercy. But Elihu is determined to be fair—or so he says! He begins by addressing the friends, or perhaps an unspecified wider audience whom he has apparently selected to join him in assessing Job's case. These are addressed as 'wise men' (ḥᵃkāmîm) and as learned or especially knowledgeable (yōdᵉ'îm). They are to listen to his arguments and assess their plausibility. Verse 3 is a variant form of a proverb quoted by Job himself in 12.11, affirming the competence of his audience. They are to settle between them what is just (mišpāṭ) and right (ṭôb).

In vv. 5-9 Elihu begins to set out his case against Job. He first cites Job's own accusations against God with reasonable accuracy as evidence against him (vv. 5-6); but then in vv. 7-8 he violates every principle of justice by launching into a violent attack on him, prejudging the issue under discussion by blatantly accusing him of having led a grossly immoral life, an accusation similar to those made by the friends in their speeches, but for which there is, needless to say, no evidence whatsoever. This accusation is sandwiched between the two citations of Job's supposedly incriminating words. Verse 5b, in which Job is cited as having accused God of condemning him without a trial, is, in fact, a quotation of Job's words in 27.2. The image of drinking blasphemy like water, however, is simply taken from Eliphaz's invective in 15.16. That Job had said that the apparent enjoyment of God's favour is no guarantee of the continuance of that favour (v. 9) is, of course, a reflection of what Job had said many times in such passages as 9.22-24.

In v. 10 Elihu sets out to demonstrate to his audience that Job's complaint against God, which he has just summarized, is not only unjustified but also blasphemous. He marks this new stage in his discourse by again calling on his audience to pay attention, and again stressing their competence to make a judgment: they are intelligent men ('anᵉšê lēbāb, literally 'men of heart'). His argument is that to charge God, the sole creator and sustainer of the world, with wickedness is a profanation. The phrase ḥālîlāh lᵉ, usually rendered by 'Far be it from...', is an extremely strong expression having the force of an oath, declaring something (usually the action of which the speaker has been accused or which he has been thought by others to be contemplating) to be unthinkable because entirely contrary to the speaker's moral character. Apart from this verse it is used only once in the Old Testament with reference to God, in Gen. 18.25, where Abraham uses it in a similar way to deter God from destroying the righteous together with the wicked. Here Elihu's point, developed in v. 11, is that it would be unthinkable that God should not render to human beings what they deserve, whether they are righteous or wicked. That God does, in fact, behave in this way was of course affirmed by the friends, notably by Bildad in ch. 8, and specifically denied in very similar terms by Job in 21.31.

In v. 12, the second line of which exactly repeats a statement by Bildad in 8.3a, Elihu reiterates what he has already said in v. 10, showing his strong feelings with a double asseverative ('ap-'omnâm). His assertion that God will not pervert justice, however, is made more specific by putting it in legal terms. Justice (mišpāṭ) was what God expected of human beings; that he himself should behave like a corrupt judge (cf. Lam. 3.35, 36) was an absurdity.

In vv. 13-15 Elihu attempts to support his contention that God cannot possibly do anything wicked or unjust by citing his absolute power and the complete dependence of all human beings on him. This is an extremely feeble argument. None of those who have spoken in the course of the book would deny God's power; but power is not always accompanied by virtue, and it has been precisely Job's point throughout that this powerful God has misused his power for unjust purposes. However, even though these verses have no persuasive power they have their theological point. Elihu's question in v. 13 is reminiscent of similar questions in Isa. 40.12-14. To a polytheist these questions might be genuine questions seeking information, since in a pantheon of deities only one would be the creator of the world, and the creator god might well have entrusted the world that he had created to a lesser deity. But from the monotheistic point of view of this book and of Second Isaiah these are rhetorical questions to which the answer is 'No one'. Verse 13b probably means 'and who entrusted the whole universe to him?'. Verses 14-15 express a belief found elsewhere in the Old Testament (Gen. 3.19; Eccl. 12.7; Ps. 104.29) that is based on the notion that it was the breath of God that gave life to 'the man' (hā'ādām) whom he had made from the dust of the earth (Gen. 2.7). The use of the word 'together' (yāḥad) in v. 15 seems to envisage the withdrawal of God's breath, which would result in the simultaneous unmaking of all living creatures ('all flesh').

Elihu now turns to address Job alone (the imperatives in v. 16 are singular). He again assumes a stance of superiority, ironically beginning with 'If you have sufficient intelligence to understand me, listen!' The argument is exactly the same as in the previous verses, though it is now inverted. God who is the Mighty One must also be the Righteous One; if he was the enemy of justice, as Job has maintained, he would be unable to rule the world (v. 17). In vv. 18-20 Elihu tries to support his case by giving examples of how God uses his power for good, showing impartiality in his dealings with human beings. As the creator of all, both rich and powerful and poor and defenceless, he treats them all impartially according to what they deserve. Elihu points out that God is able to destroy a whole people in a single moment, as he had destroyed the firstborn Egyptian children at midnight (Exod. 11.4; 12.29). Job, who is well aware of God's destructive power but also knows that he is a victim of God's injustice, is hardly likely to be impressed by such arguments.

The topic of God's judgment on the wicked is pursued further in vv. 21-30 with various covert allusions to Job. Elihu argues in vv. 21-22 that the wicked can in no way escape God's judgment by concealing themselves, because he is able to observe the actions of all human beings. This notion of God's keeping watch over human conduct is one that runs through the whole book, but it is regarded in more than one light. Job had complained of it as intolerably oppressive: he believed that God was spying on him to pounce on the slightest fault that he might commit (10.14; 13.27; 14.16). Yet later, when he looked back on his former life, in which he had enjoyed God's favour, he saw it as a benign protection (29.2); and when he came to make his formal defence of his conduct in ch. 31 he welcomed it as helping him to establish his innocence (31.4, 37). Now Elihu speaks of it as ensuring that the guilty do not go unpunished.

The unspecified subject of v. 23 is man, not God: it is not for a human being to institute proceedings (*mišpāṭ*) against God—an indirect rebuke to Job. God exercises his supreme power by making his own decisions without allowing others to question him, removing even the powerful and replacing them with others (v. 24; compare the Song of Hannah, 1 Sam. 2.7-8; Pss. 75.7; 113.7-8), as in fact he had done to Job. The wicked are struck down in public, so that others may witness their fate, like Job on his ash heap! (vv. 25-26). In vv. 27-28 Elihu again appears to be indirectly accusing Job, now of oppressing the poor. The meaning of vv. 29-30 is not entirely clear; but probably Elihu is referring to complaints that God sometimes seems to be inactive and to ignore such injustices. Elihu affirms that this does not mean that he is indifferent, and that he will not permit the wicked to triumph, whoever they may be.

Elihu concludes this part of his speech with a verdict on Job (vv. 31-37). Job has committed sinful folly, and the only hope for him is that he should confess his sin and ask God to teach him the wisdom that he lacks. There are again textual and interpretive problems in these verses. A slight textual change in v. 31a suggests the reading 'For you should say to God', followed in vv. 31b and 32 by the words that Job ought to speak. In v. 33 Elihu appears to point out that it is for Job on his own to decide whether to accept that advice or not, but points out that if he rejects it he risks divine retribution (a point that he had already made when speaking of the retribution that would befall the wicked in v. 11). He then (vv. 34-37) appeals to his audience ('men of sense', cf. v. 10) to confirm him in his judgment that Job has spoken like a fool and that even now he continues to add to his guilt.

Job 35

Elihu's argument in this chapter is not easy to follow. Some commentators have thought that the author's purpose here was to present Elihu as confused and desperately trying to find new points to make against Job. It may be that it is rather futile to try to make sense of this chapter; an attempt, however, will be made here to find some logic in it. Elihu seems to be arguing that Job has no right to demand that God should answer his complaint, because (a) it cannot matter to God whether he is innocent or not (vv. 3-8); (b) God will not listen to the complaints of evildoers (vv. 9-13); (c) Job's complaint that God never punishes the wicked is nevertheless nonsense (vv. 14-16).

The 'this' in v. 2a presumably refers to Job's verbal attacks on God mentioned by Elihu in 34.37. In vv. 2b-3 Elihu purports to cite two assertions by Job that, he claims, are mutually contradictory: on the one hand he has maintained that he has a claim (*mišpāṭ*) on God, who ought therefore to give him justice; on the other, Job has asserted that God is indifferent to his conduct (as in, for example, 9.22). Elihu then prepares to give Job his answer, and at the same time to answer the arguments of the friends, which also he evidently considers unsatisfactory. He sets out his answer in the verses that follow in the rest of the chapter. He appears to agree with the second of Job's purported remarks (v. 3) rather than with the first. In vv. 5-8 he points to the immense distance between God and human beings, and concludes from this that whether Job is sinful or innocent his conduct cannot affect God; human behaviour has consequences only for fellow human beings.

In vv. 9-13 Elihu appears to be arguing that when people are suffering from oppression they do not address their cries for help to God, and this is why he does not answer their cries. Their laments do not arise from true confidence in him but are 'empty', self-centred. They ignore his teaching, which is conveyed through the wonders of nature: it is he who gives them 'songs' (rather than strength, as in some translations) in the night, and who teaches them through (rather than 'more than') the animals (cf. 12.7). The 'songs of the night' of v. 10 may be the songs sung by the stars and other heavenly beings, who are said in 38.7 to have sung and shouted for joy when the world was created. Elihu is saying that the oppressed ought to remember their Creator (cf. Eccl. 12.1), who has many ways of teaching them wisdom, and appeal to him for help rather than to other human beings. This is a somewhat misplaced piece of advice since that is precisely what Job has done.

Elihu ends by applying his conclusions to the particular case of Job. Job's contention that God has not appeared to him and that he is still waiting for an answer to his appeal is stupid: he has failed to realize that God reveals his nature through the wonders of creation (v. 14). He is also wrong to say that God does not take notice of human sin and does not punish the offenders: if that appears to be so it is because he has not been properly approached by sincere appellants. So Job is talking ignorant nonsense.

Job 36

Chapters 36 and 37 belong together. They constitute the peroration of Elihu's discourse. There are no new ideas here, but rather elaborations of themes that Elihu and other speakers have already introduced. They are wholly concerned with the nature of God, who is depicted as just but merciful, but also as incomprehensible by human beings. The final verses of ch. 36 (24-33) and the whole of ch. 37 speak of the terrifying manifestations of God's power over the natural world, ending with a warning to human beings to put aside their pretensions to wisdom and to treat him with the reverence that is his due (37.24). This last section can be seen as a prelude to Yahweh's speeches that begin immediately afterwards with ch. 38.

Elihu begins (36.2) by giving notice to Job that he has not yet finished: he still has something to say on God's behalf. He will employ the traditional teaching acquired from of old (*l^emērāḥôq*, literally 'from afar', v. 3; compare the use of this expression in 2 Kgs 19.25 = Isa. 37.26, where Yahweh speaks of the plan he made 'long ago') to prove that it is God, not Job, who is in the right (*ṣedeq*). In v. 4 he gives a solemn assurance to Job that, like a reliable witness at a trial, he will speak what is true, supporting this assurance with the stupendous claim that it is one who is perfect in knowledge who is addressing him! Ironically, this is the exact phrase that he uses about God in 37.16. Needless to say, no one else in the book has made this claim for himself. It is not only ludicrous, underlining Elihu's egregious self-conceit, but also close to blasphemy. Later in the chapter (v. 26) he retracts this claim when he sings the praises of God, affirming that God is great and beyond human understanding.

Verses 5-12 present considerable difficulties of interpretation. God is presented as all-powerful and as a just judge who destroys the unrepentant wicked but protects the innocent and shows mercy to those who heed his warnings. The first line of v. 5 should perhaps read '(he) does not despise the pure in heart', and v. 6a is emphatic: 'he does not allow the wicked to live'. Verse 7 may mean that God sets the righteous *like* kings on their thrones. In vv. 8-12 the reference is again to the wicked: these verses speak of God's disciplining of them and his readiness to restore them to favour if they heed his instruction. The 'fetters' and 'cords of affliction' of v. 8 are metaphors for his monitory action. 'perish by the sword' in v. 12 should rather be 'pass through the River' (of death) as in 33.18. The language and thought of vv. 11 and 12 are reminiscent of Deuteronomy (especially Deut. 28.1, 15), also echoed in

such passages as 1 Sam. 12.14-15 and Jer. 22.4-5. Verses 13-15 continue
the theme of the contrast between the treatment by God of the wicked
and the (innocent) sufferers. The godless are incorrigible because they
are obdurate and do not call on God for help even when he 'binds' them
(cf. v. 8) and are doomed to an early and shameful death, while God
rescues the innocent sufferers and reveals himself (literally, 'uncovers
their ears', v. 15) to them in their troubles.

Verses 16-21 are even more difficult, and have been deemed unintelligible by some commentators. Innumerable attempts to improve the
Hebrew text have resulted in a multiplicity of quite different translations—though some commentators have declined even to offer translations of some verses. It may perhaps be accepted that the 'also' of v. 16a
associates Job with the good fortune promised to the afflicted in v. 15,
and that v. 21 is a warning to him against committing the sins mentioned
in vv. 13-14. But the intervening verses, including the reference in v.
16bc to the delicacies on Job's table, the 'ransom' on v. 18 and the
admonition in v. 20 not to long for the night, remain enigmatic.

In vv. 22-33 Elihu follows up his warning to Job in v. 21a by remind-
ing him (as if he needed the reminder!) of the nature of the God with
whom he has to do. He stresses his unlimited power and transcendence
and his incomprehensibility, but as before (e.g. vv. 5-12) he assumes—
this is precisely an assumption that Job has often disputed—that these
qualities necessarily imply that he is also supremely just. This passage is
characterized by a series of verbal repetitions and assonances that set it
apart as a structural unity. Thus 'is exalted' (*yaśgîb*, v. 22) is partially
echoed by 'extol'—that is, literally, 'make great' (*taśgî'*) in v. 24 and
saggî', 'great', in v. 26; 'who can understand?' in v. 29 echoes 'we do
not know him' in v. 26; what God has done (*pā'al*) in v. 23 is followed
up in v. 24 by his 'work (*pō'al*); the verb 'to spread' (of the clouds) in
v. 29 is repeated in the reference to the 'spreading' of the lightning in
v. 30; and there are references to the lightning (*'ôr*, literally 'light') in
both vv. 30 and 32.

Verse 22 combines the thought of God's 'exalted'—that is, unattain-
able—power with the assertion, put in question form, that he is in-
comparable as a 'teacher' (*môreh*). But this word here has nothing to do
with the kind of moral guidance to which Elihu has already referred in
vv. 10-12. The point being made is the same as that in Isa. 40.10-12, also
in question form, where the prophet asserts Yahweh's role as sole
creator of the world, who needed no one to instruct him; the same
point was made more briefly by Elihu in 34.13. Unlike the creator-gods
of other peoples who had their 'counsellors', the true God is his own
'teacher', and there are no others from whom he needed or needs to
learn. This verse together with v. 23 forms a preface to the verses that
follow concerning God's power over nature (compare Prov. 8.22, where
as here God's 'way' means his creative work). But v. 23b links this with

God's moral character: if God's human creatures are not in a position to prescribe to him how he should manage the universe, they are equally not qualified—as Job was claiming—to condemn him for acting wrongly.

In vv. 24-26 Job is urged to join in the immemorial and universal chorus of praise to God for his 'work' of creation, which is observable by all. 'Remember' in v. 24 is not so much a caution not to forget to do so as a command to do so (compare Exod. 20.8, 'Remember the Sabbath day', which is glossed in the Deuteronomistic Decalogue by '*Observe* the Sabbath day, Deut. 5.12). The reference is particularly to God's meteorological operations, which are no less marvellous because they can only be observed 'from afar'. They are beyond human comprehension, and remind us of God's eternal nature.

The rest of the chapter describes God's mysterious operations in the heavens, which provide rain on the earth (vv. 27-28) but also create the terrors of the thunderstorm, a particularly frightening phenomenon for the ancients (vv. 29-33). The latter topic is pursued in further detail in ch. 37. Clearly Elihu's intention is to put the emphasis on the more spectacular manifestations of God's power rather than on its beneficent aspects. This description is typical of a number of creation hymns and descriptions of theophanies scattered throughout the Psalms (e.g. Pss. 18.6-15; 29; 68.8-9; 104; 147; also Hab. 3.3-11), which to some extent share the same vocabulary and clearly belong to a common tradition found also in the Ugaritic literature and often associated with the storm-god Baal or, in the Old Testament, with Yahweh rather than with El as here. The mechanics of rainfall are explained (vv. 27-28) as involving successive stages: first God takes up salt water from the sea, purifies and stores it up (cf. 38.22-23) and then sends it back to earth as rain. A somewhat similar process seems to be envisaged in Eccl. 1.7.

The thought of the rainclouds implied though not specifically mentioned in vv. 27-28 leads on to the theme of the thunderstorm in vv. 29-33. (Verse 31 seems to be an interpolation, misplaced from after v. 28; *yādîn*, 'judges', there may be a mistake for a word meaning 'feeds'.) In v. 29 Elihu associates the gathering of the clouds with thunder emanating from God's 'pavilion' (*sukkâ*, literally 'booth' or 'hut')—a rather vague concept found elsewhere only in 2 Sam. 22.12 (= Ps. 18.11) apparently denoting God's mysterious presence in the midst of the dark storm clouds. Verse 30b is somewhat obscure, but may refer to the mist accompanying the storm that makes the sea invisible. Verse 32 refers to the lightning, which, though seemingly random, is seen as always reaching the target that God has determined for it. The notion of his 'hiding' the thunderbolt in his hands before hurling it is a current anthropomorphic metaphor, based on the Canaanite concept of Baal, the weather-god, hurling his thunderbolts with his bare hands; such anthropomorphism can only be metaphorical here. Verse 33 states the cause of such violent divine action: God's jealous anger.

Job 37

This chapter is a continuation of 36.27-33. After speaking of God's control over storms and bad weather it turns from v. 14 onwards to contemplate the versatility of his operations in the heavenly sphere: he creates the summer heat and the bright skies too. The chapter—and so Elihu's total discourse—ends in vv. 23-24 with a final warning to Job that this God, who is invisible to human beings and all-powerful and just must be approached with fear and humility.

The chapter begins in a similar vein (vv. 1-2); Elihu confesses his own terror at hearing God's voice in the thunder. The belief that God speaks in the thunder was a familiar one to the ancients. It is found in the Ugaritic literature, where the thunder is the voice of the weather-god Baal, and it is a major theme of Psalm 29 (vv. 3-9) and occurs also in Ps. 18.13. It persisted into New Testament times among the Jews, as is shown by Jn 12.28-29.

The emphatic injunction in v. 2 (addressed in the plural and so not to Job alone but, it seems, to humanity in general) to listen and heed God's voice in the thunder should be seen in connection with the statement in v. 5 that God does great and wonderful things beyond human understanding. In other words, his thunder is not a mere noise. As is implied in 5.9 and 9.10, the wonders of the created world sprang into existence when he spoke his commands (as in Genesis 1). The verses that follow (6-13) are examples of this creative activity (note the explicative conjunction 'For' at the beginning of v. 6). As v. 13 makes clear, these manifestations of God's power are not mere meteorological phenomena: they are his instruments, which he uses either to bestow blessings on humanity or to chastise them. It is for this reason that human beings must pay attention to God's voice even though these phenomena are in themselves beyond human understanding.

Verses 6-8 illustrate God's purpose in sending snow and torrential rain on the earth: this is to impress its inhabitants with his power. Even the animals are forced to seek shelter from the downpour. Some parts of vv. 9-12 are not entirely clear, but Elihu is here listing some other phenomena that demonstrate God's control over the climate: storm (*sûpâ*, not necessarily a whirlwind), cold and ice, constantly moving clouds— all following God's directions. Verse 12a probably refers to the constantly moving clouds that bring or withhold the rain. Elsewhere in the Old Testament (Pss. 68.4; 104.3) Yahweh's rule of the heavens is conceived in terms of his riding on the clouds as his chariot. In v. 13 the phrase 'or for his land', which appears to spoil the contrast between the positive and negative aspects of God's rule, is puzzling; it may be a gloss or an example of an irrecoverably corrupt text.

In vv. 14-18 Elihu addresses himself again to Job alone. He repeats some of the illustrations of God's control of the celestial phenomena from the earlier verses, but this time in the form of a series of ironical questions. He asks Job to think about these marvels, and then proceeds to enquire whether Job also could perform them. He thus implies that Job has spoken and behaved as though he were, in fact, equal to God. The so-called 'impossible question' is a fairly common rhetorical device, especially in the wisdom literature, and similar questions have been put earlier in the course of the dialogue with the friends (8.3; 11.7; 15.7-8; 21.22). But what is unexpected here is the close similarity of these verses to the devastating questions put to Job by Yahweh himself in the chapters that immediately follow (chs. 38–41), especially in the forms 'Do you know...?' and 'Can you...?' (e.g. 38.31-35; 39.1-2). The purpose of these questions is the same in both cases: to force Job to admit his utter insignificance in comparison with the creator-God. Yahweh's ironical taunt in 38.21, 'Surely you know it, as you were already born!' would be equally appropriate in Elihu's mouth. The proximity to Yahweh's speeches of these verses and the rest of Elihu's effusions about the creation can hardly be due to coincidence; but it is not easy to understand the reason for it. Elihu's echoing the words of God, whom he describes in v. 16 as the One who is perfect in knowledge (the precise phrase that he uses to describe himself in 36.4!), is perhaps the author's unspoken ironical comment on the pretensions of a young man who presumes to teach his elders; on the other hand, Elihu's speeches could also be seen as preparing the readers for the otherwise too sudden presentation of Job's encounter with God himself.

Verses 19-24 constitute the peroration to Elihu's discourses. Their intention is to show Job that his determination to confront God is both presumptuous and absurd. God exists in dazzling splendour and majesty; he is inaccessible to human beings, and to attempt to argue with him or to make charges against him is simply impossible. Such charges would in any case be futile since he is in fact supremely just, and can only be feared and worshipped.

The most prominent topic in vv. 19-22 is the contrast between light and darkness. God in his splendour radiates light; human beings are in darkness and so are dazzled by that light and unable even to look at it. In other words, God is unapproachable. In v. 19 Elihu appears, despite his earlier strictures, now to take his stand with Job: his question is how 'we' are to present 'our' arguments against God in court. But his appeal to Job to 'show us' how to address God is clearly ironical, and he concludes that this is impossible 'on account of the darkness'. The word 'darkness' (ḥōšek) has several quite different connotations in this book, mainly metaphorical. Here 'ignorance' is a possible meaning (as in Eccl. 2.14), but the word is also a synonym for death (e.g. Job 3.4; 10.21)— that is, nothingness. It is thus a totally negative term, and to be seen in contrast to the 'light' of God's majesty. The meaning of v. 20 is not entirely clear; but Elihu appears to be expressing a doubt whether, even if he or anyone else attempted to speak to God, his words would be heard, and to suggest that the attempt would end in his confusion (the verb's literal sense is 'to swallow up', but it is used in this metaphorical sense elsewhere, e.g. Isa. 19.3, 13; 28.7; Ps. 55.9).

The 'light' (*'ôr*) in v. 21 is probably not the lightning as in previous verses but the light of the sun appearing in the sky with undiminished brightness when the storm clouds have finally dispersed. The poet is drawing an implied analogy between the fact that human beings cannot endure to look directly at the sun and their inability to contemplate God when he appears in the fulness of his majesty. The statement in v. 22 that God comes in golden glory from the north (*ṣāpôn*) (rather than, in view of the solar imagery in v. 21, from the east as the reader might expect) has mythological overtones. In the Ugaritic literature Baal has his temple in the north, and Isa. 14.13-14 reflects a similar view that the north is God's heavenly dwelling place. In Ps. 48.2 the 'far north' is symbolically identified with Yahweh's dwelling-place in Jerusalem, and in Ezek. 1.4 the great storm wind seen by the prophet in his vision of Yahweh's glory comes from the north. The reason why the poet in Job 37.22 associates the image of the sun with the north rather than the east may be that he wished to avoid any suggestion of the idolatrous worship of the rising sun itself as is portrayed in Ezek. 8.16 (compare Job's disavowal of this in 31.26-28). In v. 24b the reference is to the 'wise of heart', not, as some translators have supposed, to those who *wrongly claim* to be wise. The phrase, *ḥᵃkam-lēb*, always signifies those who are genuinely wise (so Exod. 28.3 and comparable passages; Prov. 10.8; 11.29). The line means that even the wisdom of the 'truly wise' is not regarded as such by God, who alone is wise (cf. 28.23-27). These final verses, in which Elihu roundly asserts to Job that it is impossible to 'find' God (v. 23), may echo the thoughts of many readers who are unprepared for the shock of Yahweh's sudden appearance to address Job in 38.1.

Job 38

The two speeches by Yahweh (38.2–40.2; 40.6–41.34) are really one. The short interruption by Job in 40.3-5 is caused by Yahweh's pause and demand for a reply in 40.2. In contrast with the central portion of the book (chs. 3–37) the divine speaker in these chapters is identified as Yahweh; but 38.2 makes it clear that he is the same God as is known to the human speakers in the book as El, Eloah and Shaddai. Only in the Prologue, Yahweh's speeches and the Epilogue is he called Yahweh. The reason for this is no doubt that Job, the friends and Elihu are all non-Israelites, who, although they acknowledge only one supreme God, have not received the fuller revelation given to Israel. Chapters 3–37 report *their* words; only when God's actions and words are reported to the readers was it appropriate to identify him as Yahweh, the God of Israel.

Yahweh has, astonishingly, now appeared to Job and speaks to him; a rare privilege, granted only to the patriarchs of old, such as Noah and Abraham, and to the prophets. Since Job has constantly demanded such an interview, this speech is in a sense God's act of self-justification: God is explaining himself to Job as Job had asked him to do. But God's account of himself is not at all what Job had asked for. Far from answering Job's accusation of injustice and cruelty Yahweh embarks on a string of questions that Job is incapable of answering. It is thus Job, not Yahweh, who is forced on to the defensive from the very outset; and the purpose of the interrogation, like the questions of Elihu in 37.15-18, is to force Job in the end to recognize his utter insignificance and ignorance and so the enormity of his presumption in daring to summon God to trial.

The readers may well be astonished that throughout his speeches Yahweh only refers three times, and briefly, to the case that Job has brought against him. In 38.2 he accuses him of obscuring his 'design' (*'ēṣâ*) by speaking ignorantly; and in 40.2 and 40.8-9 of attempting to prove him in the wrong in order to vindicate himself. In fact God's argument is simply a demonstration of Job's ignorance of that 'design'. These chapters consist overwhelmingly of a mass of ironical enquiries whether Job is, or could have been, the creator of the universe. But if there are very few direct allusions to Job's words, it is even more surprising that this catalogue of creative acts includes virtually no references to human beings, whether to their creation or to God's care for them. It is restricted to only two topics: cosmology (the creation of heaven and earth and of natural phenomena) and Yahweh's care for the animals, especially the wild animals. Only in one passage (40.10-14) is there a reference to human affairs, when Yahweh challenges Job to exercise control over human society, punishing the wicked as Job has accused him of failing to do.

The general effect, then, of God's speeches is to present Job with a picture of God as universal creator and maintainer of the world that goes beyond the narrow concept of him entertained by both Job and the friends, who saw him as a God whose only duty is to dispense justice to human beings. These persons all stand revealed as utterly ignorant of his true nature. As a list of phenomena, these chapters, which have been widely acclaimed for their poetic qualities, are an adaptation of a well-known Near Eastern tradition in which an attempt was made to classify phenomena. This tradition was exemplified in the onomastica or lists of names that should probably be recognized as proto-scientific attempts to understand the nature and structure of the world. The literary form employed—a catena of questions—also has affinities with an ancient Egyptian literary tradition.

Yahweh's sudden appearance to Job (38.1) is not only an audible experience for him: it is also a visual one, as is made clear in 42.5. This experience belied the traditional belief that no human being can see God and live (Exod. 19.21). Even Moses had not seen God's face (Exod. 33.20-23). Although both Job and his friends had previously spoken confidently about God, their knowledge of him was at best hearsay, part of traditional lore. As Job later confessed (42.5), the effect of this direct meeting with God was to transform his understanding and his attitude towards God.

The great wind ($s^e\hat{a}r\hat{a}$) out of which Yahweh spoke to Job recalls the wind that carried off the prophet Elijah and transported him to heaven (2 Kgs 2.11). Other Old Testament passages associate Yahweh's theophanies or manifestations with storm imagery (e.g. Judg. 5.4-5; Ps. 18.7-15; Hab. 3). In 9.16-17 Job had envisaged God as utterly terrifying, coming in such a storm to crush him; but now he discovers that he only intends to crush him with words. Yahweh's 'Who is this?' (v. 2) is addressed to Job alone, although the friends appear also to be present (42.7). In vv. 2-3 Yahweh speaks in the manner of a prosecuting counsel, dismissing Job's arguments contemptuously ('Who is this?') as false because based on ignorance of the facts. He tells him to prepare himself for rigorous cross-questioning.

The first set of questions (vv. 4-7) concerns the initial laying of the foundations of the earth and its subsequent construction. Yahweh ironically asks Job where he was when that took place and taunts him by pretending that he must be familiar with it all. There is an allusion here to the notion, already alluded to by Eliphaz in 15.7-8, of the presence of Wisdom in the creation of the world (cf. Prov. 8.22-31). If Job was present then and familiar with all the details of the construction, he must

be, or have access to, the wisdom of God, which in ch. 28 he acknowledged to be reserved to God alone. The details of the construction follow a cosmological pattern common to the ancient Near East and employ
some of the vocabulary found elsewhere, not only in Proverbs 8 but
also in such passages as Isa. 48.13; 51.13; Zech. 12.1 and several of the
Psalms. The earth is envisaged as a building designed and constructed by
Yahweh himself as a master builder who sinks the foundations, uses a
measuring line to check the dimensions and lays the cornerstone. The
outburst of joyful song by the heavenly host on the completion of the
work (v. 7) is a splendid conceit which perhaps recalls, but on a cosmic
scale, the rejoicing at the completion of the Second Temple (Ezra 3.10-
13; Zech. 4.7). If Job had been present at that time, Yahweh implies, he
would hardly have forgotten it!

In the cosmology of the time the creation of the earth was not in itself
sufficient to make it habitable. A further step was needed: the creation
of the dry land. This stage in the process (vv. 8-11) is described in
strictly non-mythological terms in Gen. 1.9-10: there God simply commanded that the water, which covered the entire surface of the earth,
should be gathered into one place to form the sea, so that the dry land
could appear. But in the poetical allusions to this process there are
strong mythological overtones. As in 7.12, where Job complains that
God has set a guard over him as he did over the sea, the sea is still regarded as a living being that can be directly addressed by Yahweh (v.
11). Behind this language lies the myth of the hostile deity Yam, whom
God (in the Ugaritic poems, Baal) had to subdue (cf. Isa. 51.9). Other
Old Testament texts that preserve traces of this 'conflict' understanding
of the creation include Prov. 8.29; Ps. 148.4-6; Jer. 31.35-36.

In this and subsequent paragraphs the ironical questions in which
Yahweh feigns ignorance are interspersed with plain statements by
Yahweh about his creative activity. The posing of questions to which
the speaker knows the answer is a particular rhetorical device: compare,
for example, his questions, 'Have you eaten from the tree?' (Gen. 3.11);
'Where is your brother Abel?' (Gen. 4.9); 'Where have you come from?'
(Job 1.7). Their function is to put the person addressed at a disadvan-
tage—here by the use of heavy irony.

The reminder of this first of Yahweh's speeches falls mainly into two
sections covering respectively the cosmic order (38.12-38) and the animal world (38.39–39.30). In the first of these no strict order is observed,
but the main topics are the creation and function of the dawn and the
morning (vv. 12-15), the underworld (vv. 16-18), light and darkness (vv.
19-21), snow, hail and lightning (vv. 22-24), rain (vv. 25-28), ice and
frost (vv. 29-30), the sky and the constellations (vv. 31-33) and the thunder and the clouds (vv. 34-38). In v. 12 the dawn receives its orders
from the creator. There is probably a mythological background here:
in the Ugaritic literature Dawn (Hebrew *šaḥar*) was a living heavenly

being. There is a clearer reference to this myth in Isa. 14.12. The theme
of the ordering of time is reminiscent of Gen. 1.14-19 and Ps. 104.19-23.
Verses 13-15 draw out this theme in terms of the effect of the dawn on
the wicked, who are first shaken by it and then consigned to darkness,
destroying their power. Verse 14 describes the way in which the coming of the daylight restores colours to the world and brings out clearly
the shapes of objects, like a piece of clay stamped by a seal.

The mythological allusions continue in vv. 16-18: the Deep (*t^{e}hôm*),
the Sea (*yām*) and Death (*māwet*) all have such connotations. Here
Yahweh is asking Job whether he, alone of all human beings, has en-
tered the realm of the dead and returned to life. (We have noted the
preoccupation with death in various ways that runs through the whole
book.) Job is not being asked whether he is an underwater diver: the Sea
and the Deep are images associated with death (Gen. 7.11; Ps. 42.7;
69.2, 14-15; 144.7; Jon. 2.5-6). It must be supposed that the sea is the
route to the entrance gates of the realm of death that are also referred to
in Pss. 9.13; 107.18. In v. 18 the word 'earth' (*'ereṣ*) may mean the
underworld as it apparently does in Ps. 22.29; Isa. 26.19; Jon. 2.6. Verse
18 ends with another mocking demand to Job.

This is a well-organized cosmos. Just as the dawn has its proper place
(v. 12) so also light and darkness have their 'homes' (vv. 19-21). If Job
had already been born before the world was created (cf. vv. 4-7), he
would, of course, know the way to these homes. Again, Yahweh asks
Job whether he is familiar with the 'storehouses' in which snow and hail
are reserved to be hurled down to 'do battle' against human beings (vv.
22-23). The notion of the existence somewhere in the universe of such
storehouses was evidently a common one: compare Deut. 28.12; Jer.
10.13. In the same vein (v. 24) Job is asked to prove his knowledge of
the way in which the 'light' (*'ôr*, probably 'lightning' here in view of the
context) and the bitter east wind are distributed on the earth. Yahweh is
thus understood as using these phenomena threateningly as well as
beneficially.

Verses 25-27 introduce a new theme, one that is to run through the
rest of the speech: that Yahweh performs many of his activities in ways
that appear to human beings to be sheer waste, but which demonstrate
the unimaginable scope of his concerns and, by implication, the insignificance of purely human concerns in his sight. These verses, again in
the form of a question to Job ('Who has...?'), speak of Yahweh's
sending torrential rain and storms especially (by means of a heavenly
'channel') to fall on and fertilize the arid desert, which is uninhabited by
human beings because it was regarded as incapable of useful cultivation.
Verses 28-30, on the mysteries of rain, dew, frost and ice, contain a surprising number of images of procreation: father, beget, womb, give
birth. Instead of using the verbs meaning 'make' and 'create', and so on,

the author speaks of parenting. This language reflects an older theogony: in other words, the idea that these are subordinate beings born of the gods. But the language used here is poetical rather than mythological. The reason for the references to the heavenly bodies in vv. 31-32 is given in v. 33: they belong to the order of creation established by God; but it was also considered that—under Yahweh himself—they 'ruled the earth': they were heavenly beings (cf. v. 7), and they influenced the weather. The identities of those mentioned here are not entirely certain, but they are constellations rather than individual stars ('chains', 'cords', 'children').

Verses 36-38 are largely concerned with the possession of the wisdom by which Yahweh rules the created order. Job is first asked whether he can command the thunderstorm and lightning. Verse 36 is difficult, but becomes intelligible if two obscure words, often taken to mean 'the inward parts' and 'the mind', are rendered respectively as 'ibis' and 'cock', two birds supposedly possessing meteorological powers that were given to them by God, but which human beings like Job do not possess. Verses 37-38 refer again to the ability to command torrential rain as Elijah had done by praying to Yahweh (1 Kgs 18).

Verses 39-41 begin a series of paragraphs about the lives and characteristics of animals and birds which continue until the end of ch. 39. These are all, except for the horse (39.19-25) wild creatures living apart from human beings and their cities; Job is therefore as ignorant of their lives and habits as he is of what happens in the upper skies. As a catalogue of similar phenomena (i.e. wild animals) these verses have an affinity with the literary form of the onomasticon (see above, p. 158). But, far from being just a list of names, this is a remarkable poem and also astonishingly perceptive, showing a detailed knowledge that ironically belies its own message that these things are known only to God. It goes beyond the previous paragraphs in that it stresses not only Yahweh's knowledge and human ignorance but also Yahweh's loving care for those creatures that can be of no possible *use* to human beings: he provides them with food, watches over their births and cares for them generally. Its very pointed omission of any reference to human beings, with their obsession with their own problems and their demands that God should conform to their own notions of justice, cannot but be intentional; it presents a picture of the breadth of God's activities that neither Job nor his friends could have imagined. Two things in particular are emphasized: these creatures' freedom and independence from human control and God's loving concern for them.

The *lion* is generally portrayed in the Old Testament as a fierce creature that is the enemy of mankind. In vv. 39-40, however, the author's concern is with the lion cubs, whose appetites require to be satisfied;

and Yahweh speaks of himself as the hunter who forages for their food in default of human assistance, while at the other end of the scale he also ensures that the young of the ravens do not go hungry.

Job 39

In vv. 1-4 the author displays an extensive knowledge of the lives of the most timid of wild creatures, the *mountain goat* and the *fallow deer*. Job, he implies, may know something as a farmer about the lives of domesticated animals, but when it comes to the wild ones only God has knowledge of such things as the gestation period of their females. Like everything in the cosmos this follows a fixed rule (*'ēt*, 'fixed time') of which human beings are necessarily ignorant. Verse 4 emphasizes the independence of these animals: growing up in the open they learn to look after themselves; unlike the domesticated breed they do not stay with their mothers but soon leave them to live a life of untrammelled freedom. Similarly (vv. 5-8) the life of the *wild ass* is implicitly contrasted with that of the domesticated donkey. It is born free and never knows restraint. (At this point Yahweh throws aside his ironical questions and speaks of himself in the first person: 'I gave...' (v. 6). It is Yahweh who provided this animal with a broad, though barren habitat in which, nevertheless, it manages to find enough vegetation for its needs. It is again its freedom and independence that are the main point: it keeps well away from the noise of the city and so never hears the harsh cry of the ass-driver (the words *nôgēś*, 'driver', is the same word as that used of the tyrannical 'taskmasters' in the Exodus story). This contrast between the untamed and the tamed is made even clearer in vv. 9-12, the section about the *wild ox* or buffalo. Everything in these verses alludes cryptically to the life of its cousin, the domesticated ox: the submission of the latter to its life of hard labour and its attachment to its own stall; its readiness to work for its owner harnessed to the plough or the harrow; its usefulness to the farmer who exploits its great strength. All these characteristics of the domesticated ox, elsewhere regarded positively (in Isa. 1.3, for example, its docility and obedience are held up to rebellious Israel as a model) are here presented negatively: the freedom of the life of the wild ox from human servitude is clearly seen as one of Yahweh's most glorious achievements, unhindered by human tyranny.

The description of the *ostrich* (vv. 13-18) differs from the other descriptions of wild animals in that the question form used by Yahweh to address Job is lacking. Another peculiar feature is that the single reference to God refers to him in the third person (v. 17). It is no doubt implied that the ostrich is yet another creature whose habits are known only to God; but this is, in fact, a straightforward account of the bird, and so more closely resembles the genre of the onomasticon, whose primary purpose was to establish a list of phenomena belonging to a particular category—in this case the wild animals. There is also a similarity with animal proverbs, such as those in Prov. 6.6-11 and 30.24, although in contrast with those no particular moral is apparent. This could stand as a splendid poem in its own right, one that has clearly comic features, as is appropriate for a creature that has always been thought of in comic terms and about which various legends have arisen. Though no mention is made of the legend that the ostrich hides its head in the sand when alarmed, the statement that it forgets where it has laid its eggs is somewhat comparable. Unfortunately some of the lines are notoriously difficult; v. 13b should perhaps be understood as making a contrast between the uselessness of the ostrich's wings and those of the stork and the falcon, and v. 18a may refer to the ostrich's rearing itself up before taking flight—though not into the air, as the ostrich cannot fly. Although the ostrich has one remarkable advantage over other animals and birds in that it rejoices in being able to outrun the riding-horse (v. 18b), the author accounts for its eccentric conduct by saying that God deprived it of wisdom (*ḥokmâ*) and understanding (*bînâ*, v. 17). There seems to be no reason to suppose that these words are an indirect allusion to the topic of human wisdom that pervades the book: wisdom—in the sense of purposeful and appropriate behaviour—was not confined to human beings, and could be possessed by the lesser creatures, some of which were recognized as exceedingly wise (cf. Prov. 30.24-28).

The description of the *horse* (vv. 19-25) is another literary masterpiece. As so often in the book of Job there are a number of words here whose meaning is uncertain, but in general the modern translations give a correct interpretation of the author's thought. Like the poem on the ostrich this is a straightforward, though highly poetical, account; but it conforms formally to the rest of the chapter, in that it begins with questions to Job (vv. 19, 20a) asking him whether it is he who created the horse. In one important respect, however, these verses are an oddity: this horse is far from being a *wild* horse. Although it is designated by the normal Hebrew word for horse (*sûs*), it is a warhorse, specially trained for use in battle. Thus it cannot be said to live in freedom like the creatures described earlier: it has a master and clearly occupies its own stall like the domestic ox which was contrasted by implication with its wild cousin in v. 9. Nevertheless it is described in a very positive manner. This is, in some respects at least, a glorified and idealized animal rather than a real horse, and it is clearly seen by the poet as one of Yahweh's most terrifying achievements. Its capacity to inspire terror makes it comparable with the descriptions of Behemoth (40.15-24) and Leviathan (41.1-34). Between this passage and the description of the ostrich in the preceding verses there is a clear verbal link: the final line of the latter claiming that the horse is inferior to the ostrich in the matter of speed (v. 18b) is immediately followed by the line (v. 19a) which also speaks of the horse's great strength. This juxtaposition was clearly intentional, and may have been intended to make fun of the ostrich, which was capable of only one poor accomplishment in which it was superior to the magnificent warhorse. This fact perhaps tends to confirm the opinion of some commentators that these two passages together constitute a single later interpolation into the series.

The procession of wild creatures concludes (vv. 26-30) with the *hawk* (or, possibly, falcon) and the *eagle* (possibly vulture). The question about Job's wisdom in v. 26 recalls Yahweh's initial question in this speech (38.4), forming with it a framework that includes the whole catalogue, making it clear that Job cannot rival Yahweh's wisdom in respect of any of the creatures named. These two birds of prey, a complete contrast with the stupid but innocent ostrich, are equally remote from human control or knowledge. Even their nests, built on the heights far from human sight, are inaccessible to human beings; yet so sharp is their eyesight (the main reference here must be to the eagle) that they can look down and espy their prey from a great distance. This too is marvellous to human beings. But the passage ends with a gruesome fact: their prey includes not only the corpses of animals but also the 'slain' (*ḥᵃlālîm*), that is, the bodies of men killed in battle (or murdered). Yet they too were created by Yahweh in his 'wisdom'. Their young ones, too, need food just as much as the lion cubs for whom Yahweh himself goes scavenging (cf. 38.39). The inclusion of these unpleasant and even repulsive beasts side by side with the 'harmless' ones in the list of his creatures reflects a concept of the breadth of the 'wisdom' of the creator-god which leaves the reader in wonderment.

Job 40

In vv. 1-5 Yahweh breaks off his catalogue of examples of his universal rule and addresses Job with real, if rhetorical, questions. These recall the beginning of his speech (38.1) in which he had accused Job in general terms of obscuring his 'plan' through ignorance. The situation has now changed: Yahweh has given Job the unique privilege of learning from him directly the immense scope of his activities; Job can no longer claim ignorance of them. The time has come for Yahweh to pose the question again. He puts it in the legal language that Job himself had elected to use in setting up his case (e.g. *rîb*, 'legal dispute', used of God by Job (e.g. 31.35). Job had 'contended' with God and had made a legal accusation against him (*môkîaḥ* means more than 'argue with', v. 2). *He* must now respond to *God* in the light of his new knowledge. He does answer (vv. 3-5), but his answer is unsatisfactory. He cannot deny the truth of what God has said, and is, not surprisingly, overwhelmed by his sudden appearance and by the frankness of his self-revelation, and accordingly admits his utter insignificance. But he has never doubted God's power, only his justice; and even now he does not admit that he has been in the wrong or that he has been wicked as the friends have maintained, nor does he withdraw his case. He merely says that he does not know how to answer God and that he will henceforth keep quiet ('once...twice' is another example of the 'numerical saying' [cf. 5.19; 33.14] here probably meaning 'several times').

Evidently Yahweh is dissatisfied with this answer, but still hopes to gain Job's capitulation by asking even more questions about his ability to deal with the phenomena in the universe. This second part of his speech is a continuation of the first and yet also distinct from it. The introduction (vv. 6-9) consists partly of exact verbal repetition of 38.1-3 but with significant differences. Thus while v. 6 is a verbal repetition of 38.1 and 40.7 of 38.3, and Yahweh is still speaking from the storm, the contents of these verses are different. In v. 8 God no longer regards Job as ignorant of his design as in 38.2; he now deals directly with the nub of the question: Job's attempt to put him in the dock. This verse is very explicit: using the Joban language of the courts, God accuses *Job* of denying *him* justice (*mišpāṭî*, 'my rights') and of condemning him (*taršî-'ēnî*) in order to prove himself innocent (*tiṣdāq*). (The implication is that there is no middle course: this is a matter of guilt and innocence in which if one contestant is innocent the other must be the guilty one.) This verse is a riposte to earlier assertions by Job such as that *God* has taken away *his* rights (*mišpāṭî*, 27.2) and (to the friends) that they cannot be in the right (*ṣdq*) because of his own 'perfection' (*tōm*). The further question in v. 9, in which God is curiously referred to in the third person, is perhaps more closely related to what follows than to what precedes. Like much of the first part of this speech it shows God as basing his case on his unlimited power rather than offering a defence of his justice (in other words, as far as God is concerned, might is right).

In vv. 10-14, however, Yahweh does adopt—by implication—a moral stance: only he, he implies, possesses the power to subdue wickedness in human society. This, as has already been pointed out, is the only passage in either part of Yahweh's speech that touches directly on his dealings with human beings. Verse 10 continues the topic raised in v. 9. Job has been asked in v. 9 whether he can match God in power as exemplified in his sending the thunder; now he is patronizingly invited to assume the dignity and outward splendour of deity. But (vv. 11-13) this is no longer only a matter of matching God's power over the non-human features of the universe: there is a change from v. 9. What Job is now being challenged to do is to exercise that sovereignty that he has accused God of failing to exercise or of being unwilling to exercise (9.22-24; 21.7-34), a fault concomitant with his complaint of hostility to himself and to other innocent persons. The difference between the tone of these verses and the rest of Yahweh's speech has led some commentators to suggest that they have been interpolated into the original speech by an editor or reader concerned to defend God's moral character. However this may be, Yahweh is presented here as having the *power* to exercise effective judgment on errant human beings, and as pointing out to Job that *he* does not have such power. In v. 14 Yahweh assures him that if he did, he would praise him and acknowledge his superiority. (To interpret these verses as evidence that God has at last been put on the defensive is probably unjustified.)

The remainder of Yahweh's speech (40.15-41.34) is entirely taken up by descriptions of two beasts named as Behemoth and Leviathan, who have been created by Yahweh. With these the speech ends abruptly: there is no peroration, and no explicit moral is drawn. As is subsequently made clear in 42.1-3 Job is left in a state of total amazement at Yahweh's limitless power. It may reasonably be asked in what way these descriptions contribute to the effectiveness of the speech; and as this question is difficult to answer, they have been regarded by some as interesting in themselves but irrelevant to their context. However, their form (especially the address in the second person singular and the questions 'Who can...?') differs in no way from the earlier speech forms in the speech. The nature of these two creatures has been much discussed; the main problems are (a) whether they are mythological or are intended to represent actual animals; and (b) if the latter, whether these can be identified. No consensus has been reached concerning either of these questions; it may perhaps be suggested that these passages include some of the characteristics of known animals, but that these have been endowed with some mythological traits. It must be remembered that this is poetical language in which symbolism plays a large part. There can be no doubt that the intention was to present Job with a picture of creatures even more wonderful and awe-inspiring than any described in the previous chapters.

The word Behemoth, apparently the name of the creature described in 40.15-24, is the plural of $b^e h\bar{e}m\hat{a}$, the ordinary word for cattle. Here, however, it denotes a single creature; the plural form may have been employed, as is the case with some other Hebrew words, to mark the creature out from the ordinary, perhaps as a 'Great Beast', a kind of monster. Certain features of the description indeed suggest some kind of mythological character. First, though like all cattle Behemoth is one of God's creatures (v. 15), it occupies a special place in the creation, being described in v. 19 as 'the first [or possibly "best"—$r\bar{e}'\hat{s}\hat{t}$] of the creative acts [literally, "ways"] of God, who alone can control it'. This statement is curiously similar to what is said about Wisdom in Prov. 8.22, which Yahweh created as 'the first of his ways'. Secondly, it is noted that it lives in the water (as also does Leviathan, 41.1-34). This has suggested to some scholars an analogy with the sea-god Yam at Ugarit and also with an Egyptian hippopotamus deity. But if a myth lies behind this description it has been demythologized: however mighty Behemoth may be it is one of Yahweh's creatures and subject to him. The view that Behemoth is a flesh and blood animal, simply an addition to the list of animals in the earlier part of Yahweh's speech, though even more awesome, is supported by a number of features that seem to reflect knowledge of the habits of a real-life hippopotamus: its immense bulk and strength, its herbivorous nature (v. 15) and its habitat, half-concealed by vegetation, in watery marshes (vv. 21-22). The impossibility of capturing such an immense creature and dragging it away to captivity is also stressed (v. 24).

Job 41

There can be no doubt about the mythological associations of the second beast, Leviathan (v. 1), though its description, like that of Behemoth, is partly based on features of a genuine, though highly imaginative, perception of an actual reptile. Like Behemoth, Leviathan has its habitat in water, but in the sea (*yām*) and the 'deep' *tᵉhôm*, vv. 31, 32) rather than the river in which Behemoth wallows (40.23). These terms taken together point to the primaeval ocean rather than the ordinary sea, and this interpretation best fits the name Leviathan (see above on 3.8). Two of the other three Old Testament references to Leviathan (Ps. 74.14; Isa. 27.1) refer to a battle in which God defeats or kills it; Ps. 74.14 speaks of this battle in connection with Yahweh's creation of the world. In Ps. 104.26, however, Leviathan has been tamed and has become a harmless creature frolicking in the sea that Yahweh has made.

There is no sufficient reason to suppose that Leviathan and Behemoth are simply names for the same creature. Although the former is the 'king of beasts' (v. 34) and the latter is the 'first of God's ways' (40.19), the physical characteristics of the two as described here are quite different. Verses 1-11 stress Leviathan's terrifying nature, the impossibility of capturing it (cf. 40.24) and the extreme danger of tampering with it (but there is no reference to 'the gods' in v. 9 as supposed by some translations). The description of its physical characteristics begins in v. 12; and the creature that it most resembles appears to be the crocodile. These verses speak of its terrifying jaws and teeth (v. 14), the impenetrability of its interlocking scales (vv. 13, 15-17, 23) and the fact that its strength resides in its powerful neck (v. 22). On the other hand, certain features are those of the fire-breathing dragon of myth and legend (vv. 18-21; the Greek translation actually calls it a dragon—*drakon*. These verses probably reflect a current 'demonology' associated with the chaos monster. Verses 33-34, however, appear to regard Leviathan as a terrestrial creature: it is described there as the king of beasts with no equal *on earth*, and v. 33b states that it is *made*—that is, created—without fear (this does not appear in some translations). Thus as in the earlier chapters of Yahweh's speech the answer to the questions 'Can you...?' to Job (vv. 1, 2) and 'Who can...?' (vv. 13, 14) can only be 'Only Yahweh can!'

Job 42

The poem of Job, begun in 3.3, ends in 42.2-6 with Job's second reply to Yahweh. Verses 3a and 4, which clearly cannot represent Job's own thoughts, are puzzling until it is recognized that they are repetitions (with variants) of Yahweh's own words to him taken from 38.2 and 38.3b respectively, in which Yahweh had first made his challenge to Job. Job reminds himself of them in making his final response to Yahweh. In these verses more than any passage in the book—more, even, than in the prose conclusion—the author has set out his own resolution of the problem that he raised when in the Prologue he described the calamities that fell on Job. Job has capitulated; he has abandoned his aggressive attitude towards God and is content. His contentment arises not from the granting of his wishes but from a radically new awareness that human beings are not after all central to God's design and that their obsession with their 'rights' is not God's main concern.

Even before his direct encounter with God Job had been aware—as also had the friends—that God has absolute power and cannot be frustrated in anything that he chooses to do. In his first reply to Yahweh (40.4-5) he had admitted his own unimportance and the futility of his attempting to bring him to trial. This he reiterates here in v. 2. In v. 3, recalling Yahweh's words in 38.2, he now confesses that he had earlier spoken in ignorance of the wonderful acts that Yahweh has now revealed to him and that even now still surpass his comprehension. His reactions to Yahweh's speech have thus undergone a change, from a sullen recognition of his own impotence to a retraction of his case against God as having been utterly mistaken. This development can hardly be due to his recently acquired knowledge of Yahweh's creation of the monsters Behemoth and Leviathan; it must be the result of further reflection on all that Yahweh has shown him. It should be noted that no mention has been made either by Yahweh or by Job in his reply to the question of Job's guilt or innocence, nor is this referred to in the Epilogue (vv. 7-17). Job's attempted case against God is likewise ignored. These omissions suggest to the readers that the exact apportionment to human beings of what they think they deserve is not the primary preoccupation of the transcendent God.

Verse 4 emphasizes the distinction between two modes of cognition, hearing and seeing. Job has listened to God's words; but he now also further claims to have seen him. The phrase *šēma'-'ōzen*, which may be rendered by 'the hearing of the ear', does not in fact necessarily imply direct communication: the word *šēma'* usually means a report, not necessarily a true or accurate one (compare its use in 28.22). Job is here saying that only when he *saw* God for himself did he understand his true nature. The 'report' that he had 'heard' probably refers to the traditional belief about God that had been handed down to him and to his friends, who had constantly cited it in their speeches. But Job has now realized the falsity, or at least the inadequacy, of this 'report'. In v. 6 he now describes the personal consequences to him of his new experience.

The meaning of this crucial verse has been much discussed. It may be agreed, however, that the opening word 'Therefore' (*'al-kēn*) is itself important: what Job now says about his attitude towards God is a direct consequence of the experience that he has described in v. 5b. The most serious difference of opinion among the commentators and translators about the meaning of the verse centres upon the meaning of the first verb, *'em'as*. This is frequently rendered by 'I despise myself', 'I yield' or even 'I melt away'. However, by far the most frequent meaning of the verb *mā'as* is to reject. What Job rejects is not stated in the text; but in the context is is most probable that he is retracting his earlier misapprehension about God that had led him to challenge him. The probability of this interpretation is supported by the second verb, *wᵉniḥamtî*. This is often rendered by 'I repent'; but the word 'repent' has a connotation in English that is not necessarily present in Hebrew. The verb *niḥam* often simply means to change one's mind; and that is precisely what Job is doing.

Verse 6 ends with a phrase that has been understood in a variety of ways, such as 'upon dust and ashes', 'in spite of dust and ashes', 'because of dust and ashes'. It has been supposed that this is a reference to the ashes among which Job had seated himself to give expression to his grief (2.8); but this is improbable. The full phrase 'dust and ashes' (*'āpār wā'ēper*), which occurs only three times in the Old Testament, is used metaphorically in the other two instances and was probably a standard expression; it signifies humility or humiliation. It is used by Abraham in a speech addressed to Yahweh as a self-deprecatory expression signifying his insignificance, and in Job 30.19 by Job of his humiliation by God. Here it reinforces Job's confession of ignorance and insignificance with a word of humility and self-abasement.

Verse 7 resumes the narrative prose style of the Prologue. Yahweh now speaks to the friends, addressing first Eliphaz—presumably regarded as their spokesman—and then all three together. Elihu does not reappear. Nor is Job addressed; but Yahweh continues to call him 'my servant', a rare title that when used of an individual attests Yahweh's complete confidence in him. In vv. 7-9 Yahweh judges both Job and his friends according to whether the words that they have spoken—or have not spoken—about him in the course of their debate were true (*nᵉkônâ*) or not. On this basis the friends are condemned. It is important to observe that their failure to speak the truth about him is far from being seen as a matter of minor importance. On the contrary, Yahweh reacts very strongly indeed to it. He is roused to anger by it (v. 7) and speaks of it as 'folly' (*n^{e}bālâ*, v. 8). This term does not denote mere foolishness: in the Old Testament it is an ethical term reserved for the most heinous of crimes, such as rape and other sexual offences. Those who are condemned for *speaking n^{e}bālâ* (as here) are those who have spoken lies and led God's people astray (Isa. 9.16; 32.6). The friends' sin is regarded by Yahweh as so serious that they are commanded to offer propitiatory sacrifices (as Job had done in case his sons had cursed God in their hearts, 1.5). For the author, then, not to speak rightly about God is a sin worthy of death.

What was the friends' offence? The text does not define this: it leaves it to be inferred. The friends had confidently proclaimed that they knew God's true nature, and had constituted themselves instructors of Job whose notions they regarded as wicked and blasphemous. They had been strenuous in their efforts to *defend* God (that is, their own perception of him) against Job's attacks, and had perhaps expected to have their efforts applauded by him. Their condemnation is thus one of the most powerful ironies in the book; the tables are turned with a vengeance. The friends are revealed as the sinners; Job is vindicated. These verses (7-9) show clearly the fundamentally polemical character of the book. The author has already expressed his own theology through the mouth of Yahweh in chs. 38–41; this was totally contrary to that of the friends, who had constantly maintained that God always and without fail favours the righteous and punishes the wicked, and had even drawn the further conclusion that a person who had to endure misfortune and suffering was *ipso facto* a wicked person. To the author of the book this was not only untrue; it was blasphemy. It was those who held and taught this view who were *ipso facto* the real sinners. This spirit of uncompromising hostility to the religious opinions of other members of the same community, sometimes expressed, as here, in exaggerated language (*n^{e}bālâ*) is a common feature of a certain strand of Old Testament literature (cf., e.g., Ps. 73; Isa. 65).

It remains to consider in what way *Job* had spoken *rightly* about God. It is frequently supposed that this refers to what he had said during the debate. It has been argued that Job's denunciations of God as a cruel tyrant and his assertions that God had singled him out especially as a victim despite his innocence were accurate descriptions of his experience, whereas the friends had painted a wholly false picture of God. There is some truth in this explanation, but it omits too much of what Job had actually said to be entirely convincing. It is equally probable that Yahweh is here referring to what Job has *just said* in his final moment of truth in vv. 3 and 5 of the present chapter. There he has not only confessed that God and his works are incomprehensible, but has shown humility in admitting his own insignificance and ignorance. Such humility was wholly lacking in the friends, who had confidently claimed that they understood God's nature. It was perhaps especially in these final verses that Job had 'spoken rightly' about him.

Verse 9 does not specifically refer in the Hebrew text to Job's prayer for his friends: it merely states that 'Yahweh regarded him favourably'. But v. 10 states that when Job interceded for them as he had been commanded to do, Yahweh restored his fortunes, giving him twice what he had possessed at the beginning. This linking of the two events probably does not imply that Yahweh's act of bounty was dependent on Job's kindly act, though it introduces a new aspect of God's nature: his mercy. Neither his pardoning of the friends' sin nor his restoration of Job's fortunes should, however, surprise the reader, as it has now been established that God is unpredictable and behaves just as he likes (v. 2). But it must also be remembered that Job's loss and suffering had not been intended by Yahweh to be permanent, although Job was not aware of this: they were due to an experiment that resulted from Yahweh's conversation with the Satan. Now Job had won the wager: he had *not* cursed God to his face, as the Satan had predicted, and Job's final speech in vv. 2-6 of the present chapter shows that despite all that he had said he still accepted Yahweh's right to do as he pleased with his human creatures as he had in 1.21-22 and 2.10. The experiment completed, Job's rehabilitation could be said to follow as a natural consequence.

In vv. 11-17 Job's rehabilitation is described in some detail. The form and style are again characteristic of the folk-tale, in which every detail, especially the fate of the principal character, must be recorded. The doubling of the hero's wealth at the conclusion of the story is also a common motif. The reversal of Job's fortunes produces a change of heart on the part of his family and friends, who had abandoned him in his trouble (19.13-19) but now (v. 11) flock round him, bringing him gifts. This may have been a recognized custom marking a person's return to normal social life after an illness or misfortune, but there is no doubt a further ironical point here: the help that was not given to Job in his destitution is now pressed upon him when he no longer needs it. Job's new family of superlatively beautiful daughters is a detail that continues the folkloric style; their sharing the inheritance with their brothers (v. 15) gives them a privilege not normally accorded to Israelite women. The final verses (16-17) do not detract from the positive character of the chapter, but enhance it. They describe a life that was regarded as the acme of happiness and fulfilment: a lifespan double the normal one and almost approaching that of the patriarchs of Genesis (Abraham lived for 175 years according to Gen. 25.7), the joy of seeing four generations of descendants and a peaceful death in the bosom of his family (the phrase 'old and full of days' is identical with that used of Isaac in Gen. 35.29).

Bibliography

Barr, J., 'The Book of Job and its Modern Interpreters', *Bulletin of the John Rylands University Library of Manchester* 54 (1971-72), pp. 28-46.

Beuken, W.A.M. (ed.), *The Book of Job* (Bibliotheca ephemeridum theologicarum lovaniensium, 114; Leuven: Leuven University Press and Peeters, 1994).

Budde, K., *Hiob* (Handkommentar zum Alten Testament, 2.1; Göttingen: Vandenhoeck & Ruprecht, 1896).

Cheney, M., *Dust, Wind and Agony: Character, Speech and Genre in Job* (Coniectanea Biblica, Old Testament Series, 36; Stockholm: Almqvist & Wiksell, 1994).

Clines, D.J.A., *Job 1-20* (Word Biblical Comentary, 17; Dallas, TX: Word Books, 1989).

Couroyer, B., 'Qui est Béhémoth?', *Revue Biblique* 82 (1975), pp. 418-43.

Delitzsch, F., *The Book of Job* (trans. F. Bolton; 2 vols.; Grand Rapids: Eerdmans, 1961—English translation of the German 1876).

Dell, K.J., *The Book of Job as Sceptical Literature* (Beihefte zur Zeitschrift für die alttestamentliche wissenschaft, 197; Berlin: W. de Gruyter, 1991).

De Wilde, A., *Das Buch Hiob* (Oudtestamentische Studiën, 22; Leiden: E.J. Brill, 1981).

Dhorme, E., *A Commentary on the Book of Job* (trans. H. Knight, from the French of 1926; London: Nelson, 1967 [1926]).

Driver, S.R., and Gray G.B., *A Critical and Exegetical Commentary of the Book of Job* (International Critical Commentary; Edinburgh: T. & T. Clark, 1921).

Duhm, B., *Das Buch Hiob* (Kurzer Hand-Commentar zum Alten Testament, 16; Freiburg i.B.: J.C.B. Mohr, 1897).

Fohrer, G., *Das Buch Hiob* (Kommentar zum Alten Testament, 16; Gütersloh: Gerd Mohn, 1963).

—*Studien zum Buche Hiob* (Gütersloh: Gerd Mohn, 1963).

Gordis, R., *The Book of God and Man: A Study of Job* (Chicago: University of Chicago Press, 1965).

—*The Book of Job* (New York: Jewish Seminary of America, 1978).

Grabbe, L.L., *Comparative Philology and the Book of Job: A Study in Methodology* (Society of Biblical Literature Dissertation Series, 34, Missoula, MT: Scholars Press, 1977).

Guillaume, A., *Studies in the Book of Job* (Leiden: E.J. Brill, 1968).

Habel, N.C., *The Book of Job* (Old Testament Library; London: SCM Press, 1985).

Hesse, F., *Hiob* (Zürcher Bibelkommentare AT, 14; Zürich: Theologischer Verlag, 1978).

Hölscher, G., *Das Buch Hiob* (Handbuch zum Alten Testament, 17; Tübingen: J.C.B. Mohr, 1952).

Horst, F., *Hiob 1-19* (Biblischer Kommentar: Altes Testament, 16.1; Neukirchen-Vluyn: Neukirchener Verlag, 1968).

Jepsen, A., *Das Buch Hiob und seine Deutung* (Arbeiten zur Theologie, 1.14; Stuttgart: Calwer Verlag, 1963).

L'Evèque, J., *Job et son Dieu: Essai d'exégèse et de théologie biblique* (2 vols.; Etudes Bibliques; Paris: J. Gabalda, 1970).

Müller, H.-P., *Das Hiobproblem* (Erträge der Forschung, 84; Darmstadt: Wissenschaftliche Buchgesellschaft, 1978).

Pope, M.H., *Job* (Anchor Bible, 15; Garden City, NY: Doubleday, 2nd edn, 1973).

Robinson, H.W., 'The Cross of Job', in *The Cross in the Old Testament* (London: SCM Press, 1995), pp. 9-54.

Robinson, T.H., *Job and his Friends* (London: SCM Press, 1954).

Rodd, C.S., *The Book of Job* (Epworth Commentaries; London: Epworth Press, 1990).

Stevenson, W.B., *Critical Notes on the Hebrew Text of the Poem of Job* (Aberdeen: Aberdeen University Press, 1951).

Strauss, H., *Hiob 19,1-23,17* (Biblischer Kommentar: Altes Testament, 16.2/1; Neukirchen-Vluyn: Neukirchener Verlag, 1995).

Terrien, S., *Job* (Commentaire de l'Ancien Testament; Neuchâtel, Switzerland: Delachaux & Niestlé, 1963).

Vermeylen, J., *Job, ses amis et son Dieu: La légende de Job et ses relectures postexiliques* (Studia Biblica, 2; Leiden: E.J. Brill, 1986).

Volz, P., *Hiob und Weisheit* (Die Schriften des Alten Testaments, 3.2; Göttingen: Vandenhoeck & Ruprecht, 2nd edn, 1921).

Von Rad, G., 'Job 38 and Ancient Egyptian Wisdom', in *The Problem of the Hexateuch and Other Essays* (trans. E.W. Trueman Dicken; Edinburgh: Oliver & Boyd, 1966), pp. 281-91.

Westermann, C., *Der Aufbau des Buches Hiob* (Calwer Theologische Monographien, 6; Stuttgart: Calwer Verlag, 3rd edn, 1978).

Whybray, R.N., *Two Jewish Theologies: Job and Ecclesiastes* (Hull: University of Hull, 1980).

Index of References

37.6-8	154	38.14	160	40.3-5	157, 166		
37.6	154	38.16-18	159, 160	40.4-5	25, 130,		
37.9-12	154	38.18	160		170		
37.9	120	38.19-21	159, 160	40.6–41.34	157		
37.12	154	38.21	81, 155	40.6-9	166		
37.13	154	38.22-24	159	40.6	24, 166		
37.14-24	116	38.22-23	153, 160	40.7-8	25		
37.14-18	155	38.24	160	40.7	166		
37.14	24, 154	38.25-28	159	40.8-9	157		
37.15-18	157	38.25-27	160	40.8	166		
37.16	151, 155	38.25	21	40.9-14	25		
37.19-24	155	38.28-30	160	40.9	25, 167		
37.19-22	155	38.29-30	159	40.10-14	157, 167		
37.21	156	38.31-35	155	40.10	167		
37.22	156	38.31-33	159	40.11-13	167		
37.23-24	154	38.31-32	63, 161	40.14	167		
37.24	20, 151,	38.33	161	40.15–41.34	25, 167		
	156	38.34-38	159	40.15-24	164, 168		
38–41	15, 20, 21,	38.35	21	40.15	168		
	23, 27, 62,	38.36-38	161	40.19	168, 169		
	69, 116,	38.37-38	161	40.21-22	168		
	117, 125,	38.37	20, 124	40.23	169		
	155, 172	38.39–39.30	159	40.24	168, 169		
38	21, 151	38.39-41	161	41.1-34	164, 168		
38.1-3	166	38.39-40	161	41.1-11	169		
38.1	23-25, 42,	38.39	165	41.1	169		
	120, 156,	39.1-4	163	41.2	169		
	158, 166	39.1-2	155	41.4	132		
38.2–40.2	157	39.4	163	41.9	169		
38.2-3	158	39.5-30	24	41.12	169		
38.2	24, 157,	39.5-8	163	41.13	169		
	158, 166,	39.6	163	41.14	169		
	170	39.9-12	163	41.15-17	169		
38.3	166, 170	39.9	164	41.18-21	169		
38.4-7	158, 160	39.12	159	41.22	169		
38.4	81, 165	39.13-18	163	41.23	169		
38.5	21	39.13	164	41.31	169		
38.7	82, 149,	39.17	163, 164	41.32	169		
	159, 161	39.18	164, 165	41.33-34	169		
38.8-11	56, 116,	39.19-25	161, 164	41.33	169		
	159	39.19	164, 165	41.34	169		
38.10	21	39.20	164	42	21, 59		
38.11	159	39.26-30	165	42.1-6	10		
38.12-38	159	39.26	165	42.1-3	167		
38.12-15	159	40.1-14	24	42.2-6	15, 25, 117		
38.12	160	40.1-5	166		130, 170,		
38.13-15	160	40.2	157, 166		173		